Thinking Sociologically

Third Edition

Zygmunt Bauman

Tim May

WILEY Blackwell

Thinking Sociologically

in memory of
ZYGMUNT BAUMAN
(1925–2017)

Contents

Preface to the Second Edition

Writing the second edition of a book which was originally written by Zygmunt Bauman was a task that I approached with some trepidation. The original, after all, was written in a distinctive style that was attractive to numerous readers in several languages. At the same time, Zygmunt felt that a new, updated edition would benefit from my input. In the face of this, quite how I was to preserve this uniqueness, while adding my own materials, was bound to require some care.

The end result is a totally revised and expanded edition. Original chapters have been altered and we have introduced new ones, whilst materials have been added throughout the entire text: for example, on health and fitness, intimacy, time, space and disorder, risk, globalization, organizations, and new technologies. In the end, both of us believe that we have produced a book that maintains the best parts of the first edition, but adds to it in ways that significantly improve its overall appeal.

We are both concerned that *Thinking Sociologically* is attractive to a wide audience. In terms of those who are studying sociology, we have sought to anticipate the different topics that are taught within the curriculum, while writing in a way that we hope is illuminating to practicing social scientists in general. We are also keen that the book appeals to a wider audience who may wish to learn more of a discipline that is gaining greater attention for the insights it offers into society and social relations. For us, the reasons for this are clear: sociology provides a valuable and often neglected perspective on the issues that face us all in the twenty-first century.

As two sociologists, separated by two generations, we are both devoted to our subject in terms of the understanding it offers for making sense of our experiences within the social environments we inhabit. Thinking sociologically not only helps us in our understanding of each other and ourselves, but also offers important explanations for the dynamics of societies and social relations in general. We hope, therefore, that you will emerge from reading this book and agree with us that sociology is an illuminating, exciting, practical, and challenging discipline.

Preface to the Third Edition

When the publisher first suggested a third edition, I contacted Zygmunt and asked what he thought about the idea. He thought it was a good one, but it was not something he wished to undertake himself. So we agreed I would produce the third edition and he suggested we move the authorship to place me as the first author. I have not done that. The book has sold extensively and been translated into a dozen languages. It is, if not unique, certainly unusual in its format and I believe this is something to be preserved. Zygmunt devoted his life to greater understanding of the human condition and its improvement and the book is dedicated to him.

A great deal of change has happened since the last edition was published. Some of you reading this book will have grown up with and been born into an age of information technology in which assumptions of connectedness across space and time and the use of social media are commonplace. Like all epochs, those who seek to characterize them reach for new descriptions often encapsulated in acronyms. Of course there are contemporary issues requiring novel ways of understanding and these are reflected in the new edition. However, we should not forget history in our fast-paced world, for it acts as a corrective to our characterizations and enables us to learn from the past in order to inform the present and future. As we shall see, communication is enabled in new ways, but it also has the power to reinforce, reinterpret, and reconfigure our relations to each other in older ways.

Issues concerned with climate change, sustainability, advances in technology, inequality, social justice, and inclusion, to name a few, have all gained more prominence. With those and the above changes in mind, the book has been revised with new materials and discussions to reflect these and other transformations in our lives. In the face of these changes, the ability to think sociologically remains a vital component for understanding not only their contours and dynamics, but also their consequences for how we organize our societies, understand ourselves and lead our lives. This book is a route into that way of thinking.

Acknowledgments

I began writing the third edition as I started in a new post at the University of Sheffield in September 2016. The requirements of a new job, along with prior commitments, have made the time productive and intensive.

In this journey I would like to thank Beth Perry for being a supportive colleague, collaborator, and a good friend who also read through the manuscript. My thanks go to those who have been supportive of my endeavors now and in the past, including not only Zygmunt Bauman, but also Davydd Greenwood, Morten Levin, William Outhwaite, Bev Skeggs, Dorothy Smith, Carole Sutton, and Malcolm Williams. Thanks to Ken Parsons for the friendship and our frequent meetings over the years and to the "Kalkan 7" – Jane, Dave, Chris, Audrey, Steve, and Vikki – for sharing experiences, having fun, and the holidays.

My love and gratitude to Vikki, who not only read the manuscript with a keen eye and provided insights on the content, but also provided support and encouragement in the midst of her own busy life. To Cian, Alex, Calum, Nick, and Lewis, my sons and stepsons, my appreciation for their energy, zest for life, and for demonstrating that the world can be a better place through a care and concern for others. Finally, I would like to thank my new colleagues in the Sheffield Methods Institute, and express my gratitude for the support of the Mistra Foundation for Strategic Environmental Research which enables our participation in the Mistra Urban Futures Centre and the Realising Just Cities programme. Thanks also go to the editorial and production teams at Wiley Blackwell.

Introduction

Crafting Sociological Lenses

In this chapter we wish to examine the idea of thinking sociologically and its importance for understanding ourselves, each other, and our relations to the social environments we inhabit. For this purpose we are going to situate the idea of sociology as a disciplined practice with its own set of questions and ways of approaching the study of society and social relations.

Thinking Sociologically: The Distinction

Sociology comprises both ways of framing the social world and methods for understanding and explanation. It has a considerable body of knowledge accumulated over the course of its history. Sociological reflections are evident in the writings of philosophers and theologians over the course of two thousand years. The term was used in the earlier part of the nineteenth century and its development drew upon this extensive history for the purpose of studying social order and change. Now, books and journals in libraries represent the discipline as having a rich tradition of studies. They provide knowledge for the general reader, students, and those seeking to become professional sociologists; all of whom can then expand their understanding of the world in which we live. In the process we find systematic studies on such topics as: culture, economics, crime, organizations, sexuality, politics, identity, fashion, management, state, environment, media, youth, gerontology, health, housing, bio-technology, and rural and urban life. Thus, sociology is a site of continuing activity seeking to understand new phenomena and to test established ideas against experiences and data. In the process, the form and content of the discipline evolves with societal transformations.

To situate sociology there must be some distinguishing features of its practice in terms of setting questions and illuminating the social domain that are different from other disciplines. By discovering these differences we can characterize what it is to think sociologically. At this point we can think of related disciplines: for example, History, Anthropology, Political Science, Law, Social Policy, Psychology, Management and Organization Studies, Economics, Education, Criminology, Information Science, Journalism, Philosophy, Architecture, Social Policy, Archeology, Linguistics, Literature, and Geography. All of these are

Thinking Sociologically, Third Edition. Zygmunt Bauman and Tim May.
© 2019 John Wiley & Sons Ltd. Published 2019 by John Wiley & Sons Ltd.

concerned with the human world: that is, the interactions between people and with the environments of which they are a part. So, what sets them apart and why do they justify different names?

There is one simple answer: differences between these disciplines merely reflect divisions in the world that they investigate. It is human actions, or aspects of those, that differ from each other and disciplines take account of this fact. Each narrates its past and the peculiarity of its focus and constitutes its areas of inquiry. History is concerned with actions that took place in the past, whereas sociology concentrates on contemporary society. Anthropology examines human societies at different stages of development; political science focuses on actions and institutions relating to power, state, and government; economics deals with the allocation of scarce resources viewed in terms of persons acting "rationally" to maximize their individual utility, as well as the production and distribution of goods; law and criminology are interested in interpretation and application of the law and the norms that regulate human actions and how norms are articulated, made obligatory, enforced, and with what consequences. Yet, as soon as we begin to justify the boundaries between disciplines in this manner, the issue becomes problematic. After all, we are assuming that the human world itself reflects neat divisions which then become specialist branches of investigation. We now reach an important issue: like most beliefs which appear to be self-evident, they remain obvious insofar as we refrain from examining the *assumptions* that underpin them.

We now have the idea that human interactions may be divided into certain categories which are then represented in clear disciplinary boundaries. A group of "experts" who are knowledgeable and trustworthy then claim exclusive rights to study aspects of the social and material worlds and furnish us with the results of their studies and reflections. However, from the point of view of our experiences, can we divide society into economics, geography, politics, history, or social policy? We do not live separately in the realms distinguished by political science or economics, nor do we move from sociology to anthropology when traveling from parts of the global North to the South, or from history to sociology when we grow a year older!

If we are able to separate these domains of activity in our experiences and so categorize our actions in terms of the political at one moment and the economic at another, is it because we have been taught to make such distinctions in the first place? Therefore, what we know is not the world itself, but what we are doing in the world in terms of how our practices are informed by an image of that world. Our ways of knowing are frames we deploy to comprehend the world and those are forged in the relations between *language* and *experience*. Thus, there is no natural division of the human world that is reflected in different scholarly disciplines. What we discover is a division of labor between the scholars who examine the world which is reinforced by disciplinary boundaries that enable practitioners to know what belongs to their areas of expertise.

In our quest to find the "difference that makes the difference," how do the practices of these branches of study then differ from each other? There is a similarity in the ways in which they select their objects of study. After all, they all claim obedience to the same rules of conduct when dealing with their respective objects. All seek to collect relevant facts through methods of research and ensure that they are valid and then check and recheck those facts in order that the information about them is reliable. In addition, they all try to put the propositions they make about the facts in a form in which they can be clearly, unambiguously understood and tested against evidence. In so doing they seek to pre-empt or eliminate tensions or contradictions between propositions in order that no two different propositions can be true at the same time. In short, they all try to live up to a particular ideal of systematic discipline and present their findings in a responsible manner.

We can now say that there is no difference in how the task of the scholar and their trademarks – scholarly integrity and responsibility – is understood and practiced. Those claiming to be experts seem to deploy similar strategies to collect and to process their facts: they observe aspects of human actions, or employ historical evidence and seek to interpret them within modes of analysis that make sense of those actions. It seems, therefore, that our last hope of finding our difference is in the kinds of questions that motivate each discipline: that is, those that frame the points of view (cognitive perspectives) from which actions are observed, explored, described, understood, and explained by different disciplines.

Take the frames that inform the work of economists. Consideration would turn to the relationship between the costs and benefits of human action. Human action can be viewed in terms of the management and allocation of scarce resources and how these may be utilized for maximum advantage. The interactions between people would be examined as aspects of the production and exchange of goods and services; all of which is regulated by market relations of supply and demand and the desire of actors to pursue their individual preferences according to a model in which actions are subject to a prior rational calculation of means and ends. The findings would then be arranged into a mathematical model of the process through which resources are created, obtained, and allocated. Political science, on the other hand, is more likely to be interested in those aspects of human actions that change, or are changed by, the actual or anticipated conduct of other actors in terms of power and influence. Actions can then be viewed in terms of the asymmetry between power and influence and so some people emerge with views modified more significantly than other parties to the interaction. In this way its findings can be organized around concepts like power, domination, the state, authority, and psephology (the study of voting behavior).

The concerns of economics and political science are by no means alien to sociology. This is readily apparent from works within sociology that are written by scholars who may self-identify as economists, historians, political scientists, anthropologists, geographers, or who work in management and organization studies. Nevertheless, sociology, like other branches of study, has its own cognitive perspectives which inform sets of questions for interrogating human actions, as well as its own principles of interpretation. From this point of view we can say that sociology is distinguished through viewing human actions as elements of wider figurations: that is, of a non-random assembly of actors locked together in a web of mutual dependency (dependency being a state in which the probability that the action will be undertaken and the chance of its success change in relation to what other actors are, do, or may do). Sociologists ask what consequences this has for human actors, the relations into which we enter and the societies of which we are a part. In turn, this shapes the object of sociological inquiry and so figurations, webs of mutual dependence, reciprocal conditioning of action and expansion, or confinement of actors' freedom are among the most prominent preoccupations of sociology.

Individual actors come into the view of sociological study in terms of being members or partners in a network of interdependence. Sociology celebrates the individual, but the atomism, or social isolation that is assumed to exist between us that is embodied in the idea of individualism, is another matter; which is not to say that this may not be a symptom of social dislocation. Sociology is primarily concerned with a relational viewpoint: that is, we are born into and are members of a society which pre-exists us. We are forged in those relations and our experiences are influenced by social structures and our ways of seeing by cultural frames of references. We are dependent upon others and our views of ourselves are mediated in those relations. The central questions of sociology thus become: how do the types of social relations and societies we inhabit relate to how we see ourselves and each other, construct our knowledge, view our environments, and with what consequences? It is these kinds of questions −components of the practical realities that inform our everyday lives − that constitute what it is to think sociologically and which define the discipline as a relatively autonomous branch of the social sciences. Thinking sociologically encapsulates a relational way of understanding the world which also opens up the possibility for thinking about the world in different ways.

Sociology and Common Sense

Thinking sociologically has a particular relationship with what is often called "common sense." Because of its subject matter, sociology and common sense are implicated in ways that have consequences for its standing and practice. It is precisely these relations that lead to it being relevant, insightful and, at times, contentious. The physical sciences, after all, do not appear to be concerned with spelling out their relationship to common sense. Whilst there are undoubtedly social components to the practices of the physical sciences − from the ways in which phenomena may be inferred, rather than observed by scientists, to what sort of science is funded and how the findings of science have implications for how we see ourselves and the world around us − there tends to be a separation of the immediate effects of the content of the knowledge from the social contexts in which it is produced. Boundaries thereby exist with a rich yet often disorganized, non-systematic, sometimes inarticulate and ineffable knowledge referred to as common sense.

Common sense appears to have nothing to say of the matters that preoccupy physicists or chemists. The subjects they deal with do not seem to fall within the daily experiences of people. Those without knowledge and skills do not normally consider themselves able to form opinions about such matters unless aided by the scientists who focus on the domain of the content of their research. After all, the objects explored by the physical sciences appear only under very special circumstances: for example, through observed effects in giant particle accelerators or the lenses of powerful microscopes. The scientists view or infer the phenomena, subject it to experimentation under certain conditions, and then justify their findings within a bounded community of inquirers. Being the owners of the experience, the process, analysis, and interpretations remain within their control. Results have to withstand the critical scrutiny of other scientists trained in the specialist area. Their resulting knowledge does not compete with common sense for the simple reason that there is no commonsensical point of view on their subject matter.

Is the characterization of this separation as simple as the above implies? The production of scientific knowledge contains social factors which inform and shape its practice, while scientific findings can have social, political, and economic implications which, in any democratic society, are not for scientists to determine. Scientific and contextual, or indigenous knowledge, interact with one other: for example, how long people accumulate knowledge to maintain habitats for human survival in relation to plants and animals, or the increasing availability of medical information to the general population with which to question the expertise of medical doctors. We cannot, in other words, easily separate the means of scientific research from the ends to which it may be put, nor practical or local knowledge from scientific knowledge itself. How research is funded and by whom may have a bearing upon the results of that research with these interests potentially distorting results. Public concerns over the quality of the food we eat, digital storage of our personnel usage of the Internet, the protection of the environments upon which we rely and live in, the role of genetic engineering, the patenting of genetic information are just a few of the matters that science alone cannot determine. These concern not just the bounded justifications for scientific knowledge within an expert group, but other forms of justification, as well as its application and consequences for our lives and futures. After all, we are talking about the control we have over our lives and the direction in which our societies are moving.

Such matters are the raw materials for sociological investigation. All of us live in the company of other people and interact with each other. In the process we display an extraordinary amount of *tacit knowledge* that enables us to get on with the business of everyday life. Each of us is a skilled actor. Yet what we obtain and who we are depend on others. After all, most of us have lived through the agonizing experience of a communication breakdown with partners, friends, and strangers and we experience varying degrees of social dislocation, ostracization, togetherness, and belonging. The subject matter of sociology is embedded in our everyday lives and without this fact we would be unable to conduct our lives in the company of others. Yet whilst deeply immersed in our routines, informed by a practical knowledge oriented to the social settings in which we interact, we may not systematically think about the meaning of what we have gone through or the reasons for its occurrence, nor compare our private experiences with the fate of others; with the exception, perhaps, of seeing private responses to public issues paraded for consumption on television and social media. Here, however, the privatization of social issues is often reinforced thereby relieving us of the burden of understanding the dynamics and consequences of social relations within what is seen as individual reactions, rather than more general cultural expressions.

Sociological thinking takes us into a relational understanding. It sees the individual, but situated within a social milieu. As a mode of investigation, it will then ask questions such as: "how do our individual biographies intertwine with the history we share with other human beings?" Or, "how do our cultures shape what we see and do?" Sociologists themselves are part of that experience and so however hard they may try to stand aside from the objects of their study – life experiences as objects "out there" – they cannot break off completely from the knowledge that they seek to comprehend. Equally, however, this can be an advantage to the extent that they possess both an inside and outside view of the experiences they seek to comprehend through the methods of research that they deploy: from the extensive through general comparisons within and between societies, to intensive experiences of immersion in social groups to understand their dynamics. The result is a rich and insightful body of studies into the human condition whose basis of comprehension, seen from within the frames of practical reason, ranges from the proximate to the distant.

When it comes to studies of the human condition, sociology needs to understand the meanings that are attributed to human actions, artifacts, and environments before they commence their investigations with questionnaires, interviews, visual materials, or observations. Families, organizations, kinship networks, neighborhoods, cities and villages, nations and churches, and any other groupings held together by regular human interaction have already been given meaning and significance by the actors involved. As a result, sociological phenomena are already endowed with meaning and so it is implicated in the realities that make up practical reason. With fluid borders between these forms of knowledge, their boundaries also move. As with the application of the genetic scientists' findings and their implications for social life, the sovereignty of sociology over social knowledge is one of reflection, reinforcement, and even contestation. Whilst this is not peculiar to sociology and is of relevance to the social and physical sciences in general, we can consider the relations between sociology and common sense in the following ways.

In the first place sociology subordinates itself to the rules of responsible communication according to its modes of justification: that is, accepted and institutionalized ways of constituting understanding and explanation based on evidence. This is an attribute of science among a common community of inquirers that distinguishes a discipline from other forms of knowledge and ways of justification. Sociologists are expected to take great care to distinguish between the statements corroborated by available evidence and those propositions whose status is of provisional, untested ideas. The rules of responsible speech require that the procedures which have led to the resulting insights be open to scrutiny. Further, that it should relate to other works on the topic and engage with those in a manner that is argued to advance its understanding. In this way, credibility and applicability will be significantly enhanced. Indeed, the legitimacy of science is based in our belief that its practitioners have followed the rules of responsible speech whilst those scientists, in turn, can refer to the validity and reliability of the knowledge they produce according to the rigor of the production process.

Second, there is the size of the field from which sociological thinking is drawn. For most of us, our terrain is our life-worlds: that is, the things we do, the people we meet, the pursuits we follow, and the times and places in which we normally interact. We also find ourselves confronted with the experiences and viewpoints of others mediated through, for example, the Internet, television, newspapers, books, and social media. To this extent, the horizons of our experiences are broadened. However, this can be selective and reliant upon particular viewpoints which can be nothing more than the amplification of existing life-worlds where differences can turn into objects of distrust and opprobrium, rather than understanding. Thus, despite the rich and various conditions and experiences in the world, each is a particular point of view which may be partial and even prejudiced. These issues can be examined only if we bring together and compare experiences drawn from a multitude of life-worlds: that is, a disciplined viewpoint on those points of view. Only then will the bounded realities of individual experiences be revealed, as will the complex network of dependencies and interconnections in which they are entangled – a network which reaches far beyond the realm that may be accessed from the point of view of a singular biography. It is for this reason that the sociologists' pursuit of this wider perspective makes a great difference – not only quantitatively, but also in the quality and the use of knowledge. Sociological knowledge has something important to offer that common sense, for all its richness and insight cannot, by itself, provide.

There is a third way in which these forms of knowledge differ: in the ways that each makes sense of human reality in terms of how they understand and explain events and circumstances. We know from our experiences that we are "the author" of our actions; we know that what we do is an effect of our intentions or feelings even though the outcomes may not be as we intended. We normally act to achieve a state of affairs whether, for example, in order to possess an object, to receive praise, or to prevent something we do not like or help a friend. Quite naturally, the way we think of our actions serves as a model for making sense of other actions. To this extent the only way we can make sense of the human world around us is to draw our tools of explanation solely from within our respective life-worlds. We tend to perceive everything that happens in the world at large as an outcome of somebody's intentional action. We look for the persons responsible for what has occurred and once we have found them, we believe our inquiries to be complete. We assume that goodwill lies behind those events to which we are favorably predisposed and ill intentions lie behind those we dislike. In general, people find it difficult to accept that a situation was not an effect of the intended actions of an identifiable person.

Those who speak in the name of reality within the public realm – politicians, journalists, market researchers, commercial advertisers – tune in to the above tendencies and speak of the "needs of the state" or the "demands of the economy." This is said as if the state or economies were made to the measure of individual persons with specific needs and wants. Similarly, we read and hear of the complex problems of nations, states, and economic systems as the effects of the thoughts and deeds of a select group of individuals who can be named, pictured, and interviewed. Equally, governments and their spokespersons often relieve themselves of responsibility by referring to those things outside of their control, or speaking of what "the public demands" through the use of focus groups or opinion polls.

Sociology stands in tension and sometimes opposition to the particularity of such views as if they can easily translate into believing they represent some general state of affairs. It does not take for granted ways of understanding as if they constituted some natural way of explaining events that may be simply separated from historical change, or the social location from which these utterances emerge. As it starts its survey from figurations (networks of dependencies) rather than from individual actors or single actions, it demonstrates that the common metaphor of the isolated, motivated individual as the key to understanding the human world – including our own, thoroughly personal and private, thoughts and deeds – is not an appropriate way to understand ourselves and others. To think sociologically is to seek to make sense of the human condition via an analysis of the manifold webs of human interdependency – those toughest of realities to which we refer in order to explain our motives and the effects of their activation.

We should also note that the power of common sense has a twofold character. Whilst it enables us to navigate our ways through our worlds, it thereby depends on the self-evident: that is, not to question its precepts and to be self-confirming in practice. It may easily, therefore, rest upon the routine, habitual character of daily life that informs our common sense and is simultaneously informed by it. We need this in order to get on with our lives. When repeated often enough, things tend to become familiar and the familiar becomes self-explanatory; it enables us to navigate our ways through the world, presents no problems and so may arouse little curiosity. Questions are not asked if people are satisfied that "things are as they are" for reasons that are not open to scrutiny and, should they be questioned, resistance to such intrusion may easily follow. Fatalism may also play its role via the belief that one can do little to change the conditions in which we act, thereby relieving us of the burden of change.

To this extent, familiarity, and inquisitiveness can be in tension. The familiar world has the power to confirm established beliefs leaving sociology viewed as an irritant whose credibility is then to be questioned. By examining the taken-for-granted and the basis in which the life-world is constituted and sustained, it has the potential to disturb comfortable certitudes whether it sees that world as a topic for its investigations or as a resource upon which to draw for its insights. With the daily ways of life and the social conditions in which they take place under examination, they emerge as one of the accomplished ways, but not necessarily *the* only way, of getting on in our lives and organizing relations between us. Here, however, routines and the ways in which we constitute understanding between us, have their place. After all, they enable us to do things without continuously reflecting upon our actions, which could easily lead to uncertainty. Here, we may recall Kipling's centipede, who walked effortlessly on all her hundred legs until a sycophantic courtier began to praise her exquisite memory. It was this memory that allowed her never to put down the eighty-fifth leg before the thirty-seventh, or the fifty-second before the nineteenth. Having been made self-conscious, the poor centipede was no longer able to walk. Equally, *defamiliarization* has benefits. It opens up new and previously unsuspected possibilities of living one's life with more self-awareness, understanding of others, and comprehension of our surroundings in terms of greater knowledge and, with that, perhaps more freedom and control.

To those seeking to live their lives in a more conscious way through an understanding of the environments, its effect upon ourselves, our actions, and how we live together and organize ourselves, thinking sociologically is a welcome guide. When addressing, illuminating, or challenging our shared knowledge, sociology prompts and encourages us to reassess our experience, to discover new possibilities, and to become in the end more open and less reconciled to the idea that learning about ourselves and each other has an end point, rather than being an exciting and dynamic process whose aim is to enhance an understanding of the human condition in the environments we inhabit. A distance from the realms of our particular experience cannot diminish the significance of sociological insight whose justifications cannot be based within the province of practical reason alone.

Thinking sociologically is a challenge whose process can render us more sensitive to and tolerant of difference and diversity. It sharpens our senses and opens our eyes to a relational horizon beyond our immediate experiences in order that we can explore and explain. Once we understand better how the apparently natural, inevitable, immutable, eternal aspects of our lives have been brought into being through the exercise of human power and resources, it becomes a power in its own right that opens up a world of possibilities. It widens the scope and practical effectiveness of our degrees of freedom and so has the potential to make us less subject to manipulation and even more resilient to times of oppression and control. As a mode of thinking it can enable us to become more effective social actors in seeing the connections between character, action, and context and how those things which, by their fixity, claim to be irresistible to change, are open to transformation.

There is also that which lies beyond us as individuals and requires us to stand back and enter into the realm of analysis. Whilst situated in networks of social relations, our work can take us into an extensive terrain of investigation that deals with movements and changes within societies as a whole through the generation and use of different forms of data. That is important, but not to the extent that matters of concern should then be dissipated in the exercise of dispassionate indifference. Sociology stands in praise of the individual, not individualism. To think sociologically means to understand more fully the values, hopes, desires, worries, and concerns of people. In this way, we may better recognize and respect different cultures and how people practice their lives according to particular values. To this extent it also has the potential to promote solidarity between us: that is, solidarity grounded in mutual understanding and respect and in a joint resistance to suffering and a shared condemnation of the cruelties that are its causes. Going back to what we were saying about the fluidity of that which appears inflexible, sociological insight into the inner logic and meaning of forms of life other than our own may well prompt us to think again about the boundaries that have been drawn between ourselves and others. We perhaps have more in common with each other than those forces which seek to separate us. Ultimately, if this is achieved, the cause of freedom will be greatly enhanced through being elevated to the rank of common cause.

To analyze and represent sociological findings can draw attention to the extent to which individual and collective freedoms are enabled and constrained. That has a destabilizing effect on existing power relations or what are called "social orders." Charges of "political disloyalty," or questions concerning its status as a discipline, are often made against sociology by corporations, governments, and power-holders of the prevailing social order. This is very evident among those who seek to view reality in their name, or claim that an existing state of affairs is somehow natural. When we witness reactions of this type, it is often what has been revealed which is the subject of contention and sociology the means through which it has been brought into the public realm. It is here where its implications can be debated and actions decided upon, but this may also reveal the extent to which only certain voices are then heard.

Sociology can be a powerful instrument in the hands of organizations and its ideas may be drawn upon not for the furtherance of freedom, but control. No discipline can prevent this happening, but it can bring attention to its presence and effects. There is no guarantee that thinking sociologically can dissolve and disempower the "tough realities" of life for that is to over-extend its practices into realms of deliberation and action that are rightly beyond its remit. Quite simply, the power of understanding may be no match for the forces of coercion or those who mobilize people through the rhetoric of blame of particular populations which provides apparently easy solutions to feelings of estrangement induced by prevailing political and economic conditions. Without that understanding, however, the collective management of shared life conditions would be diminished further. It is a way of thinking whose value is often cherished by those who cannot take it for granted and when it comes to those who can do so, it may easily be undervalued.

Thinking Sociologically: The Content

This book has been written with the aim of helping people to understand their experiences through and with others according to the above spirit. We seek to show how the apparently familiar can be interpreted in novel and different ways. Each chapter addresses issues that are part of our daily lives, or inform our lives, even if they may not be at the forefront of our everyday understandings. They concern ways of seeing and issues we routinely encounter, but may have little time or opportunity to reflect upon. Our aim is to prompt sociological thinking, not to "correct" knowledge. We seek to expand horizons of understanding, not to replace erroneous ideas of error with some unquestionable Truth. We hope to encourage a questioning attitude in which understanding others enables us better to understand ourselves *with* others in the world. To aid this process, we provide a section at the end of the book of studies which we have drawn upon to illuminate our journey, as well as those which will be helpful in continuing this path of sociological understanding.

The book is a sociological commentary on matters that directly inform our lives and experiences. It is divided into parts and chapters with that concern in mind. In this guide our narrative will not develop in a linear manner because there are some topics to which we shall return throughout the book. For instance, issues of social identity will appear in many different guises in the chapters, for this is how the effort of understanding works in practice. We will also consider care of the environment within which we live and how we are all dependent upon it for our futures and those who will come after us. After all, as we examine new topics, they will reveal new questions and so bring to light issues we had not previously considered. This, as we have said, is part of a process in which we gain better understandings – an exciting and rewarding task without end.

Part I

Action and Understanding in Everyday Life

1

Understanding Ourselves with and through Others

We can feel isolated, alone and seemingly unable to reach out. Yet we do not stand in simple isolation from one another. We can resent being constrained by circumstances over which we feel we have no control and also assert our freedom by refusing to conform to the expectations of others. We may express frustration at the absence of instantaneous entertainment on our mobile devices, or use time to read, digest, discuss, and reflect. We need the recognition of others, but if not forthcoming or offered in a manner expected, disappointment and resentment may result. Possessing conflicting feelings or exhibiting different actions depending on the circumstances is a common part of our experiences. The human condition appears to give rise to confusing states that lead to frustration, as well as imagination and creativity.

How our actions are seen, by us and others, are constituted in these relations. Actions, self, and social identities and understandings are intimately related. These factors are informed by prevailing ideas on what it is to be human. We are, for example, free to choose and act on those choices in order to reach our goals. You can get up now and make a cup of coffee, or get a glass of water, before continuing to read this chapter. You can also choose to abandon the project of thinking sociologically and embark upon another course of study, or abandon the idea of study altogether. For you to continue to read on is a choice among the alternative courses of action that are currently available to you. Your ability to make conscious decisions in this way is said to be an exercise of your freedom.

Freedom in Living with Others

We are surrounded by particular ideas of individuals and, from there, their actions, choices, and degrees of responsibility. Adverts of all types are targeted at aspirations linked to what one wants to be in the world linked to the possession of goods. Surrounded by these techniques of persuasion into which are poured enormous resources, can we say our choices are the product of conscious decisions that we formulate in a clear, rational manner, prior to the determination of any action? Many of our actions are *habitual* and not subject to deliberate and open choice. Despite that, we may be reminded that our decisions leave us

Thinking Sociologically, Third Edition. Zygmunt Bauman and Tim May.
© 2019 John Wiley & Sons Ltd. Published 2019 by John Wiley & Sons Ltd.

responsible for their consequences. You can hear it now: "No one forced you to do so, you have only yourself to blame!" If we break rules that are meant to guide people's conduct we may be punished and those punishments can range from informal to formal sanctions: for example, breaking the norms of a group may lead to us being ridiculed or temporarily excluded, to having our liberty removed through incarceration in prison due to law-breaking. The act of punishment is one confirmation that we are held responsible for our actions. Rules, in this sense, orientate not only our actions, but coordinate interactions with others enabling an anticipation of how we and they are likely to act. Without this orientation in place, communication and understanding in everyday life would seem inconceivable.

If we are the authors of our destinies we have the power to act in controlling our lives. We have both the ability to monitor our actions *and* the capability to determine their outcomes. Nevertheless, is this really how life works for most people? It might be claimed, for example, that being unemployed is entirely the fault of the individual concerned who, if they tried hard enough and acquired suitable knowledge and skills, could earn a living. People might retrain themselves and look for work, but the area in which they live has high unemployment and they cannot afford to move, or have relatives and friends for whom they care and so, despite actively seeking employment, there is none on offer or they have limited mobility due to dependents. There are many circumstances in which our freedom to act is limited by circumstances over which we have little or no control. It is one thing to have the ability to change or modify our skills and quite another to possess the capability to reach our goals. Let us consider this in more detail.

Take conditions of scarcity. These, as well as how we are judged by others, limit our capabilities. People might seek the same goals, but not all reach them because access to what they seek is limited. In this case we might compete with each other and the outcome may be only partially dependent on our efforts. We might seek a college place, only to find out that there are 20 candidates for every place available and that most of them have the qualifications required. In addition, the college may tend to favor candidates from certain social backgrounds and those with connections to those who have attended before. Our actions are dependent upon the judgments of others over whom we may exercise limited control, but also related to our social networks and how those enable and constrain our aspirations. Others set the rules of the game and act as the referees. They are *positioned* by their institutions to exercise discretion and, in so doing, draw a boundary around the freedoms of others. Factors such as these heavily influence the outcome of our efforts. In this case we become dependent on others because they evaluate whether our efforts are good enough and consider whether we exhibit the right characteristics and background to justify our admission.

Material factors inform our capability to reach our goals. Whilst self-determination is important, what if we lack the means? We might be able to move to seek work in places where more jobs are available, only to discover that the cost of houses or of rents is far beyond our means. Similarly, we might wish to escape overcrowded and polluted conditions in order to move to a healthier location. However, we find those with more money have already done so and therefore it is not affordable, or they have created enclosures or live in high-rise buildings to secure environments separate from their surroundings. In the process house prices increase, rents go up, and the job does not pay enough to obtain somewhere to live. We can say the same thing about education and health. Some areas have better equipped schools and hospitals, yet are too far away, whilst our society does not have a public, universal health-care system and private health insurance is beyond our income. Thus, freedom of choice does not guarantee freedom to act on those choices, nor does it secure the freedom to attain our desired ends. To be able to act freely, we need more than an idea of *free will*.

Most commonly we think of being limited by the amount of money at our disposal, but we have also mentioned symbolic resources. In this case our freedom may not depend on what we do, but on who we are in terms of how others view and value us. We have used the example of a college, but we may also be refused entry to a club, or employment, because of the manner in which our qualities are judged: for example, on the grounds of class, race, sexual orientation, age, ethnicity, or disability. Alternatively, access to the club may depend on past achievements – acquired skills, qualifications, length of service, the people who we know and will sponsor us, or the manner in which we have been brought up to speak and address people. These are the lasting consequences of past choices which, when they become sedimented in more durable social structures over time, have an effect on individual actions. Freedom to act in the present is thus informed by past circumstances, accumulated experiences, and the value accorded to those by others.

How we are positioned in these ways interacts with how we feel about and act in the social situations into which we enter. Let us return to our college example. We may find that a mode of speaking and particular accent is expected during the interview, but it is one with which we are unfamiliar. Coming from a working-class background, we may feel uneasy among middle-class students, or our sexual orientation is not judged to be "normal" and so we experience a sense of isolation and an absence of others seeing our choices as valid. Perhaps, being a Catholic who follows orthodoxy, we cannot accept divorce and abortion as the choices that others have a right to make.

Here we come to a possibility: those groups with whom we feel most at ease may actually limit our freedom by restricting the range of opinions we can hold. Informal and formal groups are often constituted by the expectations that they place upon their members and in so doing exclude those who are presumed not to live up to those requirements or ways of life. When these gaps in understanding occur between groups, they are frequently filled by stereotypical assumptions which are prejudicial and inaccurate, but enable a separation between "us" and "them." The very fact that we may be adjusted to the conditions of action inside our group circumscribes our freedom by preventing us from engaging with experiences beyond the confines of that group. Having been trained in the ways of our groups, we practice a freedom whose price is to limit engagement with other ideas and practices.

We are both enabled and constrained in the everyday practices of freedom. At one level we are taught that there are types of desires that are acceptable and achievable within a group. Appropriate ways to act, talk, dress, and conduct ourselves provide an orientation to get us through life within the groups to which we belong. We judge ourselves according to those expectations and our self-esteem is directly informed in these ways. Groups enable boundaries that orientate us through common interests and/or by proximity and these advantages may become problems as we traverse from one group to another and find ourselves in environments where different ways of being and forms of evaluation are promoted. Alternative ways of conducting ourselves may be seen as appropriate and the connections between other people's conduct and their intentions are not familiar to us and appear alien. The French sociologist Pierre Bourdieu referred to this gap as the "Don Quixote" effect: that is, between our dispositions and the social contexts in which we find ourselves.

One way in which we can gain a sense of the appropriateness of conduct is through our physical presence with others and hearing what they say and seeing how they act. However, if one is exposed to the reactions of online communities, there may be no way to see the actions of others over time and their utterances may be anonymous. As a result, their actions are not constrained by the consequences of being judged by those who are in physical proximity. As we move from one setting to another, whether in virtual or real space, the background understanding that allowed us to navigate and belong in one group can appear as a limitation. Where a disjuncture occurs between our expectations, experiences, and actions, it may be because of the unintended consequences of intentional actions. In other words, despite intentionally seeking one outcome, another arises because circumstances unfolded in a way we did not anticipate, or there were factors we did not know about and over which we had no control.

When it comes to the factors that inform our dispositions, or ways of being in the world, the reference groups to which we belong are not ones we have opted for out of free choice. Quite simply, we can be members of a group because we are born into it. The group that defines us and orients our actions may not be one that we have consciously chosen. When we first joined it or were seen by others to be a part of it, it was not an act of freedom, but a manifestation of dependence. We do not decide to be French, Caribbean, white, or working or middle class. Such apparent fate can be accepted with equanimity or resignation, or it can be transformed into our destiny through an enthusiastic embrace with the identity of the group and what it stands for – being proud of what we are and the expectations placed upon us as a result. If we want to transform ourselves, however, it will require a great deal of effort against the taken-for-granted expectations of those who surround us. Self-sacrifice, determination, and endurance will take the place of conformity to the values and norms of the group. The contrast is one between swimming with the tide, or against the current. This is how, despite not always being conscious of it, we are dependent upon others: even though we may swim against the current, we still do so in a direction that is oriented or informed by the expectations or actions of those who lie both inside and outside of the familiar group. How we act and see ourselves is informed by the expectations of the groups to which we belong. This is manifested in several ways.

First, there are the *ends* or goals that we assign with particular significance and so consider worth pursuing. These vary according to such factors as class, ethnicity, age, and gender. The work of caring for others is often, but not exclusively, provided by women and so there is a clear tendency to gravitate to particular occupations in which caring for others is rewarded: for example, teaching, nursing, and social work. This is based on assumptions about divisions of labor in terms of the types of characteristics that men and women are expected to exhibit. These are tendencies, not simple determinations, which have cultural variations. Yet they are ones that circumscribe not only what is seen to be acceptable, but the recognition and rewards offered to different occupations and to those within them.

Second, how we are expected to achieve these ends is influenced by another manifestation of group expectations: the accepted *means* employed in the pursuit of ends. We are concerned here with the forms of conduct that are taken to be appropriate in everyday life. How we dress, use our bodies, our forms of talk, display our enthusiasm and even how we eat, are just part of the ways in which groups inform our conduct in the pursuit of ends. What are acceptable and unacceptable means for the attainment of ends may saturate individual concerns with the consequences of actions in situations where people wish to belong or fear the consequences of acting against the prevailing order. Indeed, persons deploying unacceptable means may not be positively sanctioned, but ignored as long as they are succeeding in the attainment of ends. These forms of justification can normalize actions and were certainly believed to be apparent in the culture of the banking sector that led to the global financial crisis of 2007–2008.

Third, groups also seek to identify themselves through acts that distinguish them from those outside of their formal and informal networks of relations. The resulting phenomenon is called the *criteria of relevance*. Here we are taught to distinguish between those objects or people who are relevant and irrelevant to the life-projects we embark upon. Inscriptions on objects may have different meanings between groups depending upon how those objects are accorded significance and relevance in a culture. Identifying allies, enemies, rivals, what to wear, who to listen to and who to disregard is part of this process. Thus, we owe the ends which we pursue, the means employed in their pursuit, and how to distinguish between those who may and may not assist us in the process to the groups to which we belong.

Sociological Lenses: Viewing Ourselves with Others

An enormous amount of practical knowledge is gained through our belonging to groups without which we would be unable to conduct our daily activities and orient ourselves and impute significance and value to our actions. In most cases this knowledge is "tacit": that is, knowledge that orients our conduct by establishing meaning and connections between things, persons, and places without us being able to express it, or how and why it operates in particular ways. If asked, for example, the form of codes we use to communicate with others, how we decipher the actions of others and attribute meaning to objects, we may not even understand the question. How do we explain the rules of speech that enable communication, when we necessarily take them for granted in our communicative competency? Yet that knowledge is required to perform our tasks and practical skills. A branch of sociology – ethnomethodology – is concerned with studying the minutiae of everyday interactions and provides for fascinating insights into those things that we take for granted: for example, taking turns in conversations, how we begin and end sentences and attribute characteristics to people on the basis of their mode of dress and bodily deportment in everyday, routine gestures.

We may begin sociological understanding of the relations between the individual and society with the background knowledge that informs practical reasoning and actions. The resulting studies become those areas of social life where we might feel secure in our actions and which inform the reproduction of the social order whose routines we rely upon for navigating our way through the world. That very reproduction can rely upon our forgetting, or simply taking for granted, the origins of the ways that can exert a powerful grip upon us. It comes in the form of a *natural attitude* that micro-sociologists turn into the objects of their investigation. Resulting studies on social knowledge and everyday life enable us to know more about our interactions with each other and the bases of our understandings in time and place.

One of the central figures who provided much insight into the formation of our self and social identities was George Herbert Mead. Who we are, our "selves," is not an attribute that we are born with, but one acquired over time through interaction with others. In order to understand how this occurs, our sense of self can be seen in two parts: the "I" and the "Me." Mead held that our minds seek an "adjustive relationship" with the world in which we find ourselves. However, that does not mean we simply reflect the expectations of groups because we have a reflexive capacity to act on the world and learn in new social contexts. For this purpose we come to know ourselves through others via symbolic communication. Language is the medium through which we speak, but also how we hear ourselves and evaluate our actions and utterances according to the responses of others. Communication is a generator of our subjectivity – it does not simply describe a world that is external to us, but constitutes the meaning and understanding of that world. The "I" is an "internal" conversation where language acts as a medium that enables us to conceive of ourselves as a "whole." The "Me," on the other hand, is the organization of the expectations of others within our actions. We respond to others in terms of how we see ourselves and that is constantly modified according to the different social settings we inhabit and act within.

The above takes place in three stages of development. First, there is a *preparatory stage*. Here our sense of self is passive in that it is made up of the actions and utterances which others display towards us. Awareness is built up and we respond to others with the symbols of the group, enabling us to define our conduct in terms that are appropriate to the setting. In this way, a growing awareness of ourselves is derived via the responses of others. At this stage we cannot experience ourselves directly, only through others, but this commences the process of being able to judge our performances in our interaction with others.

We then, as children, enter the *play stage* by acting out different "others" in roles. However, these are not connected and lack an overall organization. We should also note that some children may be placed in contexts where "play" itself is not possible or even seen as desirable. Learning language and attaching feelings to particular roles are central at this stage and so responses to performance are important for understanding what is seen as "appropriate" play. Through a third, *game stage*, the organization of the attitudes of the group begins to be consolidated. Roles are learnt along with their relations to one another. Although a variety of "parts" are played, the rules that govern the game become more apparent. Our reflexive character is then built up by treating ourselves as objects of our own actions as they are understood through the responses of others to our utterances and actions.

The formation of the social self is not a passive process. Activity and initiative mark both sides of the interaction. After all, one of the first skills that a child learns is to discriminate and select, which cannot be acquired unless supported by the ability to resist and withstand pressure; in other words, to take a stand and act against external forces. Because of the contradictory signals from various significant others, the "I" must stand aside, at a distance, looking at the external pressures *internalized* in the "Me." The stronger the "I," the more autonomous becomes the character of the child. The strength of the "I" expresses itself in the person's ability and readiness to put the social pressures internalized in the "Me" to the test, checking their true powers and their limits and so challenging them and bearing the consequences. In the course of this acquisition, we ask questions of ourselves and the first reflexive question of selfhood is, as the French philosopher Paul Ricoeur put it, "Who am I?" Here we experience the contradiction between freedom and dependence as an inner conflict between what we desire and what we feel obliged to do because of the presence of significant others and the expectations placed upon us. Images and meanings of acceptable behavior become part of our "internal" conversations as we reflexively consider our "being" and "doing."

At this point we meet the interactions between the biological and the social. A great deal of money is being spent on trying to determine the genetic bases of different aspects of human behavior and neuroscience can easily lapse into seeking the basis of the social in the structure and function of the brain. Interpretations among those influenced, for example, by Darwin's theory of evolution differ on whether we are competitive or cooperative by nature. Equally, we know that actions and how they are evaluated differ between cultures. As the geneticist Steve Jones put it, the most problematic word in genetics is "for" – as if finding a gene meant that it then stood *for* a particular form of behavior. Whilst vast sums of money are being poured into genetic research that produce potential gains in the treatment of diseases, the control of that knowledge and for what reasons remains a vital issue for us all.

When it comes to explanations for society according to biological drives or instinct, Sigmund Freud, the founder of psychoanalysis, suggested that the whole process of self-development and the social organization of human groups may be interpreted in the light of the need and the practical effort to contain sexual and aggressive instincts. Freud suggested that these instincts are never tamed, but "repressed" and driven into our subconscious. Thus, they are kept in limbo by the "superego" as the internalization of the perceived demands and pressures of the group. It is for this reason that Freud described the superego as a "garrison left in a conquered city." The ego itself is then suspended between two powers: the instincts that have been driven into the subconscious yet remain potent and rebellious and the superego which presses the ego to keep the drives subconscious to prevent their escape from confinement.

Nancy Chodorow, the American feminist sociologist and psychoanalyst, modified such insights utilizing object relations theory. Examining gendered differences in emotional attachment, she argues that a son exhibits a "primary love" for his mother, but that desire is then repressed. As a result, he moves out of the relationship into a realm in which a tie with the mother is severed and that love then repressed. The son becomes the "other" and his autonomy is achieved via a repression of desire. A daughter, on the other hand, tends to experience more of an alignment resulting in her sense of self being formed not through a process of distinction from her mother, but a relational attachment. A gendered emphasis upon empathy and less of a concern among women to differentiate themselves from the world of which they are a part is characterized by the American psychologist, Carole Gilligan, as an "ethic of care."

Other sociologists have followed up Freud's hypotheses. Norbert Elias, who fused these insights with comprehensive historical research, suggested that the experience of the self we possess arises from a double pressure to which we are all exposed. Our attitude towards our selves is the result of the ambivalent position in which the pressures of instinct and conformity act in opposite directions. The fact that all societies inform the predispositions of their members is beyond question. There is, however, no conclusive evidence that human beings are naturally aggressive and so must be tamed by overt control. What tends to be interpreted as outbursts of natural aggression is more often than not an outcome of callousness or hatred. To deploy Ernesto Laclau's terminology, we can see these as born of situations in which the logics of equivalence (we share broad similarities) and difference (our group affiliations emphasize differences) tilt to extreme points of view: we are identical and we are fundamentally different. Both of these are traceable to their social, rather than genetic, origin. Thus, whilst groups undoubtedly inform the conduct of their members, it does not follow that they make such conduct more humane and moral. It means only that the conduct better conforms to the patterns recognized as acceptable within a group.

If we take the struggle between autonomy and conformity into the realm of what is termed the "imaginary" – the meanings that inform particular social structures – psychoanalysis can be deployed in the service of heightened self-criticism as a condition for our autonomy to emerge in situations where consciousness ("ego") increasingly takes the place of instinctual drives ("Id"). Cornelius Castoriadis examined imaginary institutions of society in this way. However, he was not suggesting these were fictions; on the contrary, they are rationalizations for the ways in which societies work. These forms of significations enable the reproduction of society and inform the psyche of their individuals, but there is never complete formation between individual socialization and society. To understand this further, let us turn to the process of socialization.

Socialization, Significance, and Action

How our selves are formed and how instincts may or may not be suppressed is often given the name *socialization*. We are socialized to become capable of living in society through the internalization of norms and values from society in general and significant others in particular. Who are those significant people with whom we interact and who socialize us in this way? We have seen that the force that operates in the development of the self is the child's image of the intentions and expectations of significant others. A freedom to select from these expectations is not complete, for some may force their views into the child's perception more effectively than others within their worlds, but there is no avoidance of choice, even if the demands themselves are contradictory. After all, some of them must be paid more attention than others and so assigned greater significance in our lives.

The need to assign differential significance to the expectations of others is not restricted to children. We experience this as a matter of routine in our daily lives from families, friends, and work colleagues. We risk the displeasure of some in order to placate others. Whenever we express political views, there will be those who care about what we say and listen and others who say that issues of politics, religion, or money, for example, should not be subject for discussion. Assigning significance whether through our utterances or actions means, unavoidably, assigning less importance and even irrelevance to other views. The risks of this process grow to the degree that the environments we inhabit are heterogeneous, that is, characterized by different views, values, and interests, or homogenous, where expectations of conformity via an unquestioning individual allegiance are strictly enforced through group surveillance and pressure.

Here, *reference groups* play a significant role in our lives. This is a group, expressed through common interests, values, and activities that enables us to assign significance to our actions and provides the standards by which we judge ourselves. How we dress, talk, feel, and act in different circumstances are informed in these ways. The Canadian-born American sociologist, Erving Goffman, a wonderful observer of everyday life whose books provide a fascinating insight into our actions, wrote of the importance of "face work." Face is defined as the value that a person attaches to their action in terms of the attributes they display. In turn, those they seek to identify themselves with value those attributes. A good professional performance is one instance in which a person's self-esteem and standing among their group may be enhanced by what Axel Honneth has characterized as our "struggle for recognition."

As we have said in respect to communication, what we intend and what actually occurs may not be aligned and this leads to frustration and misunderstanding. Groups may be unaware of our efforts to imitate their modes of conduct and even mock those who attempt to do so. Some of the groups are normative reference groups in that they set the norms for our conduct without being present at each and every interaction, or are not in physical presence, as in the case, for example, of online communities. Particularly prominent among these are family, friends, teachers, and employers and managers at work. Yet even when these people are in a position to respond to our actions, it does not follow that they become reference groups. They do so only when we assign them with significance. Disobedience at work may occur when we disregard the normative pressures placed upon us by our managers and choose to follow other standards. We might also "play it cool" when the group is actually calling for a strength of involvement and passion.

A further influence beyond the immediate contexts of our actions is comparative reference groups. These are groups to which we do not belong, because either we are beyond their reach or they are beyond our reach. We "see" the group without being seen by them, and closely follow their activities. Assigning significance in this case is one-sided. Because of the distance between us and them, they are incapable of evaluating our actions and so can neither correct deviations nor lavish praise upon us. In recent times we have increasingly moved towards situations in which we gain increasing amounts of knowledge through description rather than acquaintance with others through various forms of media. Groups seeking influence spend a great deal of time and resources and deploy a variety of means to influence our frames of reference, spending patterns, and beliefs. As a result, the role of these forces in shaping our sense of self becomes more pronounced.

Summary

Socialization never ends. It brings with it changing and complex forms of interaction between ideas of freedom and dependence. We move across spaces and places and bring with us our histories: for example, those brought up in small rural communities may find themselves lost in a strange city in which the indifference of strangers leads to feelings of helplessness; all of which is exacerbated by the volumes of traffic, rushing crowds, and forms of architecture. Equally, there are those at home in the city whose anonymity may provide for ease of movement across cultures as a source of their cosmopolitan identities. Our feelings of risk and trust then mix in differing degrees. There are also those situations over which we may have no control. Sudden economic depression, the onset of mass unemployment, floods, famine, and the outbreak of war, are just some examples. These changes have the potential to place in doubt our patterns of socialization and require a radical restructuring of what we have taken for granted.

In the absence of such major upheavals, each of us confronts problems on a daily basis that call for reflexive examination and perhaps question our modes of being or expectations: changing schools or jobs, entering and graduating from university, starting a new relationship, acquiring a place to live, becoming parents, and experiencing the death of those close to us. Relations between experiences of freedom and dependence do not then reach a final destination, but are part of processes of change, learning, resistance, and negotiation that start at birth and end only with death. Our freedom is never complete, but a struggle in which we are routinely engaged and which defines us. Present actions are informed by past actions and each has an embryonic sense of the future in our performance.

Freedom for some may be bought at the cost of greater dependence for others. We have spoken of the role that material and symbolic resources play in making choices viable, realistic propositions and that not all people enjoy access to these in order to realize their ends. While people are free and bound to take responsibility for what they do, some have more degrees of freedom than others. A consequence of this can be to restrict the horizon of opportunity for others. We can say that the ratio between freedom and dependence is an indicator of the relative position a person, or a whole category of persons, occupies in a society. What we call privilege appears, under closer scrutiny, to be a higher degree of freedom and a lesser degree of dependence. Societies and groups then seek orders of justification that legitimize these outcomes. How we see others in these processes is the subject of the next chapter.

2

Sustaining Our Lives

We have discussed issues of social identity and group belonging and how these relate to the conception we have of ourselves in interaction with others. How groups influence our conduct, how we interact with others, and what groups we belong to and are excluded from as a result, are part of everyday life. The outcomes of this process, whether intended or not, contribute to the social relations that characterize our societies. We continue our journey of understanding in this chapter by considering these issues in more detail and examining the consequences that these processes have for social relations.

Interaction, Understanding, and Social Distance

What of all those people whose actions inform our everyday lives? Who puts the coffee in the cup? Who provides the power, water, and food upon which we rely? Who are the people who make decisions about how, where, and when to move what is estimated to be the $650 trillion to $1.2 quadrillion invested in global derivatives markets? Who decides to deploy technology, using advances in robotics, for the purpose of manufacturing and in the places where we buy our food and obtain our goods? Who puts the additives in our foods, for what reasons, and is it what we want and good for our health or for profit? These people are part of an unknown multitude that affects our ability to sustain ourselves, obtain employment, and lead healthy and fulfilling lives. There are also those who, in a preoccupation with their own ends, produce foul air, over-consume finite resources, and create waste with consequences for our health, environments, and wildlife in general.

Compare these people with those who you have met, recognize, and can name. Now consider that among those who influence how you conduct your life and the choices you can and cannot make, the people you actually know are a small proportion of the population as a whole. Indeed, how those people appear to us may be different from the roles they perform in other parts of their lives. When we get to know people well we talk to each other, share understanding and discuss matters of common interest. Others may be casual acquaintances, or those we meet on just one occasion. We also meet in the places that Erving Goffman calls the

Thinking Sociologically, Third Edition. Zygmunt Bauman and Tim May.
© 2019 John Wiley & Sons Ltd. Published 2019 by John Wiley & Sons Ltd.

"interaction order": that is, those "spaces" that are not "personal" as such, but the regions and social situations in which we interact with others. The content of the interactions within these places may be functional: for example, when obtaining money from a bank, visiting a doctor, or buying food from a shop. Relations are driven by our purpose and we are often not interested in the people we meet except in terms of their ability to perform those functions. Intimate inquiries are out of place in such circumstances and often regarded as an unwarranted intrusion into what we see as our privacy. Should an intrusion occur, we might resist it as a breach of the unwritten expectations of the relationship – a relationship that is, after all, concerned with an exchange of services. Of course, those relations may change over time to become more expressive as we build up understanding and familiarity leading to those places taking on a different meaning.

Proximity informs interactions and, despite the global age, these include those defined as economic which are bound up in social relations. Taking measures of economic output or number of interactions utilizing digital analytics in online research tells us about the numerated self that enables selective advertising, access to networks, and frequency of use. However, it does not tell us about the experiential self in terms of quality among participants. Some will claim that their "net friends" – those with whom they communicate over the internet – are just as much their friends as those whom they have physically met. From an individual point of view, Alfred Schutz suggested that all other members of the human race may be plotted against an imaginary line: a continuum measured by social distance which grows as social intercourse shrinks in volume and intensity. That line ranges from personalized knowledge to knowledge limited to an ability to assign people to particular types: the rich, football hooligans, soldiers, bureaucrats, terrorists, politicians, journalists, and others. The more distant such persons become, the more stereotypical may be our awareness and reactions to them.

Aside from contemporaries there are those who fall within our mental maps as predecessors and successors. Our communications with them may be one-sided and incomplete, but can assist in seeking to solve tensions in current identities. We can see this in acts of recollection. Here, ceremonies seek to preserve historical memory and even adherence to particular interpretations of past acts in order that they may be reproduced in present generations. With successors it is different, for we provide imprints of our existence but do not expect them to answer back. We might project imaginary futures into present actions as in the case of sustainability being based on meeting present needs, but without compromising the needs of future generations. Whilst we cannot know such things in advance, it is not unknown for modern-day scientists to be motivated by the genre of science fiction and for technological advances to be financed by the imaginative possibilities they hold for certain visions of the future. Those who manage organizations "re-engineer" them through the projection of an efficient, economic, and effective future that is constituted in contrast to an existing reality whose process invokes the power of a mechanical metaphor as if it had a machine-like quality, with each of its members being components in an engine.

These present–future practices have the possibility of relieving their authors of responsibility because the effects of their decisions are contained within some imaginary future. Equally, the sustainability example is about living according to a contemporary ethic for the preservation of future generations. Whether talking about the influence of the past or imagining possible futures in the present, they are not fixed over time. People change locations, move from one category to another, travel towards and away from a point on the continuum, and shift from being contemporaries to predecessors. In the process the capacity for empathy – an ability and willingness to put oneself in another person's position – changes. Our self-identity is bound up with the social identities that we portray to others, those we encounter in our everyday existence, the places in which we interact, and the dynamics between past–present–future relations.

"Us" within the "Other"

Our ability to make distinctions and divisions within the world includes those between "us" and "them." One stands for the groups to which we feel we belong and understand. The other stands for a group that we cannot access, do not believe we understand, nor wish to belong to. Our vision of this is often but not always vague, fragmentary and, due to poor comprehension, strange and even frightening. We may be reinforced in our beliefs and feelings by suspecting that "they" have the same reservations and anxieties about "us." The result is a gap in understanding whose consequences can range from curiosity, bemusement, and envy to prejudice and hostility.

The distinctions between "us" and "them" are sometimes presented as one between an in-group and out-group. These opposites are inseparable, for there cannot be one without the other. They sediment our map of the world on two poles of what can be an antagonistic relationship. Such fixities in assumptions render the groups "real" to their respective members and provides for the inner unity and coherence they are taken to possess. As our identities are bound up with the groups to which we belong, some scholars, notably Michel Foucault and Jacques Derrida, have argued that we only possess an "essence" to whom we are because we exclude any negative elements that make up our identities: in this case, the assumed characteristics of "them." Self-identification is enabled by the resources that we draw from our environment and there is no fixed "core" to our identities. Oppositions become tools that we draw upon to chart and navigate the world. Examples include the distinctions made between the "deserving" and "undeserving" poor, "respectable" citizens and the "rabble" who defy rules and are characterized as disliking all forms of order. Our respective characteristics and investment of emotion may easily derive from a mutual antagonism.

From these observations we can draw out the following: an out-group is precisely that imaginary opposition to itself that the in-group needs for its self-identity, for its cohesiveness, for its inner solidarity and emotional security. A readiness to cooperate within the confines of the group thereby requires, as its prop, a refusal to cooperate or join with an adversary. It is as if we needed the fear of a wilderness in order to feel the security of order. The ideals that sustain this include solidarity, mutual confidence and what might be termed, following Émile Durkheim, a "togetherness" or "common bond." It is how one would expect the members of an ideal family to behave towards each other and parents towards their children in terms of their patterns of love and care.

If we listen to the rhetoric of those who wish to evoke a mutual loyalty in their audience, we often hear the metaphors of "sisterhood," "brotherhood," "nationhood," and all being in one "family." Expressions of national solidarity and a readiness to sacrifice oneself for a greater good are peppered with references to a nation as "our mother" or "the fatherland" and often accompanied by a common enemy who have taken away something from a past of triumph and certainty. Nostalgia mixes with protection and the invocation of a collective identity for those who share the same beliefs. The imaginary rules of in-group life make us perceive relationships in this context as emotionally safe, suffused with mutual sympathy and the potential to inspire loyalty, as well as a determination to defend interests against those who would undermine them. The feeling of community becomes paramount and exists as a pleasant place that precedes dialogue and reflection. In this place times may be difficult, but one can always find a solution in the end. People can seem harsh and sometimes selfish, but one can count on their help if the need arises through the invocation of common interest. Above all, one can understand and be more confident of being understood.

We do not necessarily have to be in the physical presence of those people with whom we identify in order to evoke these feelings and engage in activities and beliefs that link us to them. There are face-to-face groups and online communities, as well as those which are large and widespread to which we can relate. Class, gender, and nation are typical examples of this second category of in-group. Though we often consider them as if they were like the small, intimate groups we are familiar with, they are imaginary communities. Although often characterized by similar language and customs, they are also divided in their beliefs and practices. These cracks are thinly plastered over by a "we" image that appeals to a sense of unity. Indeed, the speeches of nationalist leaders so often refer to either the burying or eradication of differences in a spirit of commonality that is oriented towards a collectively held ideal and goal.

There is work to do in making classes, genders, ethnicities, sexualities, and nations' in-groups by themselves because they lack the social cement of groups that are familiar to us in everyday interactions. One consequence of this process may be to suppress or dismiss evidence that runs counter to their ideal image as being false or irrelevant. A process of purification demands a disciplined and resourceful body of activists whose practices add plausibility to a unity of interests and beliefs. Indeed, those technicians of desire who seek influence, power, and control can mobilize strong reactions among people with disastrous consequences for those who are the victims of their prejudice. Despite the work that goes into this process, the hold on reality remains fragile. Why? Because it lacks the substance that can derive from networks' daily interaction and so no effort to induce loyalty in large groups stands a chance of success if there is not an accompanying practice of hostility towards an out-group, or those within who are targeted as having transgressed the codes, norms, and values of the group.

For those groups who actively seek to protect their boundaries against the threat of those who do not hold their beliefs, vigilance becomes a necessity. Prejudice – as the refusal to recognize any virtue that outsiders may possess, along with an inclination to magnify their vices to add to processes of internal coherence and solidarity – prevents one from accepting the possibility that their intentions may be honest. Prejudice also manifests itself in double moral stand-ards. What the members of an in-group believe they deserve as an entitlement will be an act of grace and benevolence if granted to members of an out-group. One's own atrocity against out-group members may not seem to clash with moral conscience, whilst severe condemnation can be demanded in cases where much milder acts have been perpetrated by outsiders. Prejudice prompts people to approve of the means used in the promotion of their own cause, often accompa-nied by denigration of the "other"; means that would not be similarily justified if employed by the out-group in pursuit of their own purposes.

Prejudicial dispositions are not uniformly distributed. They can manifest themselves in, for example, racist attitudes and actions or, more generally, in xenophobia as the hatred of everything "foreign." People who entertain high lev-els of prejudice and demand an authority that is beyond any question are ill pre-pared to endure deviations from strict rules and are likely to endorse coercive means to keep people "in line." Theodor Adorno characterized such people as having "authoritarian personalities." These reactions are closely related to expres-sions of insecurity generated by drastic changes in habitual conditions. What people have learned as effective ways to go about their daily lives suddenly becomes less reliable in what Ulrich Beck termed "risk society." The result can induce feelings of losing control of the situation accompanied by resentment and resistance.

The result of these transformations may be the need to defend, or return to, "the old ways." Targets become the newcomers who represent new ways of being, or those that do not believe in the old ways and so cannot belong to a journey that seeks the unity embodied in nostalgic calls. Pierre Bourdieu wrote of this process within what he called "fields" of social relations in terms of people pursu-ing strategies of "orthodoxy" or "heresy" depending on the fit between their dis-positions and social context. The stakes for those involved then become the conservation or subversion of established relations. An influx of "outsiders" pre-sents a challenge to the way of life of the "established," to deploy Norbert Elias's terms, whatever the objective difference between the newcomers and the old inhabitants. Tensions arise out of the necessity to make space and recognize the newcomers. Anxieties can become hostile feelings with the established inhabit-ants tending to possess better resources to act upon their prejudices. They can also invoke the rights they have acquired by their sheer length of habitation as encapsulated in such phrases as "this is the land of our forebears."

Taking a historical view of tolerance captures this two-sided character in terms of those who have the power to tolerate others and how and why? Is it that there must be an "other" who is to be tolerated by "us," but not accorded the same rights, or are there good reasons to accept such tolerance due to a recognition of the limits of the world views that "us" have about "them"? The consequences of these two views are very different. The former depends on the exercise of good will and can lead to second-class citizenship, whilst the latter assigns the same rights to an out-group with the result that they have equal status. We can see these differences historically in, for example, the Huguenots in France being granted rights under the Edicts of Nantes in a largely Catholic country. Rainer Forst's studies on tolerance and justification show how they were second-class citizens who had to practice their religion in specific places and could only hold certain offices and attend particular schools and universities.

Such changes need to be understood in their socioeconomic context. The birth of modern anti-Semitism in nineteenth-century Europe and its wide reception can be understood as the result of a coincidence of factors: that is, between the high speed of change in a rapidly industrializing society and the emancipation of the Jews, who emerged from the ghettos or separate Jewish quarters and closed communities to mix with the Gentile population of the cities and enter "ordinary" occupations. Changes in the industrial landscape of postwar Britain generated widespread anxiety which was subsequently focused on the newcomers from the Caribbean countries or Pakistan, whilst male resistance to women's claims of equal rights in employment remains a feature of the political landscape.

Gregory Bateson suggested the term "schismogenesis" for the chain of actions and reactions that follows these processes. Each action calls for a stronger reaction and control over the situation is gradually lost. He distinguishes between two types of schismogenesis. First, "symmetrical schismogenesis," in which each side reacts to the signs of strength in the adversary provoking a stronger reaction. Think, for example, of the slogans "deterrence must be credible" or "the aggressor must be shown that aggression does not pay." Second is "complementary schismogenesis," that develops from opposite assumptions, but leads to identical results. The schismogenetic sequence of actions is complementary when one side strengthens its resolve at the sign of weakness in the other side, while the other side weakens its resistance when confronted with manifestations of growing strength in the opposite side. Typically, this is the tendency for any interaction between a dominant and a more submissive partner. The self-assurance and self-confidence of one party can feed on symptoms of timidity and submissiveness in the other.

We can think of a gang terrorizing an entire neighborhood into submission and then, convinced of its omnipotence via an absence of resistance, raises demands beyond the capacity of its victims to pay. Victims are driven to desperation, their rebellion ignited, or they are forced to move away. On the other extreme, one can think of the patron–client relationship. The dominant majority (national, racial, cultural, and religious) may accept the presence of a minority on condition that the latter studiously demonstrates an acceptance of the dominant values and an eagerness to live by their rules. The minority may be keen to please, but may discover that the necessary concessions tend to grow with the dominant group's confidence. The minority will be driven to escape into its own territory, or to change its strategy to symmetrical schismogenesis. Whatever the choice, a negative consequence for the relationship is a likely outcome.

Returning to our point on tolerance, there is another way: reciprocity. That combines features of symmetrical and complementary schismogenesis, but in a way that neutralizes their self-destructive tendencies. In a reciprocal relationship, single cases of interaction may be asymmetrical, yet over long periods the actions of both sides balance each other, because each has to offer something that the other side needs: for instance, the resented and discriminated minority may possess skills that are lacking among the population as a whole. Arguably, some form of reciprocity characterizes most frameworks of interaction and global demographic changes are likely to lead to recognition of a need for such skills. However, if rich countries simply take the workforce from poorer ones without sufficient investment or large corporations exploit the existence of cheaper labor for financial gain without any investment in the social infrastructure upon which they rely, a more negative relationship can emerge.

Boundaries and Outsiders

We are dealing here with boundaries between identities. Boundaries are an important feature of social life and so of sociological research. They do not just define differences, they also create them. In other words, their operation can create negative feelings between "us" and "them." We can divide these into what Michèle Lamont and Virág Molnár call symbolic and social: the former boundaries being the ways in which people categorize objects, events, and others and the latter the ways in which unequal access to resources are then manifest in the opportunities that are open to groups. Sets of divisions within society then follow, but there is a group that can defy ready categorization: the "stranger." What they oppose is the opposition itself: that is, divisions of any kind in terms of the boundaries that guard them and thus the clarity of the social world that results from these practices. By their sheer presence, which does not fit easily into any established categories, the strangers deny the very validity of the accepted oppositions. They expose the apparent "natural" character of boundaries and so lay bare their fragility. Whether we desire it or not, these people sit firmly inside the world that we occupy and show no signs of leaving. We note their presence because it simply cannot be ignored and because of this we find it difficult to make sense of them. They are, as it were, neither close nor distant and we do not know exactly what to expect of them and ourselves.

Constructing boundaries that are as exact, precise, and unambiguous as possible is a central feature of the human-made world. All our acquired skills and knowledge would be rendered questionable, useless, harmful, and even suicidal, were it not for the fact that well-marked boundaries send us signals as to what to expect and how to conduct ourselves in particular contexts. Yet those on the other side of these boundaries do not differ so sharply from us in a way that relieves us from mistaken classifications. Because of this, a constant effort is needed to maintain divisions in a reality that knows of no sharp, unmistakable contours. When symbolic, social, and state-enforced boundaries mix, groups can find themselves subject to what Imogen Tyler terms "abjection." Here, anxiety and fear heighten among the population and minorities find themselves subject to negative categorization and control leading to resistance to these processes of stigmatization.

Among human preoccupations, a crucial role is played by the never-ending task of making the human-made order "stick." For Mary Douglas, in her work *Purity and Danger*, boundaries are not simply negative, but also positive because rituals enact forms of social relations which enable people to know their societies. To achieve this outcome, the ambiguity that blurs boundaries needs to be suppressed. Consider some examples of this process. What makes some plants into "weeds," that we seek to control and uproot, is their tendency to question the boundary between a well-kept garden of borders and defined plants and the chaos of a wilderness. The same may be said about "dirt" and how companies market similar cleaning products for bathrooms and kitchens. Amplifying concerns about purity and eradication through advertising can easily add to obsessive behavior that is devoted to the constant need for total cleanliness. One outcome may be that our immune systems are less able to cope with infections. A desire to render the world orderly in the face of the threat of those things that signify disorder easily results in a cost for us, as well as those things that threaten the idea of harmony.

The boundary of a group can be threatened from both outside *and* inside. Within the group ambivalence on the part of its members might be expressed and that leads them to be branded as deserters, detractors of values, and enemies of unity. It can also be attacked and eventually pierced from the outside by people who demand parity and who move about in spaces where they are not so easily identifiable. "Neophyte" (someone who converted to our faith), "nouveau riche" (someone poor yesterday, who made a sudden fortune and today has joined the rich), and "upstart" (someone of low social standing quickly promoted to a position of influence) are just some of the changes that elicit anxiety and uncertainty and produce contempt in contexts where values are taken to be homogenous. Their existence raises questions which we do not know how to answer because we have had no occasion and saw no reason to ask them ourselves: "Why do you do it this way? Does it make sense? Have you tried to do it differently?" The ways we have lived, the kind of life that gave us security and made us feel comfortable, now find themselves open to what we view as a challenge and we are called upon to explain and justify our actions. This can be advantageous for the outside observer seeking to uncover the dynamics of a social scene, but it can lead to conflict among those in the group who prefer established prerogatives to be beyond question. Even if newcomers refrain from asking awkward questions, the way they go about their daily business will still raise issues. Those who have come from other places and are determined to stay will wish to learn ways of life and try to become "like us." However hard they try to mimic, they cannot help making mistakes in the beginning because the assumptions upon which the ways of life are built need to be learnt over time.

Members of the group are led, by a newcomer's presence, to examine their own assumptions, habits, and expectations. Although never having been open to explicit questioning, their comforts have been disrupted and resistance will result, or the newcomer is ignored or denigrated. In terms of possible responses to such situations, the first is to seek a restoration of the status quo. Boundaries require a return to clarity. They can be sent back to where they are presupposed to have originated from – even though such a place may not exist! Life is therefore made uncomfortable for them by, for example, turning humor into ridicule and denying them recognition in terms of the rights that are granted to existing members of the group. However, even if they leave, when a group is based upon such fragility, new targets will need to be discovered in order to sustain themselves.

At a national level, the form of this process changes and attempts may be made to force them to emigrate, hide, or make their lives so miserable that they themselves would treat exodus as a lesser evil. If such a move is resisted, the stakes are raised and genocide may follow; thus cruel physical destruction is charged with the task that attempts at physical removal failed to fulfill. Of course, genocide is the most extreme and abhorrent method of "restoring order." Less odious and radical solutions may be chosen, with one of the most common being separation. This may be territorial, spiritual, or a combination of both. Its territorial expression may be found in ghettos or ethnic reserves: that is, parts of cities or areas of the country reserved for the habitation of people with whom the more powerful elements of the population refuse to mix. Sometimes walls and/or legally enforced prohibitions surround the allocated land. Alternatively, movements to and from these spaces is not punishable and nominally free, but in practice its residents cannot or will not escape their confinement because the conditions "outside" have been made intolerable for them, or because the standard of living in their own, often derelict, areas is the only one they can afford. Recent work on refugees and the right to move demonstrates a dynamic between what is regarded as inside and outside. As Reece Jones documents in his book *Violent Borders*, distinctions between natives and foreigners are "integral" to the reproduction of the state as an institution as migrants are viewed as threats to established cultural, economic, and political systems.

In cases where territorial separation is incomplete or becomes altogether impracticable, interactions between groups can be reduced to strictly business exchanges with social contact being avoided. Efforts, conscious and otherwise, can be made to prevent or reduce physical proximity from turning into a source of awkwardness or recognition and understanding of difference. Resentment or overt hostility is the most obvious among such efforts. Barriers of prejudice may be built that prove far more effective than the walls whose presence signifies separation and repression. Active avoidance is bolstered by the fear of contamination from those who "serve" but are not like "us." Resentment spills over into everything one can associate with the strangers: their ways of talking, their ways of dressing, their rituals, the way they organize their family life, and even the smell of the food they like to cook. Layered upon this is their apparent refusal to engage in the natural order of social relations and so they do not accept responsibility, as "we" have to do, for their actions. The order that produced this state of affairs is not questioned, but instead finds its target in those who fail to adhere to its unquestioned justification.

Segregation and Movement in the City

We have spoken to the boundaries between groups that enable particular ideas of identity and group belonging. These cannot be separated from wider forces of social change whose effects create ambivalence and ambiguity within and between boundaries. These social, economic, cultural, and political forces mix with the spatial and temporal elements of our everyday lives. The societies in which most of us live are urban: that is, people live together in great density, travel continuously, and in the course of their daily business they enter diverse areas inhabited by different people. In most cases, we cannot be sure that people we meet uphold our standards. Almost constantly we are struck by new sights and sounds that we do not fully comprehend and, perhaps unfortunately, hardly ever have the time to pause, reflect, and make an honest attempt to understand these people and places. We live among strangers and to whom we are strangers ourselves. They cannot be simply confined or kept at bay, but instead become a reminder of other ways of life.

Despite these interactions within the city, practices of *segregation* still take place through territory and the wearing of salient, easily visible marks of group membership. Law may enforce such a group-ascribed appearance, so that "passing for someone else" will be punished. Nevertheless, it is often achieved without necessarily resorting to the law for enforcement. Those who have more disposable income than others can afford to dress in particular ways and these act as codes for classifying persons by the splendor or peculiarity of their appearance. Yet relatively cheap copies of admired and highly praised statements of fashion are now produced in mass quantities which renders distinctions blurred. The result is that they may hide, rather than disclose, the cultural origins and mobility of their owners and wearers. This does not mean that appearance does not set the wearers apart, for they are public statements concerning the reference groups they have chosen. Equally, we may disguise our origins by dressing in different ways in order to subvert or disrupt the social forms of identity classification; the overall effect being that the valuations used by different groups in interactions are disrupted or diminished.

If appearance becomes a means of identity classification, this is not so for segregation by space, where particular contexts emerge over time and then exhibit a mix of the historical and contemporary. To be "local" in Suzanne Hall's study of everyday life in London is to see two dispositions: cosmopolitan and parochial. Here, people demonstrate ingenuity, but also exhibit a frailty in their sense of belonging to a place. With land and rent mixing at the urban margins with factors such as class and migration, she uncovers the origins of the owners of the independent shops which demonstrates an extraordinary diversity, but against a backdrop of control of the urban poor. Practices of territoriality and insularity mix with housing tenure to produce an urban landscape where boundaries are crossed, but they also serve to contain populations. The territory of shared urban spaces is thereby divided into areas in which one kind of person is more likely to be found than others, but there are those whose resources enable them to move across those areas.

Segregated areas provide an orientation to everyday conduct and inform expectations through practices of exclusion: that is, by being selective and limiting admission. Exclusive residential areas, policed by private security companies, are one example of this phenomenon in which those with the financial means exclude those who do not enjoy capabilities that are derived from income and wealth. However, whilst security guards at the gates of exclusive residences are visible, there are also those in large shopping areas where our time is easily lost in acts of consumption – ably assisted by the absence of clocks. There are also box offices and receptionists and in each the criteria of selection employed will vary. In the case of the box office, money is the most important criterion, though a ticket may still be refused to a person who does not meet some other requirement as a condition of entry. These tests of entitlement set a situation in which entry is denied to all as long as they remain total strangers. Ritual acts of identification transform a faceless member of the gray, indiscriminate category of strangers into a "concrete person" who is recognized as being entitled to enter. The uncertainty entailed in being in the presence of people "who can be anybody" has now, locally and temporarily, been reduced for those who identify themselves with such places.

The power to refuse entry to a place or event and so demarcate boundaries according to the perceived characteristics of their entrants, is deployed to secure a relative homogeneity. These practices seek a reduced ambivalence in selected spaces within the densely populated and anonymous world of urban living. It is a power practiced on a small scale whenever we take care in controlling those spaces identified as being private. We trust, however, that other people will use their powers to do a similar job for us on a grander scale in the enclosures between which we move as a matter of routine. On the whole, we try to minimize the time spent in intermediary areas by, for example, traveling from one closely guarded space to another. One clear example of this is to travel in the isolation of the hermetically sealed shell of a private car while even complaining about increased road congestion.

Our mobility within these areas can meet with the gaze of strangers who have the potential to disrupt our self-identities. In these cases the most we can do is to try to remain inconspicuous, or avoid attracting attention. Erving Goffman found that *civil inattention* is paramount among the techniques that make life in a city, among strangers, possible. Characterized by elaborate modes of pretending that we do not look and do not listen, or assuming a posture that suggests that we do not see and do not hear, or even care, what the others around us are doing, civil inattention may become routine. It is manifested in the avoidance of eye-contact which, culturally speaking, can serve as an invitation to open up a conversation between strangers. Anonymity is thereby assumed to be given up in the most mundane of gestures. Yet total avoidance is not possible, for a simple passage in crowded areas requires a degree of monitoring in order to avoid colliding with others. We must be attentive, while also pretending that we are not looking or being seen.

Newcomers who are not used to urban contexts are often struck by such routines. Viewing masses of people commuting by train and moving from station to station with little or no verbal interaction between them may signify a peculiar callousness and cold indifference on the part of the population. People are tantalizingly close in a physical sense, yet remote from one another. Lost in the crowd, there is a feeling of abandonment to our own resources leading, in turn, to loneliness. Loneliness appears as the price of privacy. Living with strangers becomes an art whose value is as ambiguous as the strangers themselves. Yet there is another side to this experience.

Anonymity can mean emancipation from the noxious and vexing surveillance and interference of the other who, in smaller and more personalized contexts, would feel entitled to be curious about aspects of our lives that we would prefer remain private. The city provides for the possibility of remaining in a public place while keeping our privacy intact. Invisibility, enabled by the application of civil inattention, offers a scope for freedom that is unthinkable under different conditions. Here is fertile soil for the intellect and, as Georg Simmel pointed out, urban life and abstract thinking are resonant and develop together. After all, abstract thought is boosted by the immense richness of an urban experience which cannot be grasped in all its diversity, while the capacity for operating under general concepts and categories is a skill without which survival in an urban environment may be inconceivable. One result being that in order to preserve what is particular to us in a generalized, metropolitan environment we may exaggerate our uniqueness in order to accentuate our self-identity.

There are two sides to this experience and there appears to be no gain without loss. Together with the cumbersome curiosity of others, their sympathetic interest and willingness to help may disappear. With the exhilarating bustle of urban life, there comes cool human indifference fueled by many interactions that are driven by exchange of goods and services. What is lost in the process is the ethical character of human relationships. A wide range of human intercourse which is devoid of significance and consequences now becomes possible, because so much routine conduct appears free from judgment by some standards of morality. After all, a human relationship is moral when a feeling of responsibility arises within us for the welfare and wellbeing of the "other." This does not derive from a fear of being punished, nor from a calculation that is made from the point of view of personal gain, or even the obligations that are contained within a contract we have signed and are legally bound to fulfill. Neither is it conditional on what the other person is doing or what sort of person they may be. Our responsibility is moral as long as it is totally selfless and unconditional. We are responsible for other people simply because of their personhood and so they command our responsibility. Our responsibility is also moral insofar as we see it to be ours alone and so it cannot be passed on to another human being. Responsibility for other human beings arises simply because they are human beings and the moral impulse to give help that follows from this and requires no argument, legitimation, or proof beyond that.

As we have seen, physical proximity may be cleansed of its moral aspect. People who live close to one another and affect each other's conditions and wellbeing may well not experience moral proximity. In this way they remain oblivious to the moral significance of their actions. What follows may be to refrain from actions that moral responsibility would have prompted and to engage in actions that it might have prevented. Thanks to the rules of civil inattention, strangers are not treated as enemies and most of the time they escape the fate that tends to befall the enemy: that is, they are not targets of hostility and aggression. Yet not unlike the enemies, the strangers (of which we are all, at some time, a part) are deprived of the protection that moral proximity offers. It is a short step from civil inattention to moral indifference, heartlessness, and even disregard for the needs of others.

Summary

There can be little doubt that the search for contentment, happiness, wellbeing, and meaning has informed not only a spiritual quest in human history, but has also become big business. As William Davies in his study of the happiness industry documents, blending neuroscience with psychology and behavioral surveillance leads to the belief we can predict human actions and that becomes a self-fulfilling prophecy. Yet a great many of those who are hailed as gurus of the human condition focus on interiorization: that is, increased contentment is given within ourselves, not with and through others. The relational dimension evaporates in an extraordinary abstraction whereby there is only the isolated individual. Reference groups, cultures, social contexts, and societies evaporate in the process. Their influence on who we are and how we see ourselves does not diminish, it is denied or ignored.

We have spoken about the importance of social distance, boundaries, and space in our everyday lives. These boundaries are symbolic and physical, but they interact in complex ways. We are all bound up with the routines, decisions, and consequences which provide for the knowledge and conditions that enable us not only to monitor our actions, but also to have the capability to act. While there are clear differences in the access that people have to the means to pursue their ends, we are all implicated, at different levels and with different effects, in the processes we have described in this chapter. They provide us with our social identities, our self-identities, and ways of viewing others. In the next chapter we continue our exploration by examining in more detail the role of communities, groups, and organizations in our lives.

3

Social Bonds

Speaking of "You" and "We"

In this chapter we shall examine the processes through which each of us, as individual subjects, are brought together within larger configurations of people and objects. How does this occur, under what circumstances and with what effects? These are just some of the issues we will consider. Such issues are brought to our attention every day through the use of such terms as "all of us," "we demand," and "we would agree," as well as references to "us" and "them." Such things are written in blogs, tweets, books, and through various media, expressed by business people and religious leaders and invoked by politicians seeking votes from those to whom they wish to appeal by invoking the "other" as alien and whose presence is assumed to detract from established and homogenous ways of life. We interact with others in our everyday lives and can differentiate between ourselves and them – "I" and "you." Who, therefore, is this "we" and how is it constituted?

Communities: Proximity and Distance in Consensus and Conflict

A collection of people, who are not clearly defined or circumscribed, but who agree to something that other people reject and bestow an authority or value upon those beliefs, may be referred to as a *community*. It might be defined spatially in terms of physical proximity, or through some common interest, as in the case of online communities. What we find is a sense of "togetherness" whereby encounters may oscillate between presence and absence, but exhibit degrees of constancy over time. Individuals may wish to differentiate themselves from other groups in order to maintain a social identity, but for this to work they need to do so in a way that is recognized by significant others and so is part of a more general social group. These culturally available repertoires seek to position, justify, or explain a place in a community through senses of belonging and perhaps even an idea of unity that transcends the individual. Without this in place, there may be no community. Agreement or, minimally, recognition and acts or rituals of such belonging are assumed to be the underpinnings of the community. The unifying factors are taken to be stronger and more important than anything that may divide it, while the differences between members are secondary in comparison to a belief in shared similarities.

Thinking Sociologically, Third Edition. Zygmunt Bauman and Tim May.
© 2019 John Wiley & Sons Ltd. Published 2019 by John Wiley & Sons Ltd.

Contemporary times are often characterized as fragmented as traditional ties of community belonging are loosened: for example, the power of distant interactions with others via social media undermines our immediate familiarity with each other. Nevertheless, the continuing power of social bonds should not be underestimated. They relieve people of the need to explain and convince one another of "who" they are and enable shared views to be constituted as truth and deserving of belief and respect. Faced with a polyphonic world which can appear alien, the draw to a monophonic space may appeal in the desire to relieve anxiety and enhance a sense of identity and belonging. We might even say that belonging to a community is at its strongest and most secure when we believe that we have not chosen it on purpose and that we have done nothing to make it exist, nor can we transform it through our actions. For the sake of effectiveness, their images and postulates, as implied by phrases such as "we all agree," are never given in detail or come into question; they may never be written down in a formal code or turned into objects of conscious effort aimed at *demarcation* and *maintenance*. Their hold is stronger when they stay silent as taken-for-granted orders that remain unchallenged. The bond that unites may appear at its fullest among those who conduct their lives, from birth to death, in the same company and who never venture into other places and are not visited, or infiltrated, by members of other groups. With these conditions in place, occasions to reflect upon their own ways and means and to see them in need of justification become reduced.

Situations such as these rarely exist and do not imply a harmony of consensus and the absence of conflict. Instead, community is a postulate, an expression of desire and a call to mobilize and close ranks, rather than a reality. In the memorable words of the Welsh critic and novelist Raymond Williams, "the remarkable thing about community is that it always has been." Even assuming that it had existed, it no longer exists and its moment has passed. Nevertheless, the unshakeable power of "natural" unity is often evoked when people confront the practical task of creating unity, or rescuing through conscious effort its ideal – an ideal that may be no more than a crumbling edifice of the past in the face of the uncertainties of the present. The confluence of such forces often raises its head. As Benedict Anderson suggests in relation to nationalism, it is not a connection between a common language and particular territory that creates bonds, but a sense of fatality concerning linguistic diversity, coupled with changes in capitalist production and technological advancements that leads to ideas of the past that inform "imagined communities." A great deal of effort may go into the mobilization of such images. Therefore, representations and narratives via social media are no stranger to such attempts.

Any reference to a natural state within the idea of community is itself a factor in rendering appeals to unity effective. Most powerful are those assumed to be beyond human interpretation and control in which we see allusions to such things as "common blood," shared hereditary character and a timeless link with the "land." These work to bind people to a common past and even a sense of destiny over which they have little or no control. At its extreme, it creates exclusionary practices via ideas of a purity which is to be protected from external contaminants. More prosaically, common religions and the unity of nations are appealed to in terms of the objective "facts of the case" that place elements of selection and arbitrariness involved in the choice and interpretation of events, processes, and characteristics in the background of everyday considerations. Such can become the weight of the invoked "we" that those who question interpretations are seen to commit acts that betray their own "essence." They become renegades, engaged in acts of disloyalty in their denial of reality.

Allusions to those things beyond our grasp are often accompanied by a desire for greater control over our destinies. Speaking of genetic similarities for the purposes of creating unity, for example, does not relieve the speaker of the burden of choice in their translations. Why? Because aside from difference in opinion, when it comes to understanding the relations between genes and human behavior any assumed inevitable connection is highly problematic. In an age in which genetic engineering is a reality and vast sums of money are spent on research for technological advancement, the search for genetically determined solutions through a belief in scientific certainty continues. However, as the feminist psychologist and social theorist Lynne Segal puts it, we still face a choice: we can look backwards in order to examine the "constraints in our genetic heritage that determine our fate." Or, we can look forward by putting our faith in the "new Genetic Gods" and the freedoms that are assumed to be provided through rendering our natures "infinitely malleable."

In the face of this latter possibility reference to the unifying power of genetic determinism is limited. Another route is open through the creation of a community of belief or faith by converting (proselytizing) people to new ideas. The aim here is to create a community of the faithful among those who are unified in their attachment to a cause that is revealed to them by a saintly founder or a perceptive, far-sighted, spiritual and/or political leader. In this kind of exercise, the language employed is not that of sacred traditions or historical fate, but one of the good news that comes with being "born again" and above all, of living according to *the* Truth. Appeals are not made to situations in which people have no choice but, on the contrary, to the noble act of embracing the true faith through a rejection of doubt. Overt acts of joining are seen as acts of liberation and the beginning of new lives. This is not fate at work, but an act of free will that is read as the first true manifestation of a new-found freedom. What is concealed at this time, however, are the pressures that will be exerted on converts to remain obedient to the newly embraced faith and subsequently to surrender their freedom to what the cause may demand. Therefore, the demands upon their adherents may be no less excessive than from those who invoke historical tradition or genetic predisposition to legitimize their practices. Sociologists thus study what are called New Religious Movements with such issues in mind. Ideas of "brainwashing" mix with freely chosen courses of action and payments to those who offer techniques to counter such processes.

Communities of faith cannot limit themselves to the preaching of a new creed intended to unite future devotees. Devotion would never be secure unless supported by ritual: that is, a series of regular events and gatherings – festivals, meetings, services, and forums – in which the faithful are called to participate so that their common membership may be reasserted and devotion reinforced. However, there will be variations in the stringency and volume of demands that are made upon members. Political parties – with the important exception of those that treat their members as fighters thereby demanding loyalty and subordination – may seek no more unity of thought than is necessary to secure regular electoral support at particular moments in time. After this the army of volunteers may be forgotten until, of course, they are needed again. In other words, a pre-occupation with the private lives of members is not apparent through the intent to control the entirety of their everyday existence.

A religious sect tends to be more demanding in expectations concerning the conduct of its members. They are unlikely to settle just for participation in periodic rituals with the whole of their members' lives coming into a domain of concern with the reproduction of its existence. Sects are, by definition, minorities and as such exposed to pressures from outside beliefs that are considered to be problematic to their maintenance. With this in mind, they can be seen to require devotion that others may see as unwarranted intrusions into privacy. The whole of a life becomes a profession of faith and appropriate actions and utterances a manifestation of *loyalty*. Sectarian communities will attempt to defend their members' commitment against the skepticism or outright hostility of the environment and may be able to mobilize considerable resources to that end. In extreme cases, attempts will be made to cut off the community altogether from the "ordinary" flow of social life with "normal" society being censured for its sinfulness, temptations, and the irredeemable failings of its population.

Which of the many possible contaminants originating from the outside are invoked to maintain internal boundaries depends upon the form of life that the community wishes to promote. Members may be invited to run away from the abominations of mundane life to a solitary existence, or they may be enjoined to opt out of a "rat race" and enter into relations that are based solely on mutual intimacy, sincerity, and trust. Members may be asked to turn their backs on the attractions of consumerism, reconcile themselves to a life of modesty and austerity or socialize and seek employment only with those who are existing members of the same community. Some communities, often described as communes, confront their members with the task of belonging without legally enforced contractual obligations. These may, however, be invoked if animosities or a lack of consensus threatens its existence. So we find a variation in the extent to which conduct is seen to constitute a threat and so they differ in terms of the uniformity demanded of members. In most cases, however, stipulations tend to be diffuse, ill-defined, and impossible to determine in advance, with boundaries becoming apparent only when significant moments of commitment from outsiders become apparent. Even if the advocates of unity declare neutrality regarding non-spiritual aspects of members' lives, they still claim priority for the beliefs they advocate. Potentially, such a claim may lead to interference in matters that were previously regarded as neutral if they subsequently appear at odds with the underlying shared creed.

Constituting and Organizing "We"

Relations between distance and proximity inform our capacity to be reflexive: that is, to think not only about the relations into which we enter, but the ways in which they constitute us and others through how we are seen and exist in the world. Our use of mobile and other devices leaves a trace of communications and preferences. In *Weapons of Math Destruction*, Cathy O'Neill notes that two-thirds of American adults have a Facebook page and spend 39 minutes on the site each day – estimated to be only four minutes less than the average daily time spent in face-to-face interactions. She documents how Facebook have access to a huge human laboratory in which it is possible to use varying updates to influence people's actions. Knowledge by direct acquaintance with others then mixes with knowledge of others through descriptions mediated by data sources that are produced for specific purposes. A digitized version of who we are emerges through the control of information. Such forms of representation organize individual behavior into collective resources with the result that issues of privacy become paramount when public and private worlds starts to blur and, with that, consequences for how we interact and the knowledge we have of each other and the world around us. A great deal of money is to be made in the buying and selling of such information for advertising purposes. The "we" that emerges is one of a population of consumers who exchange goods and services in the marketplace.

In organizing a "we" boundaries become blurred and simple distinctions between the individual and group are placed in question. With sects we saw that they require a discipline from their members which, from an outside point of view, eradicates the individual, promotes the boundary of the group from "others," and does so with what those outside the group often see as unacceptable invasions of freedom and privacy. With a distance from their contexts, the consequences seem clear. More proximally, however, we find ourselves in communities that bring people together for the aim of pursuing defined tasks. The purpose of these groups is taken to be limited from the point of view of the individual and thus the associated claims on their time and ways of being in the world. They are clear in their orientations and in terms of their overall purpose with specific performances where discipline and commitment are expected. In this sense we can speak of *organizations* whose distinctive feature is a deliberate and openly declared self-limitation vis-à-vis control of the everyday lives of its members.

Organizations can have written statutes that detail the *rules* to which members must adhere. Such rules enable organizational members to clarify expectations of their actions, orientate themselves to what is deemed appropriate behavior, and even deal with uncertain situations. Rules may vary according to different parts of the organization and there may be toleration of their transgression if someone is a new recruit who needs time to understand and orientate themselves. All aspects of the members' lives may not be covered by rules and to that extent they remain free from organizational control. If the presence or absence of self-limitation, rather than of consensus of beliefs, is taken as the main difference between communities and organizations, then some of the communities discussed above are, contrary to their own claims, counted among organizations.

The idea of individuals following the same rule enables a "we" to emerge as each person acts according to what is commonly prescribed. Rules may operate in the background to the extent that behavior is informed by them without the individual necessarily being aware of them and so the organization has a life beyond its particular members and may reproduce itself over time. There may also be awareness and they orientate actions and even provide a justification for their occurrence should one be required. In cases where we find partial involvement in organizational activity, we can speak in terms of playing different role – a word drawn from the language of the theater. Indeed, the works of Erving Goffman are characterized as "dramaturgical" because he assigned particular significance to performance in interactions. A stage play has a plot decided in advance and written up in a narrative that assigns parts and lines to every actor in the cast and thereby enables a pattern through which the organization may run its life. We can see theater as a prototype in another respect: stage actors do not necessarily "exhaust" the entirety of their being in the roles they have been assigned for they "enter" the prescribed character only for the duration of the performance and are able to leave it behind after the play has ended.

Organizations exhibit different specializations according to the tasks they perform and, with those, the associated training, knowledge, skills, and status of their personnel. They are recruited according to attributes possessed measured against the goals of the organization. We find specialized divisions of labor where member's roles are not only set apart, but also related to, other roles performed in the same organization. Matters of *coordination* and *communication* become paramount. Yet these skills and attributes are different from those required by the roles we play in other contexts. For instance, as parents, friends, and carers, voluntary members of a charitable society, a local branch of a political party, or an ad-hoc committee set up to contest developments that are seen to have negative impacts on localities. As we perform these roles, others may not be interested in those we undertake in other contexts and, indeed, what we know of each other is obtained through observation of and interaction in these "performances." Understanding comes, therefore, not from seeing people in isolation, but from the roles they occupy and the performances they undertake. In this respect we can see *professions*, characterized not only by the roles they perform, but the knowledge and skills they possess. A professional body may then control the boundaries through associated periods of training and education that are recognized as being legitimate to enable entry into its ranks.

Let us repeat: unlike an enclosed community, which we think of as a group to which its members belong (or ought to belong) "body and soul," the organization seems to absorb only part of the persons involved. People involved in an organization are expected to embrace their roles in order to dedicate themselves to their performance while working in and for the organization. Yet there is an expectation of distance in order that they can not only reflect upon their performance in order to improve it, but also not confuse the rights and duties attached to a particular role with those belonging to another activity or place. To this extent, organizational roles need a relative stability in order that people can identify the expectations made of them; furthermore, while the incumbents may come and go, the roles themselves remain the same. People join and leave the organization, are hired and fired, admitted and expelled, but it persists. People are interchangeable and what counts are not them as whole persons, but the particular skills they possess and the effectiveness of their performances.

What we see here are concerns on the part of the organization with calculability and predictability in the pursuit of formal goals. The German sociologist Max Weber regarded the proliferation of organizations in contemporary society as a sign of the continuous rationalization of everyday life. Rational action, as distinct from traditional and affective action – those triggered by habit, custom, and momentary emotion perpetrated without due consideration of the consequences, respectively – is oriented towards clearly stated ends. Actors are then enjoined to concentrate their thoughts and efforts on selecting suitably effective and efficient means towards those ends. For Weber, the characteristics of organization, or more specifically what he called a "bureaucracy," represent the supreme adaptation to the requirements of rational action. Here, we see the most effective means to pursue ends and Weber listed the principles which must be observed in members' actions and in relations between them in order that an organization could be an instrument of rationality.

According to this analysis, it is important that all those within the organization must act solely in terms of their "official capacity" as given by the rules attaching to the roles they perform. Other aspects of their social identities, such as family connections, business interests, private sympathies, and antipathies, should not be allowed to interfere with what they do, how they do it, and with the way others judge their actions. To achieve this, a truly rational organization must split tasks into discrete activities, so that each participant in a common effort becomes an expert in doing his or her own job. Each person must be responsible for an element in the overall task, so that no part of the whole remains unattended. That means clarity in the authority structure so everyone knows who is in charge and it is ensured that competencies are directed towards common goals. Ambiguity would detract from the rational pursuit of ends and so is to be avoided.

Weber added further characteristics of bureaucracy to those above. In the actual performance of their respective roles, the officials ought to be guided by abstract rules in order that there is no regard to personal peculiarities. The officials themselves should be appointed to their offices and promoted or demoted solely according to a criterion of merit considered in terms of the "fit" of their skills and attributes to those required by the office. Any considerations that fall outside of this judgment such as being of noble or plebeian origin, political or religious beliefs, race, and sexual orientation, must not interfere with this policy. The individual role incumbent is thereby able to orient their actions according to clear roles and expectations and match their abilities and skills to the tasks that are accorded to the position. The organization, on the other hand, is bound to adhere to a set of rational rules in the selection of such persons and be bound by the precedents – decisions made in the past in its name – that were made by them in those positions, even if they have left or moved on to other roles within the organization. The history of the organization is made of practices whose records are stored in its files apparently independent of personal memories or the loyalties of individual officials.

To ensure the rational coordination of activity, the roles must be arranged in a hierarchy that corresponds to an internal division of labor oriented towards the pursuit of the overall goal of the organization. The further down one moves in the hierarchy, the more specialized, partial, and focused are the tasks, while the higher up one moves, the wider becomes the vision and more of the overall purpose comes into view. To achieve this situation, the flow of information must be from the lower to the higher rungs of the hierarchical ladder and commands must flow from the top to the bottom becoming, as they do so, more specific and unequivocal. Control from the top needs to be reciprocated by discipline from the bottom; thus power, as the capability to influence conduct throughout the organization, is also *hierarchical*. In this manner, there is a clear and expected difference between strategic planning and operational matters.

Returning to our theme of the unity of groups, the key factor here is the postulate that everybody's decisions and behavioral choices must be subordinated to the overall goals of the organization. The organization as a whole should surround itself with thick and impenetrable walls with just two gates being left open: the "inputs," through which the goals and subsequent tasks the organization has to perform in pursuit of those are fed in, and the "outputs," which provide for the results of that organizational processing. Between the feeding in of the tasks and the production of results in terms of goods and/or services, all outside influences ought to be barred from intervening with the strict application of organizational rules and the selection of the most effective, efficient, and economical means in the pursuit of the declared end.

In deriving these characteristics of rational organizations, Weber was not suggesting that all organizations were, in practice, like this. What he was proposing was an "ideal-type" in which increasing aspects of our lives are subject to rules and procedures aimed at calculability and predictability via routinization. This is the process that the American sociologist George Ritzer has characterized as the "McDonaldization" of society. In Weber's work we find that actions which are informed by absolute values, without due regard to the possibility of their success in these terms, form an increasingly smaller part of our lives in the unfolding of history; all of which led him to write of increasing "disenchantment" with the forward march of modernity and its calculations concerned with ever-increasing elements of our private lives.

Although there are organizations that proximate Weber's ideal model with consequent effects on their employees and customers it remains, by and large, unfulfilled. The question is can it ever be fulfilled? A person reduced in their orientations to just one role, or to a single task unaffected by other concerns, is a fiction that no reality can match. This, however, is not to suggest that idealizations of efficiency, effectiveness, and economy in the pursuit of goals do not inform the strategic management of organizations as they seek to control the everyday, operational goals of its employees. Indeed, we might reasonably characterize the practice of management as the continual attempt to marry the formal and informal aspects of organizational life in pursuit of sets of organizational imperatives. Therefore, managerial practices move according to trends in pursuit of solutions to this general issue; ably assisted by the armies of organizational consultants and so-called management "gurus." In this process we see the continual invention of ideas as solutions to the issue of orienting the actions of individual members towards collective ends: for example, "total quality management," "business process re-engineering," "human resource management," management by "objectives," and a concern with getting the "right culture" in an organization.

In terms of the informal aspects of organizations, as opposed to the rules and procedures that make up the formal dimension, members of organizations are naturally concerned with their own, as well as the wellbeing of significant others, which may be adversely affected by the risks involved in certain forms of decision-making. A tendency to avoid taking decisions on dubious and/or controversial matters may then arise: for example, the idea of the "hot potato" as a popular name for eluding responsibility by shifting an urgent file or matter for decision onto somebody else's desk. So, relieved of the burden, it becomes someone else's problem. A member of an organization may also find that a command received from superiors cannot be squared with her or his moral beliefs, leaving a choice between organizational obedience and loyalty to moral principles. Other members may believe that the requirement of secrecy put to them by superiors may endanger public welfare or some other cause they believe to be equally valid or even more important than organizational efficiency. In such cases we have witnessed the practice of "whistle-blowing." Here a person or group within an organization takes matters into the public arena in the hope that such attention may stop what they see as dubious organizational practices.

The reasons for resistance to managerial edicts may also lie in the imbalance of power that comes with hierarchical structures. For Michel Foucault, because power is always enacted on free persons, resistance is bound to result. Therefore, we can say that managerial intentions in implementing organizational policies will not always correspond to their actual effects on practices. In addition, we might observe that organizational members bring into their work the prejudices they hold in their daily lives. A man, for instance, might find it difficult to accept commands coming from a woman and despite widespread denials that "glass ceilings" do not exist in organizations, women remain disproportionately under-represented in managerial positions and tend to be paid less for performing similar work. From this point of view, the idea of organizational "merit" is routinely informed by the mirroring of prejudices which are found in societies in general.

From this last observation we can question the idea that the boundaries between an organization and its environment are fixed. Instead, they are fluid and constructed according not only to the strategies of those in positions of power, but also to the pressures and influences coming from places ostensibly unrelated to its tasks and hence denied authority in organizational decision-making. There may, for example, be an anticipatory concern with its public image that places limits on taking courses of actions that are calculated in technical terms alone, or which lead to obsessive secrecy, thereby placing limitations upon the flow of communications. These can be concerned with matters that might arouse public concern and anger, or that are related to preventing a rival learning of new technological developments yet to be patented and commercially exploited.

These are just some of the practical limitations of the model. Let us both suppose, however, that the conditions for its implementation have been met. Here we find that the persons involved in the organizational division of tasks have been reduced to the roles they have been assigned, while the organization as a whole has been effectively fenced off from all concerns and influences irrelevant to its declared purpose. Regardless of how improbable these conditions might be, would they guarantee the rationality of organizational activity if put in practice? Would an organization that fully conforms to the ideal model behave as rationally as Weber suggested it would? There are strong arguments that this would not happen because this ideal recipe would produce numerous obstacles to the realization of such a form of rationality.

For a start, equal weight is ascribed in the model to the authority of the office and that of the relevant technical skill. Would these two differently grounded authorities coincide and remain in harmony? In fact, it is more than likely that the two will tend to clash, or at least be in tension. One may, for example, place a professionally trained person, such as a doctor, in a managerial position in which there is an expectation that costs are uppermost in their decision-making. What if they are then faced with a patient who is very ill and there are drugs available, at some cost, which would cure the condition? There is a clear clash here between their ethical duty as a doctor and their accountability for budgetary matters. Another tension arises in the model concerning the minute division of labor that is calculated according to tasks. Allegedly, this is a factor that boosts efficiency but, in fact, tends to produce a "trained incapacity." Having acquired expertise in the quick and efficient performance of narrowly circumscribed tasks, members can gradually lose sight of the wider ramifications of their job. Therefore, they will fail to note the adverse consequences of their activities, which have become mechanical routines, for both their overall performance, those with whom they work, and the organizational goals in general (this is a frequent criticism that strategic managers make of their operational counterparts who, in turn, accuse them of failing to understand the technicalities of their work).

Because of the narrowness of their skills, members can be ill-prepared to adjust their routines to changing circumstances and to react to unfamiliar situations with the necessary speed and flexibility. In other words, the organization as a whole falls prey to the pursuit of perfect rationality. It becomes stiff and inflexible and its methods of work fail to adapt quickly enough to changing circumstances. Sooner or later, it may well turn into a factory of increasingly irrational decisions. From an internal viewpoint the ideal model is also subject to *goal displacement*. For the sake of their effectiveness, all organizations ought to reproduce their capacity to act. In other words, come what may, an organization must be continuously ready to make decisions and take actions. Such reproduction calls for an effective mechanism of self-perpetuation that is immune to outside interference. The problem here is that the goal itself may fall among these outside interferences. There is nothing in the model to prevent that mechanism from outliving the task that the organization had been called to fulfill in the first place. On the contrary, everything points to the likelihood, and even desirability, that the concern for self-preservation will prompt the endless expansion of organizational activities and the scope of its authority. It may happen, in effect, that the task originally seen as the reason to establish the organization is relegated to a secondary position by the all-powerful interest of the organization in pursuit of self-perpetuation and self-aggrandizement. The survival of the organization then becomes a purpose in its own right and so a new end against which it will tend to measure the rationality of its performance.

There is another trend that we can identify from those above. We have spoken about the partial demands of organizations in terms of role expectations and performance. This presupposes that social and self-identity are, in some senses, separate from organizational existence. In situations tending towards total embrace, the organization would exhibit the characteristics of the kinds of communities we described as being of religious origin: that is, they demand of their members an allegiance in all aspects of their lives. As organizations respond to the increasingly rapid nature of change, complacency and an unwillingness to alter are taken as signs of an absence of competitive advantage. Therefore, that employees should be flexible, dynamic, and innovative is taken to be of paramount importance. Organizations have thus become more interested in the whole person in terms of their temperament, attributes, dispositions, skills, knowledge, and motivations. A series of quasi-scientific practices and concerns with areas hitherto regarded as being of little interest to organizations have now fallen under their routine gaze. Technology plays its role as smart-card entry systems and computer logs enable the monitoring of activities and mobile phones can be assumed to provide for constant communication without regard to the private lives of individuals who, in turn, may internalize such expectations on their time as "normal." As these practices proliferate, a blurring of boundaries between public and private elements of our lives then increases. Organizations expect more of their members' time and may even make provision to do their shopping and buy presents for their families – if one occupies a sufficient rank in the hierarchy.

In this process we have seen a questioning of the ideal model and its ideas of rationality as being the bracketing of the emotional aspects of our lives. Now, the idea of unlocking something called "emotional intelligence," the psychometric testing of candidates, and concerns with the aesthetics of office design may fall within the gaze of organizations. Depending upon the sector about which we are speaking and the nature of the role within the organization, a greater concern with what were, hitherto, private aspects of employees' lives is more commonplace. Seen as part of what Luc Boltanski and Eve Chiapello call a "new spirit of capitalism," the realm of meaning and the imaginary are drawn into the promotion of growth and opportunity. That spirit can be seen in knowledge management, brand marketing, corporate culture, the entrepreneurial self, social media, and the practice of human resource and knowledge management. This may extend to the routine surveillance of organizational members where we see a fusion of affect and rationality in the pursuit of organizational ends.

In his studies of the surveillance society, David Lyon noted how organizations utilize computer software to monitor emails and to inform them if an employee violates company policy; how active badges alert a central computer where someone is located in a building in order to enable them to locate the nearest phone and screen for their "convenience"; how routine drug testing is employed and private detectives are used to research all aspects of a person's identity to ensure they are of good character. In the process, the way in which identities are constructed changes, whilst we find resistance to the routine surveillance of space and time and impositions into areas that are not recognized as relevant to work activities. In response to these trends we see increasing means being available to protect people's privacy and remain anonymous in their digital presence.

Because of such things as resistance to the demands placed upon people, both models of human groupings are wanting. Neither the image of community nor the model of organization adequately describes the practice of human interaction. The two models sketch artificially separated, polar models of action, with separate and often opposite motives and expectations. Real human actions, under real circumstances, resent such a radical division and so manifest a tension in the expectations that are routinely placed upon people's actions. By representing and seeking to impose a representation on their members, communities and organizations display an inherent tendency to streamline complex and convoluted actions. The response may then be to seek to purify the action further, but our interactions are torn between two gravitational forces, each pulling in an opposite direction. Ideas and material reality clash as one seeks to configure the other in its image and pockets of resistance and gaps and cracks in control appear.

Our interactions are mixed: they are *heterogeneous* by being subject to tensions. For instance, the family often does not meet with the idealizations that many have of it and there are tasks to be performed, as in any other group of people seeking to understand each other and cooperate. Therefore, it too exhibits some of the criteria of performance that comes with organizations. On the other hand, in every organization the members can hardly avoid developing personal links with people with whom they join forces for a protracted period. Sooner or later, informal patterns of interaction will emerge which may or may not overlap with the official chart of formal relationships of command and subordination. Sociologists have long recognized these relations and how they develop and coincide or lie in tension with the formal requirement of the organization.

Contrary to what the ideal model would suggest, it is found in practice that the task-oriented performance may considerably benefit if the interaction is not reduced to specialized roles. Companies set about soliciting the deeper commitment of their employees through bringing more of their concerns and interests within the orbit of the organization. The people in command of the organization may utilize the fusing of the formal and informal aspects of organization. This strategy has witnessed the "cultural turn" in management theory with its emphasis upon values, commitment, motivation, and teamwork and mission statements. Organizations can offer, for example, recreation and entertainment facilities, reading groups, and even living accommodation. None of these extra services is logically related to the explicit task of the organization, but all of them together are hoped to generate "community feelings" and to prompt members to identify themselves with the company. Such emotions, apparently alien to the organizational spirit, are deemed to boost the members' dedication to the ends of the organizations and thus neutralize the adverse effects of the purely impersonal setting suggested by the criteria of rationality.

Communities and organizations often act as if freedom was presupposed in their members, even if their practices do not live up to their own expectations. Members may then, of course, leave or act in ways contrary to dominant expectations. However, there is one case when the organization explicitly denies freedom to leave and the people are kept under its jurisdiction by force. They are what Erving Goffman called "total institutions." Total institutions are enforced communities in which the totality of members' lives is subjected to scrupulous regulation, with their needs being defined and catered for by the organization. Actions are then explicitly sanctioned by organizational rules. Boarding schools, army barracks, prisons, and mental hospitals all approximate, in varying degrees, the model of total institutions. Their inmates are kept under routine surveillance at all times so that deviations from the rules are visible and then subject to prevention or punishment. People, in Erving Goffman's terms, are stripped of their normal "economies of action." Neither spiritual dedication nor the hope of material gains can be appealed to in order to elicit desirable behavior and secure the members' will to stay together and cooperate. Hence we find another feature of total institutions: the strict divide between those who set the rules and those who are bound by them. The effectiveness of coercion, as the only substitute for commitment and calculation, depends on the gap between the two sides of the division remaining unbridgeable. That said, personal relationships do develop inside total institutions and span the gap between supervisors and the inmates.

Summary

Manuel Castells writes in *The Information Age* that we are witnessing the growth of networks, markets, and organizations that are increasingly governed by "rational expectations." Yet if this is the summary of a dominant trend in contemporary Western societies, in our survey of the bonds that unite what is most striking is also the diversity of human groupings. They are all forms of human interaction in which the group exists by virtue of being a persistent network of the interdependent actions of its members. The assertion that "there is a college" refers to the fact that a number of people come together to engage in a routine called a lecture: that is, a communicative encounter whose purpose is learning and which is temporally and spatially structured in such a way that one person speaks while others, facing that person, listen and take notes. In their interactions, group members are guided by an image of what is the right conduct that is specific to the setting.

We have also seen that constituting the "we" involves invoking a sense of common identity and a belonging based on the past, or an offer of an imaginary future. We may be cognizant of the processes and their effects through acquaintance, they may also happen at a distance and not necessarily with our awareness. Computers and mobile devices leave a trace of our digital selves whose use can be deployed for targeted advertising, as well as contribute to the idea of numerated groupings of apparently like-minded people. During times of elections it is possible to obtain information to target groups with particular ideas and images to influence their voting behavior.

As in life, we have seen the relation in this chapter between continuity – through rigidity of conformity and hierarchy – and uncertainty produced by societal change and a resulting ambiguity and inability to control all aspects of our lives and where attempts to do so lead to resistance to its effects. Factors such as sexual identity, religious affiliation, race, class, and nationalism all play their roles in these dynamics and are manifest in different places at varying points in time.

These produce struggles to be afforded the same recognition and rights that may be assumed by dominant groups. As a result they challenge the power to provide an unambiguous prescription for who we are. The frameworks that we invoke to inform our being are constantly being interpreted and reinterpreted and this provides for new orientations and expectations. Our practices cannot but feed back into the images and idealizations that inform the desire for collective identity and so each inform and transform the other.

Part II

Choices, Contexts, and Challenges

4

Values, Power, and Choice

In the last chapter we saw that we are informed not only by our interactions with others in social spaces, but by different forms of communities and organization, the control and production of information, and the symbolic resources that are deployed to understand each other and ourselves. With these dynamics and others in place, there is no shortage of questions that arise in our daily lives. These types of questions may concern matters that do not, ordinarily, preoccupy us, but which still inform issues about who we are and how we make sense of the world around us. Sometimes, these will raise further questions about why and how events and processes occurred. When we engage in this type of thinking, we are on shared ground with scientific activity in terms of explaining events as "effects of a cause." How such matters relate to and inform our understandings and actions is the subject of this chapter.

Decisions: Chosen, Influenced, and Caused

When it comes to seeking explanations as the result of a cause our curiosity is, by and large, satisfied when we conclude that the event was inevitable or, at the very least, highly probable. Why was there a fire in the house down the road? Because there was an electrical short-circuit. Why did no one hear the burglar breaking the window? Because everybody was sleeping and people may not be awoken by sounds when they are asleep. Our search for the explanation ceases once we have found either that one event is always followed by another, or that it follows in most cases. With the former we speak of "laws" because there are no exceptions whereas, in the latter, we are dealing with probability because it happens in most, but not all, cases. In both cases we do not tend to speak of choices because one event is *necessarily* followed by another.

Such a form of explanation becomes particularly interesting when applied to the realm of human conduct. After all, these are explanations in relation to events that appear to be the product of causes beyond human control. Actions are conducted by people who are assumed to be responsible because they are faced with choices in their everyday conduct. Because there are different ways of acting, the events cannot be seen as inevitable. Therefore, due to variation, contexts informed by human choice cannot be characterized as having any degree of

Thinking Sociologically, Third Edition. Zygmunt Bauman and Tim May.
© 2019 John Wiley & Sons Ltd. Published 2019 by John Wiley & Sons Ltd.

certainty or predictability. We can, of course, try to comprehend such things retrospectively: that is, with the benefit of hindsight, we can interpret the action in terms of certain rules, or dispositions within that context, that people must have followed to perform the action in the first place. Nevertheless, there still seems to be something missing, for we know from our own experiences that people undertake actions with a purpose and they are infused with meaning. As such, there are "motives" in creating or responding to a situation which, for one reason or another, lead to particular actions. As a result we attribute to ourselves and each other the capacity to choose between courses of action. Driving a car and stopping at a red traffic light may be observed to be a regulated form of behavior, yet it is still a demonstration of a preferred course of action informed by a reason – in this case, for example, the avoidance of accidents and not wishing to break the law.

So, do we explain human actions according to causes or do we seek to understand the meanings that inform actions and the contexts in which they take place? Human actions may vary under similar conditions even when informed by shared motivations. People may interpret those conditions in different ways and form alternative conclusions as a result. Equally, their motives may not be seen as legitimate, particularly in cases where that involves law-breaking or what others see as deviant actions, or the context is discarded as irrelevant for understanding. If we wish to know why this rather than that form of action has been selected, we might turn our attention to an individual's perception of the situation and how that related to their decision-making process. Although attractive as a solution, this is still not adequate, for it assumes that such decisions are formulated according to a connection between perception and conscious choices about explicitly stated ends with the importance of understanding the role of social context removed. Given that, we need to understand actions in a dynamic encounter between individuals, social contexts, and the meanings informing those.

To examine these relations and their effects, we might first consider *habitual* actions. We get up, clean our teeth and perform a morning routine while still half asleep. Indeed, we may not make conscious decisions, but instead perform a routine and even think of other things whilst doing so. We may eat at regular times and develop all sorts of habits that become part of our actions without any conscious planning. In cases where routines are broken by unexpected interruptions, we have to make decisions because habit suddenly becomes a poor guide. Habitual conduct is thus the sedimentation of past experience or learning. Thanks to regular repetition, it relieves us from the need to think, calculate, and make decisions in many of our actions just as long as the circumstances we encounter appear in a regular pattern. Our actions can become so habituated that it can be difficult to describe how they occur and our reasons for performing them. They come into our attention when things go wrong: that is, when regularity and orderliness break down.

Our next type of action can be characterized by an intensity that might bracket reflexive consideration of what we are doing at that moment in time and arises from strong emotions. *Affective* actions are characterized by a suspension of the rational calculations that inform what are assumed to be the purpose and possible consequences of actions. Such actions are regarded as impulsive, emotionally driven, and deaf to the voice of reason. Following actions informed by such intensity and with the passage of time, passions may cool and deliberation interrupt the act. These forms of action may result in hurting those we love and cherish. Nevertheless, if the act is premeditated it would not be affective because it was the outcome of a calculated decision that is designed to hurt, intimidate, or silence. We can now say that an action is affective insofar as it remains unreflective, spontaneous, unpremeditated, and is embarked upon prior to any weighing of different courses of action or contemplation of consequences.

Both habitual and affective actions are often characterized as "irrational." Yet this does not imply that they are foolish, ineffective, wrong, or even damaging. Nor does it suggest any evaluation of the utility of the act. After all, habitualized routines can be effective and useful and relieve those who engage in them of the simultaneous, conscious monitoring of their actions. Indeed, they enable us to accomplish those practical activities that make up our everyday lives and spare us of prior contemplation of weighing up the pros and cons of our varying courses of action. Similarly, an outburst of anger might be helpful in getting people to understand how we might feel about an event, action, or issue. From this point of view, it is a mistake to assume that rational actions are necessarily superior to irrational ones. Emotions are part of our lives and what make us human. As Christopher Lasch put it in *Cultures of Narcissism*, our emotional maturity lies in recognition that others are not projections of our own desires, but are independent of us and have desires of their own.

A *rational* action is taken to be different. It is one characterized by a conscious choice being made from among several alternative courses of action which are oriented towards the achievement of an explicit end. This is an "instrumental–rational" view of action whereby the *means* are selected according to the pursuit of a given *end*. Another form of rational action will also necessitate the choice of means towards ends, but in this case those ends are considered to be more valuable than others. "Value–rational" action is thus motivated by considerations such as what is "dear to one's heart," attractive, desirable, and most closely connected to the felt need of the moment. What they both have in common is a choice of means whose efficacy is measured against given ends and that the fit between these is the ultimate criterion in the choice between a right and wrong decision. Furthermore, that the act of choosing is voluntary insofar as the actor has exercised a free choice without being goaded, pulled, pushed, persuaded, or bullied into it, nor did it arise habitually or via a momentary outburst of passion.

In choosing courses of action through conscious and rational deliberation, there is an anticipation of their probable outcomes. That necessitates taking stock of the context in which the action will take place and the effects we expect to attain as a result. In approaching action from this point of view, we have two components: the values that inform our conduct and the resources we draw upon to realize our goals. In terms of these resources, Pierre Bourdieu divides the forms of capital that are employed in our actions into the following: symbolic, cultural, and economic. Symbolic capital refers to the power to confer meaning upon objects, attributes, and characteristics; cultural capital is the skills and knowledge that we possess and draw upon in our actions and economic capital refers to our access to wealth and material resources. These resources can be turned to many uses and they differ from each other by carrying varying degrees of attractiveness and being attractive to others who occupy similar social contexts, for alternative reasons.

Symbolic capital confers meaning upon objects and attributes. In this way it produces assessments of what is valuable and for what reasons. If we have the recognized skills, we may then turn to the pursuit of those things that promise to be most useful, or which may increase the volume of resources at our disposal and so enhance the range of our choices. Ultimately, it is the combination of our values and the resources at our disposal that preside over the decision to spend extra cash on a new mobile phone, a holiday, or to purchase sociology books. Taking stock of our resources and values shows us the degrees of freedom we enjoy: that is, what we can do and how we can pursue our goals, as well as what is out of the question. To return to a theme in an earlier chapter, a key ingredient of the possibilities available to us is how we are seen by others. As those such as Imogen Tyler have shown, fear and anxiety mix with beliefs and prejudices sedimented in history concerning particular "problem" populations. These forms of devaluing people remove from vision their positive attributes and place symbolic and material barriers in the way of their aspirations.

Power and Action

We are now in the terrain of contexts which inform our capability to act which, along with our ability to monitor our actions and formulate goals, comprise the dimensions of social action. We may possess the ability to monitor our actions, but the range of freedoms that we enjoy in order to be capable of engaging in actions oriented towards particular ends is differentially distributed. Quite simply, different people have different degrees of freedom. The fact that people differ in their freedom of choice refers to social inequality; a more recent term that has been employed in a broader context is "social exclusion." That is manifest in the inverse relation that exists between need and access to and use of resources. Danny Dorling charts in his meticulous study of inequality (*Injustice: Why Social Inequality Still Persists*) that we find in affluent societies, characterized by significant inequalities, people feel disenfranchised and experience a lack of control over their lives. There we find a minority of people enjoying a wider range of choice due to their access to more resources.

We can study these dynamics in terms of *power*. To refer to power is contentious because it brings to attention the importance of social context, structure, and culture for our understanding. It refuses to see the individual in isolation from social context that is the personification of an abstract individualism. We may see power in terms of pursuing chosen ends and commanding the necessary means towards the realization of those ends. Power is an enabling capacity. The more power people have, the wider is their range of choices and the broader the scope of outcomes they may realistically pursue. Being powerless means a relative absence of such choices. To have power is to be able to act more freely and this has consequences for those who have less power. If it is to command resources, it means those with less power will have their freedom of choice limited by the decisions made by those who have the capability to control them. One person exercising their autonomy can result in the experience of heteronomy by another. The devaluation of the freedom of others in pursuit of the enhancement of freedom may be achieved by the following methods.

The first method is *coercion*. Coercion comprises the manipulation of actions in such a way that the resources of other people, however large they may seem in other contexts, become inadequate or ineffective in that context. An entirely new game is created by the manipulation of a situation in such a way that those doing the manipulating can then assume the advantage: for example, whether the victim of a mugger is a rich banker or a powerful politician, their respective resources, which assure them a large degree of freedom in other contexts, lose their "enabling" capacity once they are confronted in a dark and deserted street with a knife, or the sheer physical power of an assailant. Similarly, to force a reconsideration of cherished values may result in people feeling that their practices are now more subject to evaluation and questioning by those whose authority they do not recognize. Other values then come to predominate in reaction to this situation. In the extreme conditions of high security prisons characterized by violence, for instance, the value of self-preservation and survival may well overshadow other choices. In organizations subject to a change in ownership and purpose, from a service ethos to one concerned with profit maximization at all costs, employees can find themselves having to adjust to a very different culture manifest in individual targets linked to performance-related pay.

The second method consists of the strategy of *enlisting* the desires of others towards one's own ends. What characterizes this form is a manipulation of the situation in such a manner that other people may attain the values they pursue only if they follow the rules set by the power-holder. Thus, the zeal and efficiency with which the enemies are killed is rewarded by enhancing the social standing of the brave soldier with medals and honorable citations. Factory workers may secure improved living standards (wage rises) provided they work with more dedication and intensity and comply, with no dissent, to managerial edicts. The values of subordinates become the resources of their superordinates. They are not valued as ends in themselves, but as means deployed in the service of ends set by those with greater power. Yet for those subject to such manipulations, they have no other choice but to surrender a considerable part of their freedom.

The actions of others affect the values that inform the ends we seek and our evaluation of how realistic it is that we shall attain these ends. What we call "realistic" and what we call "dreams" are all given by the relations we have with others and the resources we can hope to deploy in our actions. However, where do these values come from in the first place? After all, why do we place a particular premium upon some ends and disregard or downgrade others? Are the values that inform our orientations matters of free choice? For example, we wish to go to university straight from school. However, our friends have decided otherwise and in arguing about our respective choices, they convince us that more fun will result from starting work immediately rather than being condemned to three years of self-study and debt. We then change our minds and seek work for an instant income and, for a while, enjoy the benefits that this provides. Management then announce that they are going to reorganize the office and make people redundant, but our job will be secure and the prospects for promotion remain promising. As members of a union, our colleagues vote for strike action and the management respond by announcing that in the event of a strike, important orders will be lost with the result that everyone will be made redundant. Understandably, we seek to avoid such a prospect, but most of our colleagues in voting for such action have appeared to place solidarity above the security of their own jobs. In reflecting upon our position, we recognize that our interests are bound up with our colleagues and so we vote for a strike. The consequence is now the possibility that the job will be lost along with the freedoms that the income enabled us to enjoy.

What is happening here? The values that people adopt in orienting and justifying their actions transform in the course of social interaction within different contexts. We are influenced in particular ways and values are manifest through an alteration in the hierarchy of importance we attach to them. Consciously or by default, some ends are selected above others. The consequence is that the ends which have been assigned priority may be justified by us in terms of being more satisfying, dignified, morally elevating, and rewarding. In this way we become attuned to the sense we have of what is proper and improper conduct in our lives and the cultures and social contexts we inhabit inform those judgments.

Assumed to be separate spheres of activity, the spheres of culture and the economy have increasingly blurred in recent times. We have seen a movement away from technological advancement manifest in the tangibility of material objects or strict adherence to costs and benefit, to a concentration of knowledge, creativity culture. In what Luc Boltanski and Eve Chiapello term the *New Spirit of Capitalism*, it leads to the realms of meaning and identity being drawn together with the realms of growth and opportunity. We can see this in the rise of brand marketing, corporate culture, the entrepreneurial self, and the use of social media. Indeed, an increasing concern with wellbeing is symptomatic of these trends as private concerns become more public. Algorithms capable of capturing how much happiness is expressed in a 140-character tweet have been designed to analyze the estimated 500 million tweets a day. We become part of a living laboratory in our individual actions that captures inventories of happiness which, as William Davies charts in *The Happiness Industry*, is related to the global economic management of whole populations. With such increased surveillance and forms of evaluation of behavior among populations, values are bound to be influenced and even altered as a result.

In the face of such trends we should recognize that whilst values inform issues of consensus, conflict and coercion, they are not always consciously chosen. As we have said, many of our actions are habitual and routine. As long as the actions remain habitual, we seldom pause to ask about the values they serve. Habitual action does not need justification as long as we are not called to account by others or by abrupt changes in the circumstances in which we act. These discursive justifications – those *about* our actions – may be difficult to embark upon. If pressed, we might allude to tradition: "this is the way things have always been done," or "this is how it is." What we are doing here is to suggest that the length of time in which these habits have persisted lends them an authority that is not normally the object of questioning. We have learnt from the actions of the past and placed them, without reflection, in the present. Action thereby remains habitual as long as it is not called upon to legitimize itself in the sense of requiring reference to the values and purposes it is supposed to serve. It goes on repeating itself, by and large according to the same pattern, on the strength of habit alone. The values that inform these actions act at a subconscious level and we become aware of their influence only when it comes to the making of deliberate choices. These may occur in situations where the values we obey are challenged, defied, and questioned and so called upon to legitimize themselves.

Those who occupy positions of command over others, where those positions are circumscribed by rules, may be said to exercise authority. Clearly, this has an influence upon conduct, but the particular form of this relationship is given by the rules that surround the relations that exist between the subordinate and superordinate. Returning to our discussion on bureaucracy, we can see how rules informing a hierarchical division of labor were said to provide for its authority. To be accepted as legitimate, however, requires not only that the relationship conforms to particular rules, but also that it is justified by the beliefs that all those who are subject to them share and, further, that they willingly consent to that relationship. To have all three conditions in place – rules, justifications, and consent – means that someone submits themselves to the authority and the values that underpin its existence. Two elements, in particular, underpin such arrangements. First, differences between the dominant and subordinate are based on differential access to resources according to their position. Second, those differences are justified on the basis that subordinates see the advantages which they derive from these arrangements despite an unequal access to resources.

To become an authority for us, a person or an organization must produce legitimation, based upon the second element, which demonstrates why their position and decisions ought to be recognized and accepted. One form of legitimation, already encountered, is that based upon being time-honored and tested. History binds its heirs and what it united should not be set apart lightly. Allusion to past is another route: those who seek popular acceptance for the values they preach will go to some lengths to dig out genuine, or putative, historical evidence of their antiquity. Historical imaginary is selective and the deference that people feel for it may be enlisted in the service of contemporary contestations over values. Once accepted that certain values were held by common ancestors, they are less vulnerable to contemporary criticism. These *traditionalist legitimations* can become particularly attractive in times of rapid change, characterized by uneasiness and anxiety, as they seem to offer a safer, less agonizing set of choices; albeit ones that can have consequences for others.

Another means is to defend new values as a form of revelation and this is associated with *charismatic legitimation*. Charisma was the quality first noted in the study of the deep and unchallenged influences exerted by the church upon the faithful. The concept of charisma then refers to the conviction of the faithful that the church is endowed with a privileged access to truth. Charisma, however, need not be confined to religious beliefs and institutions. We can speak of charisma whenever the acceptance of certain values is motivated by the belief that the preacher of values is endowed with privileged powers and that these guarantee the truth of their visions and propriety of their choices. Therefore, the reason of ordinary people possesses no means of evaluating these claims and so no right to doubt the power of their perception. The stronger the charisma, the more difficult it is to question their commands and the more comforting it is for people to follow their orders when exposed to situations of risk and uncertainty.

We are said to live increasingly in an age of anxiety in which the relations between trust and risk are ever changing. Through a process of detraditionalization it is suggested that the control over our lives that is associated with traditional societies has passed to external agencies whose distance increases feelings of powerlessness. As we learn more about the effects of anthropogenic climate change through scientific findings being filtered through the mass media, the more people are aware that contemporary actions have profound consequences for the future. Ulrich Beck, the German sociologist, wrote about these trends in modern society under the theme of "risk society."

Ulrich Beck captures a dynamic between power and action in terms of the possibility of us having a degree of certainty concerning what we know and then the capacity to act on that knowledge. Increasingly, however, we find ourselves exposed to ever greater amounts of information, and traditional domains of knowledge, bounded by professional groups, are now open to scrutiny. Medical diagnoses can be placed into search engines to reveal an enormous wealth of often contradictory interpretation and experience. There is so much information out there, but what exactly do we do with it? Does it allay our concerns or heighten them? Does it inform our capacity to act, or induce a crippling fear? Where once traditional authorities were to be trusted, we find differences in interpretation between scientists and scholars, whilst politicians and the mass media fluctuate between declarations that risks are minimal and then dramatize them in order to mobilize support and draw in audiences and boost viewing and circulation figures. An increasing circulation of knowledge then mixes with a more individualized sense of responsibility for how to act and this can induce greater uncertainty.

We might observe that in times of rapid change and heightened uncertainty, people may turn to those who apparently promise simple solutions. Thus, such conditions can be accompanied by a demand for charismatic solutions to these shifting problems of value, with some political parties and social movements stepping in to provide a substitute service. A collective skepticism regarding any form of authority over knowledge can then ensue. Those organizations can then turn themselves into collective carriers of charismatic authority and place influence and the desire for certainty on a different basis. Yet whilst, in more recent history, the center of charismatic authority may have tended to move away from the religious and the political arenas, there is still a strong pull to both, with political leaders deploying nationalist rhetoric to bolster their support and sects demanding total obedience. Various media certainly have a role to play in this process. Routine, mass exposure to particular personalities is a powerful influence in this trend. People may then look to those with high-profile, public personalities to provide solutions to perceived risks and the uncertainties they generate and that adds power and strength to their positions.

Traditionalist and the charismatic forms of legitimation share a similar tendency: that is, they both imply the surrender of our right to make value choices and can be associated with the transfer of responsibility. Choices have been made for us, or we give the power of choices over to others. There is a third type, however, to which we have already alluded: the *legal–rational*. This implies that some organizations, and those positioned to speak on their behalf, have the right to tell us what sort of actions ought to be undertaken and it is our duty to obey without further argument, or face the consequences. We are dealing here with a relationship between obligations whose transgression has clear negative consequences and a sense of duty to which people feel an absolute commitment. In this space, the moral quality of the advice recedes in that it can become law and, as such, subject to a command that selects the authority to determine actions. In this way, legal–rational legitimation separates action from choice and appears to render it free from value. The executors of a command need not scrutinize the morality of the action they have been ordered to perform, nor do they need to feel responsible if the action fails a moral test. One reaction to retrospective scrutiny of actions could be: "I was only carrying out the orders I received from my superiors."

Legal–rational legitimation can be said to hold societies together and yet carry with it potentially sinister consequences due to the tendency to absolve people from responsibility for their choices. The mass murder and genocide of the Second World War and those since that time, such as the Korean, Vietnam, Congo, Bosnian, and Gulf wars, provide the most conspicuous, though by no means unique and exceptional, examples of such consequences. Those who have perpetrated murder refuse to accept moral responsibility, pointing instead to the legal determination of their obedience to command. In so doing they reject the charge that their decision to obey was, in fact, a moral choice on their part.

Removing the values which the actions serve from the sight of the actors by the simple expedient of extending the chain of command beyond the vision of the executors renders the action apparently value-free and exempt from moral judgment. The actors are offered, so to speak, escape from the burden of their freedom, which always comes complete with the responsibility for one's actions. In this way moral duty mixes in a tension with a desire for self-preservation that is derived from membership of a group. This group identity (as we have seen) may be achieved with disastrous consequences for those who are defined as the other. These issues, in their turn, vary according to the situations in which we find ourselves and what are regarded as the values to which we aspire. Whilst we can take the exceptional and clearly tragic consequences of war as our barometer, everyday life in society can also lead to *adiaphorization*: that is, exemption from the realm of moral evaluation. To consider this further, we turn to matters of competition, exclusion, and ownership.

Needs and Action

Most, but not all, of our actions are motivated by our needs. We have basic needs, in terms of survival, and another set of needs that relates to the meaningful constitution of social reality that provides for a degree of satisfaction, or what André Gorz referred to as "qualitative needs" – those that make up a meaningful life in terms of such factors as communication and creativity. The fulfillment of those needs, as we have suggested, is dependent upon the degree of autonomy we have in relation to our actions and, in turn, on our ability to monitor, understand, and reflect upon our actions, as well as having the resources and capability to act. In *Development as Freedom* the economist Amartya Sen asks: should removing poverty come before any guarantee of rights and liberties? This, he suggests, is the wrong starting point as the interconnections between them are essential and democracy a vital part of their realization.

These elements can become fused and obscured in consumer societies. After all, we might say we do not "need" an object, but "want it"! Whether such utterances occur in situations in which relative affluence or poverty is manifest is of prime significance. In the Western world, lifestyle now seems bound up with the ability to consume, the purpose of which is rarely reflected upon and, when considered, may be justified according to the satisfaction of unmet needs. What become bound together in such utterances are the realms of value, affect, and identity, along with the capability to acquire something. We can move when these realms are fused, from the satisfaction of an expressed need, to feelings of absence which produce a state of deprivation in which our lives would be incomplete, flawed, and even intolerable.

Such fusion brings together the quality of an object being needed for survival or self-preservation with a cultural desire that is manifest in the wish to acquire a "good." As Gilles Deleuze, the French philosopher, and Félix Guattari, a psychoanalyst, have written, as soon as desire and acquisition are fused, we can feel a significant "lack" in our lives. We fill this gap with the desire to acquire: commodities to be bought in exchange for money or the furthering of debt: for example, silence in the street at night through purchasing properties elevated above and distanced from the noise of urban life and domes built in polluted cities filled with filtered air. Our needs cannot be satisfied unless we are able to gain access to the goods in question, either through being allowed to use them, or by becoming their owners. Yet this always involves other people and their actions. However self-concerned our motivations, our ties with other people are required and, even if not acknowledged, we are rendered more dependent upon other people's actions and the motives that orient them.

This situation is not evident upon first glance. On the contrary, the idea of holding goods in terms of ownership is widely accepted as a "private" matter. It seems that the object (the property) is somehow invisibly connected to its owner; it is in such a connection that we suppose the essence of ownership rests. If one is the owner of something, then at the same time there is a right as to its use determined by the will of its owner. Of course, that right is circumscribed in particular ways. Thus, trees in our garden subjected to preservation orders may not be felled without official permission and neither can we set fire to our houses without the risk of being prosecuted. Nevertheless, the fact that a special law is needed to forbid us to dispose of our property in such a manner only bolsters the general principle that self-determination and property are inextricably linked. Problematic issues arise at this point in our discussion through a trend towards short-circuiting the social via a focus upon individualized pleasure, consumption, and ownership.

Property, labor, and entitlement to its use and disposal are not free from influences in relation to gender, ethnicity, and class. We have long equated the entitlement to property through the labor we exert in its acquisition and this is apparent in the work of the seventeenth-century philosopher John Locke. Here we find ideas of property rights being laid down by the first laborer who appropriated them and then being handed down through subsequent generations – a principle that survives to this day. Locke argued for a "social contract" so that order could be brought to what would otherwise be a chaotic social and political world. In his argument he then made a leap. As women were held to be "emotional" and exhibit a "natural dependence" upon men, he argued that they do not then possess such rights. Marriage was a contract that women entered into so that they could produce sons who inherited the property. The contract of marriage thus ensures that property rights are stable within society and men have sons in order to perpetuate their lineage. Aside from assuming that the ability to be rational inheres in the individual man prior to his membership of a society (and we have seen how groups form our social identities in contrast to a position that removes people from the societies of which they are a part), this same ability was then denied to half the human race on the basis of a prejudice that exists to this day: women are emotional and men are rational. The result is to exclude women from the social contract, but also to add to the idea that freedom comes from the absence of dependence upon others.

The issue of the exclusion of women and the construction of particular forms of what is assumed to be acceptable sexual identity brings us on to another problematic issue. Popular descriptions of the property relation leave out a central aspect of its exercise. It is, more than anything else, a relation of *exclusion*. Whenever we say "This is mine," we are also implying that it is *not* somebody else's. Ownership is not a private quality; it is a social affair that conveys a special relation between an object and its owner and, at the same time, a special relation between the owner and other people. Owning a thing means denying others ownership. At one level, therefore, ownership establishes a mutual dependence, but it does not connect us with things and others as much as it divides us from people. The fact of ownership sets apart, in a relation of mutual antagonism, those who own the object from those who do not. The first can use and abuse (unless specifically constrained by the law) the object in question, while the second are denied such a right. It may also (remember our discussions of power) make the relationship between people asymmetrical: that is, those who are denied access to the object of ownership must obey the conditions set by the owner whenever they need or want to use it. Therefore, their need and their willingness to satisfy that need put them in a position of dependence on the owner.

All ownership divides and distinguishes people. Ownership confers power only if the needs of the excluded require the use of the objects owned. For instance, ownership of the tools of work, of raw materials to be processed by human labor, of technology, and the sites on which such processing can take place, offers such power. This is not so with the ownership of goods to be consumed by the owner. Owning a car or a washing machine may make our lives easier or more enjoyable and may even add to our prestige, but they do not necessarily give us power over other people. Unless, of course, other people wish to use these things for their own comfort or enjoyment, in which case we might set the conditions of use to which they must conform. Most things we own do not offer power, but independence from the power of others by removing the need to utilize their possessions. The larger the part of our needs that we can meet in this way, the less we have to conform to the rules and conditions set by other people. In this sense, ownership is an enabling condition because it can extend autonomy, action, and choice, thus ownership and freedom are often taken to be fused together.

Returning to our earlier discussions, the principle underlying all ownership is that the rights of others are the limits of our own rights and therefore the promotion of our freedom requires that others are restricted in the exercise of their freedom. By this principle, the enabling condition of property always comes together with varying degrees of constraint. The principle assumes an irreparable conflict of interests in terms of being a zero-sum game. Thus, nothing is assumed to be gained by sharing and cooperation. In a situation in which the capability to act depends on control over resources, to act reasonably will mean to follow the commandment "everyone for themselves." This is how the task of self-preservation can appear to us in cultures of individualism.

Pierre Bourdieu wrote that politics begins with the "denunciation of the established doxa." What he called "doxic acceptance" encapsulates the idea that there are many categories of thought that we routinely employ in our understandings, but rarely reflect upon in our practice. One of the most powerful, if not *the* most, is the idea of self-preservation based upon competition. Competitors are moved by the desire to exclude their actual or potential rivals from using the resources they control, hope to control, or dream of controlling. The goods for which the rivals compete are perceived as scarce: it is believed that there are not enough of them to satisfy everybody and that some rivals must be forced to settle for less than they would wish to possess. It is an essential part of the idea of competition, and a basic assumption of competitive action, that some desires are bound to be frustrated and hence the relations between the winners and the defeated must be permanently marked with mutual dislike or enmity. For the same reason no competitive gains are considered secure unless actively and vigilantly defended against challenge and contest. Competitive struggle never ends; its results are never final and irreversible. From this, a number of consequences follow.

First, all competition contains within it a tendency towards monopoly. Large corporations are now becoming even larger through mergers involving vast sums of money. In the process, the winning side tends to make its gains secure and permanent by seeking to deny the losers the right to challenge their gains. Paradoxically, this can be the case when it is suggested that ownership is not the future, but openness! Computers and computer systems store vast amounts of information that, as we have seen, are routinely collected, analyzed, and sold by large corporations who have power and reach, such as Google and Facebook. When Francis Bacon said knowledge is power, intellectual property and information transactions on these scales were inconceivable. What Evgeny Morozov describes in *The Net Delusion* is often old inequalities in apparently new spaces. The ultimate purpose of the competitors remains the same: to abolish the competition itself with the result that competitive relations have an in-built tendency to self-annihilation. Whilst there are those still only too happy to sell simple technological solutions to social problems, we can detect the same trend: resources concentrate on a few, large corporations. A resulting polarization of resources gives the winning side the ability to dictate the rules of all further interaction and leave the losers in no position to contest the rules; this is ably assisted by the atomization of users deploying their mobile devices and computers. Gains in such a case would be transformed into a monopoly and so attract more gains still and further deepen the gap between the sides. It is for reasons such as these that the economist, John Kenneth Galbraith, wrote that government action is necessary to prevent the "self destructive tendencies" of the economic system.

Second, the polarization of chances brought about by monopolistic activity tends to lead in the long run to the differential treatment of winners and losers. Sooner or later winners and losers solidify into "permanent" categories and the digital world in which we live reproduces these same outcomes. The winners blame the failure of the losers on the latter's inherent inferiority and so the losers are declared responsible for their own misfortune. This is a triumph of the type of thinking that believes social problems have individual, biographical solutions. These people may be described as inept, wicked, fickle, depraved, improvident, or morally contemptible: that is, lacking the very qualities that are assumed to be necessary for the competition that contributed to this state of affairs in the first place. Then, so defined, the losers are denied legitimacy for their grievances. The poor become defined as lazy, slovenly, and negligent, as *depraved* rather than deprived. Assumed to be lacking in character, shirking hard labor, and inclined to delinquency and law-breaking, they can be seen as having "chosen" their own fate. Similarly, in societies dominated by a particular conception of what is acceptable, degrees of recognition and value vary: for example, women are blamed for their oppressed state, leaving their confinement to what are assumed to be less prestigious and desirable functions to be explained by excessive emotionality or a lack of competitive spirit, whilst those whose sexuality does not fit within particular categories can be subject to suspicion, ostracization, and violent reaction. Societal social orders are underpinned by values and those, in turn, are produced and reproduced by the actions of their members. They do not saturate in their reach into actions and those seeking being valued and valuing other ways of being may find themselves in conflict.

Expediency and Morality

Part of understanding these dynamics is to consider the importance of morality and ethics in our lives. In his historical study of debt (*Debt: The First 5000 Years*), David Graeber writes of the changing roles of honor and degradation. In contemporary society, defamation of the victims of competition is one of the most powerful means of silencing recognition of an alternative motive for human conduct: moral duty. We also find social media performing a reproduction of value for different populations who are regarded as being "less" for reasons over which they have little or no control. Friendship itself becomes something that can be monetized and infused with other values. Whilst it is difficult to research, for example, the role of Facebook in these relations using the software that they deploy, Bev Skeggs and her colleagues have sought to examine how these relations of value and valuing are manifest in these digital infrastructures. These new modes of communication and formation of social relations reflect an old issue: how varying forms of value and moral motives clash with those of gain. Moral action, after all, requires solidarity and disinterested help. Solidarity is recognition of having something in common with another; it is a willingness to assist those who are in need without asking for, or expecting, remuneration. It is an expression manifest in consideration for the need of others and often results in self-restraint and a voluntary renunciation of personal gain.

The differences between ethics and morals are often described in terms of the former being concerned with publicly acceptable standards of conduct as given by, say, professions, whilst the latter concerns an individual's sense of what is right and wrong. The boundaries between the public and private blur over time due to different forces. Max Weber observed that the separation of business from the household is one of the most conspicuous characteristics of modern societies. The overall effect is to isolate the spheres in which gain and moral duty are, respectively, the dominant considerations. When engaged in a business activity we are often, but not exclusively, separated from the network of family bonds. Put another way, we may feel freed from the pressures of moral duties. Thus, considerations of gain may be given the sole attention that successful business activity demands while, ideally, family life and those communal forms whose patterns follow different values and obligations ought to be free from the influence of gain.

We might also observe that business activities should not be affected by the motives prompted by moral feelings and so instrumental–rational action prevails. Efficiency, economy, and effectiveness are the goals: that is, the amount of labor or materials for a given output; a concern with overall costs and delivering according to the objectives of the business. We have noted that one idea of organization is the attempt to adjust human action to the ideal requirements of rationality. We see again that such an attempt must involve, more than anything else, the silencing of moral considerations via every task being reduced to a simple choice of obeying or refusing to obey a command. It is also reduced to a small part of the overall purpose pursued by the organization as a whole, so that the wider consequences of the act are not necessarily visible to the actor. The organization puts discipline in place and as long as a member of an organization performs well according to the rules and commands of a superior, that person is offered freedom from doubt. A morally reprehensible action, unthinkable under different conditions, can suddenly become a real possibility.

The potency of organizational discipline to silence or suspend moral reservations was dramatically demonstrated in the notorious experiments of the American psychologist Stanley Milgram. In these experiments, conducted in the 1960s, a number of volunteers were instructed to deliver painful electric shocks to the objects of a fake "scientific research." Most volunteers, convinced of the noble scientific purpose of their cruelty and relying on the expertise and authority of the scientist in charge of the research project, followed the instructions faithfully – undeterred by the cries of anguish of their victims. The tendencies revealed in the experiment may be said to be present in breathtaking dimensions by the practice of genocide during the Second World War and thereafter. The murder of millions of Jews initiated and supervised by a few thousand top Nazi leaders and officials was a gigantic bureaucratic operation that involved the cooperation of millions of "ordinary" people. They drove the trains that carried the victims to gas chambers and worked in the factories that produced the poisonous gases or crematoria appliances. The consequences of their actions were so remote from the simple tasks that preoccupied them on a daily basis that the connections could escape their attention or be barred from consciousness.

Even if the functionaries of a complex organization are aware of the ultimate effect of the joint activity of which they are a part, that effect is often too remote to worry them. Remoteness may be a matter of mental rather than geographical distance. Because of the vertical and horizontal division of labor, the actions of any single person are, as a rule, mediated by the actions of many others. In the end, our own contribution pales into insignificance and its influence on the final result seems too small to be seriously considered as a moral problem. These "techniques of neutralization," as the American sociologist David Matza termed them, enable perpetrators to relieve themselves of the responsibility for their actions. After all, they could have been doing things as innocuous and harmless as drawing blueprints, composing reports, filing documents, conducting research, or switching on and off a machine that mixes two chemical compounds.

Forms of organization, including those defined as bureaucratic, can easily lead to indifference. Drudgery and routinization can serve ends that are not intended and as Michael Herzfeld puts it in the *Social Production of Indifference*, it does not emanate from the barrel of a gun, but that which too readily become habitual. Employed in the service of inhuman ends we have seen its power to silence moral motivations not only in employees, but also well beyond the boundaries of the organization itself. It achieves this by appealing to the motive of self-preservation and even the cooperation of its victims and the moral indifference of its bystanders. In many cases, an anticipatory compliance may appear in the sense that victims go out of their way to please the oppressors by guessing their intention in advance and implementing it with zestful passion. In such fashion, the managers of genocide can attain their ends.

As for the bystanders, their compliance, or at least their silence accompanied by inactivity, may be secured through setting a high price for any expression of solidarity with the victims. Choosing morally correct action would mean inviting an awesome punishment. Once the stakes are raised in this way, the interests of self-preservation may push aside those of moral duty and techniques of rationalization and forms of justification are left to perform their purpose. Historically, such rationalizations have been assisted by those scientists who, in separating the means and ends of their inquiries, provided the dominant ideology with scientific evidence for the inferiority of those persons subject to horrific crimes. Subjects can be transformed into inferior "objects," rendered non-human and in this way their manipulation and destruction become not a moral matter, but one of technical know-how by those whose power can alleviate perpetrators of any responsibility for inflicting suffering and those who witness their atrocities, a power of empathy with the victims.

To speak of genocide is an extreme illustration of the opposition between self-preservation and moral duty, but the processes we describe are still with us when it comes to refugees and, more proximally, attitudes to those who exhibit differences from what is taken to be "normal." It is, therefore, an opposition that leaves its imprint on the everyday human condition. After all, extinguishing moral obligations may be facilitated by the statistical treatment of human actions. Viewed as numbers, human objects can lose their quality and so be deprived of their separate existence as bearers of human rights and moral obligations. What then matters is the category to which they have been designated. The classification itself can then sharpen the focus on selected shared attributes of the individuals in which the organization has expressed its interest, as well as form a basis of evaluation for the populations as a whole. Such categorization can license a neglect for all the other attributes of the person and thus for those very characteristics that form them as moral subjects and unique and irreplaceable human beings.

For Michel Foucault, as populations grew and social life became more complex, so the care of its citizens became a central concern of the state. A new regime arose in the art of government, with everyday life becoming an object of intervention in the desire to predict and control populations; all ably assisted by developments in statistical reasoning. People became regulated and categorized according to the strategies that were pursued with these ends in sight. The productivity of labor was very important in these rationalizations. What were once houses of confinement became hospitals in which those who were unable to work for physical or non-physical reasons became the objects of medical interventions. At this time, the idea of "psychiatry" was born. However, if such means were employed, for what purpose and with what consequences? Now, not only governments, but large corporations, including marketing and insurance services, classify populations for the purpose of collecting information and generating revenue. We have seen that business matters can be in tension with moral purpose. Why? Because people are treated as means to the pursuit of those interests and not ends in their own right.

There is another silencer of morality: the crowd. It has been noted that people who find themselves tightly packed together in confined spaces with great numbers of other people whom they do not know – who they have not met under other circumstances, have not interacted with before, and with whom they are "united" at present only by a temporary, accidental interest – are prone to behave in a way they would not deem acceptable in "normal" conditions. The wildest of behavior may suddenly spread through the crowd in a fashion which can be compared only with a forest fire, wind blast, or contagion. In an accidental crowd, for instance in a congested marketplace or in a theater in the grip of panic, people overwhelmed with the desire for self-preservation may trample over their fellow humans, push others into the fire, just to secure a breathing space for themselves or to get out of danger. In a crowd people may be able to commit deeds no single perpetrator would be morally capable of committing if alone. That happens in both mass physical proximity and its absence: for example, outpourings of moral condemnation on Twitter. If the crowd commits acts that its individual members might abhor, it is because of its "facelessness"; people lose their individuality and "dissolve" into the anonymous gathering and lack significant others to whom they feel accountable for their actions. The crowd may disappear as quickly as it gathers and its collective action, however coordinated it may appear, neither follows nor generates interaction of any degree of permanence. It is precisely the momentary character of the crowd action which makes possible the purely affective conduct of its individual members. For a fleeting moment, inhibitions may be removed, obligations rendered void, and rules suspended.

The rational conduct of the bureaucratic organization and the riotous eruptions of a crowd's anger seem poles apart. Yet they both tend towards "depersonalization" and so may reduce the propensity for moral action through a faceless anonymity. After all, people remain moral subjects as long as they are acknowledged as *humans*: that is, as beings eligible for the treatment reserved for fellow human beings alone and considered appropriate for every human being. This assumes that the partners to our interactions possess their own unique needs and that these needs are as valid and important as our own and so ought to be paid attention and respect. That, as Richard Sennett notes in his study of respect in an age of inequality, is a complex interaction between social structure and character. Whenever certain persons or categories of people are denied the right to our moral responsibility, they are treated as "lesser humans," "flawed humans," "not fully human," or downright "non-human." To guard against this, as Simone de Beauvoir put it, necessitates not treating someone we meet as a member of a class, nation, or some other collectivity, but as an individual who is an end in their own right.

In the universe of moral obligations not all members of the human species may be included. Many "primitive" tribes gave themselves names which meant "human beings." An accompanying refusal to accept the humanity of strange tribes and their members lingered on in slave-owning societies in which slaves had been assigned the status of "talking tools" and considered solely in the light of their usefulness to the accredited task. The status of limited humanity meant in practice that the essential requirement of a moral attitude – respect for another person's needs that includes, first and foremost, the recognition of their integrity and sanctity of their life – was not seen as binding in relation to the bearers of such status. It looks as if history consisted of a gradual, yet relentless extension of the idea of humanity – with a pronounced tendency of the universe of obligations to become ever more inclusive and in the end coterminous with the totality of the human species.

This process has not been straightforward. For as the boundaries of humanity extended, the propensity to regard the non-human as means to our ends has consequences. We can see this exemplified in the *anthropocene*, whereby human activity becomes the dominant influence on the environment with resulting climate change that may well remove basic needs for future generations. Our past is littered with the appearance of highly influential worldviews that not only expropriated vital and limited resources from our environment, but called for the exclusion of whole categories of populations – on the grounds of class, nation, race, sexuality, and religion – from the universe of obligations. These forces cannot be confined to the past, but remain. Those standing up to the perfection of the promise of the rationally organized world embodied in technological advancement may be readily denigrated as standing in the way of progress and efficiency. Whose progress? Whose idea of efficiency and with what consequences for how we live?

Summary

A combination of factors – suspending moral responsibility offered by the technology of management and the presence of worldviews ready and willing to deploy what it seems to offer – easily slips into a confinement of the universe of obligations. That has opened the way to such diverse consequences as the mass terror practiced in communist societies against the members of hostile classes and persons classified as their helpers; persistent discrimination of racial and ethnic minorities in countries otherwise proud of their human-rights record, many of whom practiced overt or surreptitious apartheid systems; the sale of arms to countries subsequently castigated for their lack of morality and who may then have been subject to a declaration of war only to be shot at by those same weapons; the numerous cases of genocide, moving from the massacre of Armenians in Turkey, through the annihilation of millions of Jews, gypsies, and Slavs by Nazi Germany, to the gassing of Kurds or the mass murders in Cambodia, the former Yugoslavia, and Rwanda. The boundaries of the universe of obligations remain to this day a contentious issue.

Inside the universe of obligations, the authority of the needs of others is recognized and acted upon. Everything should be done to secure their welfare, expand their life-chances, and open their access to the amenities that society has to offer. Poverty, ill health, and differential life expectancy, mobility, and chances constitute a challenge and an admonition to all other members of a society who occupy the same universe of obligations. Faced with such a challenge, we feel obliged to excuse ourselves – to supply a convincing explanation of why so little has been done to alleviate their lot and why not much more can be done; we also feel obliged to prove that everything that could be done has been done. Not that the explanations provided must of necessity be true. We hear, for instance, that the health service offered to the population at large cannot be improved because "money cannot be spent until it is earned." What such explanations may readily conceal, however, are forms of categorization that seek to naturalize differences, but are themselves the product of dominant social forces. Thus, the profits made by private medicine used by well-off patients may be classified as "earnings," while the services provided for those who cannot afford private fees are counted among "expenditures." Such explanations conceal a differential treatment of needs depending on the ability to pay and a social contract that came about as a result of recognizing the limitations of private provision of health. The very fact that the explanation is thought to be needed at all, however, testifies to the recognition that the people whose health needs are neglected remain, to some degree, inside the universe of obligations.

Self-preservation and moral duty often stand in tension. Neither can claim to be more "natural" than the other or better attuned to the inherent predisposition of human nature. If one becomes dominant over the other, the cause of the imbalance can usually be traced back to the social context of interaction. Self-interested and moral motives become prevalent depending on the circumstances over which the people who are guided by them may have only a limited control. It has been observed, however, that two persons may act differently when faced with the same circumstances. The power of social circumstances is evident and in order to understand ourselves and each other, it is an essential ingredient. Yet it does not necessarily saturate conduct which itself is influenced by the past, present, and future. The choice between courses of action can therefore remain open, whilst our individual actions are bound up with the actions of others upon whom we are dependent. A moral predisposition in our actions towards others is also a precondition of our self-esteem and self-respect.

5

Gifts, Exchange, and Intimacy

In our discussions on power and choice, we examined issues that inform our daily lives and the decisions which we routinely face in our interactions with others. Some of these we are aware of as we engage in our daily activities, whilst others are forged in the structures that shape our lives. In both cases they are informed by various circumstances and forces of which gift and exchange are a part and these bring form and meaning to our lives. In this chapter we continue our journey through an examination of these issues and those concerned with intimacy and care for others.

Gift, Exchange, and Expectation

In *The Nature of Money*, Geoffrey Ingham argues that the distinctiveness of the economic system that we call capitalism resides in the structural links to be found in the relations between states, banks, and companies and how private debt has become "monetized." Money, after all, is a social relationship of credit and debt involving a "promise to pay." It also structures the global economy which is based upon debt. As Ann Pettifor documents in her study *The Production of Money*, total global Gross Domestic Product (GDP) – broadly defined as a measure of the goods and services produced within an economy over a particular period of time – was $77 trillion in 2015, whilst the burden of debt was 286% of that figure.

At an interpersonal level, debt may be an occasional visitor, or daily preoccupation inducing overwhelming feelings of anxiety and impotence. Some may seek remedies without unduly altering the material and symbolic aspects that make up the routines and exceptions of their lifestyles. For others, it requires daily attention to fulfill obligations to children, family, and friends. It is not an occasional visitor, but a permanent resident requiring continual attention and activity in seeking to ameliorate its worse effects. It appears to meet a need that has varying consequences depending on whether credit comes from banks, those loan institutions with exorbitant rates of interest, or those who operate outside of any regulatory control.

Reminders from creditors flood into the places where we live. We do not use the term "home" here because that signifies some permanence and security

Thinking Sociologically, Third Edition. Zygmunt Bauman and Tim May.
© 2019 John Wiley & Sons Ltd. Published 2019 by John Wiley & Sons Ltd.

which, as Matthew Desmond's study of poor US families *Evicted* shows, can never be taken for granted, with one utility company alone disconnecting energy from some 50,000 households in one year. We sort through money demands and prioritize as best we can. After all, some may be urgent because the creditors are threatening to remove a valued piece of furniture, possession, or our accommodation in order to recover the debt. What can be done? We could go to a close relative and ask them for a loan – if they have the means to help us. We could then explain the situation and promise to pay the money back as soon as circumstances improve. They may have the means and refuse, or perhaps grumble a little and inform us of the virtues of foresight, prudence, and planning and not living above our means but, if able, reach into their pockets to help. Others, from families of sufficient means, may be more fortunate in the levels of financial support they routinely receive and a gift may move from an event to expectation and even sediment into a sense of entitlement.

There may be another option open to us. We could go to a bank or a credit agency. Would they be interested in how we are suffering as a result of our situation? Would they care? The only questions they might ask would refer to the guarantees that could be offered in order to ensure the loan would be repaid. They will inquire about income and expenditure in order to ascertain whether the capital repayments and interest on the loan can be met. Supporting documentation will be required and if they are satisfied that we are not an excessive risk and that the loan is likely to be repaid – with the interest that ensures a good profit – we may then be lent the money. Therefore, depending on to whom and where we turn to solve our financial problems, we can expect two different kinds of treatment. Our close relative may not inquire about matters relating to solvency as the loan is not a choice between good and bad business. What counts is that we are in need and so have a claim to help. Someone representing a credit agency, on the other hand, is not required to be concerned with such matters; they simply want to know whether the loan is likely to be a sensible, profitable business transaction. In no way is there an obligation, morally, or otherwise, to lend us the money.

In this case we see human interaction being influenced by two principles: *exchange* and *gift*. In the former case, it is self-interest that is predominant. Although the person who has the need for the loan may be recognized as an autonomous person with legitimate needs and rights, these are subservient to the satisfaction of the potential lender's own interests or the organization they represent. The lender is guided by preoccupations with the risks involved in making the loan, how much will be paid back and what material benefits may be derived from the transaction. These and similar issues will be asked of the prospective action in order to evaluate its desirability and to establish the order of preference between alternative choices. Parties to these interactions will bargain about the meaning of equivalence and deploy all the resources at hand in order to obtain the best possible deal and so tilt the transaction in their favor. It is one based upon a particular view of human action in which calculation and the maximization of self-interest are assumed to be the guiding principles. It takes the acts in which we engage and defines those in terms of acquisition and thereby saturates any alternative values.

As the French anthropologist Marcel Mauss recognized in the 1920s, the idea of the gift is another matter. Studies in economic anthropology have increasingly drawn attention to forms of action that cannot be described in the above terms or reduced to competitive instinct. What we see is more of a reciprocal economy in operation whereby it is obligation that motivates the exchange of gifts in terms of the needs and the rights of others. These gifts have symbolic value for the group to which the parties to the interaction belong and take place within belief systems in which reciprocity is praised. Thus, in the act of giving, we also give something of ourselves and this is prized above the instrumental calculations that inform a system of exchange relations which are governed by abstract systems based on extracting profit through debt. Such rewards are not a factor in the calculation of desirability of action. The goods are given away with the services being extended merely because the other person needs them and, being the person they are, they have a perceived right to their needs being respected.

The idea of the "gift" is a common name for a wide range of acts that differ in their purity. "Pure" gift is, as it were, a liminal concept – a sort of benchmark against which all practical cases are measured. Such practical cases depart from the ideal in various degrees. In the purest of forms, the gift would be totally disinterested and offered without regard to the quality of the recipient. Disinterestedness means a lack of remuneration in any shape or form. Judged by the ordinary standards of ownership and exchange, the pure gift is a pure loss. After all, it is a gain solely in moral terms and this is a basis for action that its logic cannot recognize. The value of the gift is not measured by the market price of the goods or services offered, but precisely by the subjective loss they constitute for the donor. The only qualification considered when the gift is offered is that the recipient belongs to the category of people in need. For this reason, generosity towards members of one's own kin or close friends, which we discussed earlier, does not in fact meet the requirements of the pure gift: it sets apart the recipients as special people selected for special treatment. Being special, the recipients have the right to expect such generosity from others with whom they are bound by a network of special relationships and the absence of such generosity may meet with disapproval. In its pure form, the gift is offered to anyone who may need it simply because, and only because, they need it. The pure gift is thus the recognition of the humanity of the other with no expectation of reciprocity.

There are those who suggest the future of business is giving away things for "free." Chris Anderson in his book *Free: The Future of a Radical Price* is one of those for whom the digital age is apparently an open one. The idea being that the digital age is cheaper because it is not about production costs using raw materials. Those developers producing open source software might be characterized as living in a culture in which the idea of the gift is core to their motivation. Whilst this may only be part of the reasons for such production, gifts offer the donor that elusive, yet deeply gratifying, reward of moral satisfaction in which the act of giving is also an act of giving something of themselves. The act embodies an experience of selflessness, of self-sacrifice for the sake of another human being. In sharp contrast to the context of exchange or gain seeking, such moral satisfaction grows in proportion to the degree of self-sacrifice and the resulting loss. The philosopher, social critic, and social policy analyst Richard Titmuss wrote, for example, about the British context of giving blood to the National Health Service for no reward except that inspired by *altruistic* motives. He spoke of the gift of blood having attributes that distinguished it from other forms of giving in that it was "a voluntary, altruistic act." To replace such altruism with a system that encourages and legitimizes giving in terms of being the exchange of a good would undermine its basis in values accorded to strangers and not what isolated individuals expect to gain from society.

Research conducted on human behavior under extreme conditions – war and foreign occupation – has shown that the most heroic cases of gift-giving, in terms of sacrificing one's own life in order to save another whose life was threatened, were on the whole performed by people whose motives came very close to the ideal of pure gift. They considered helping other human beings as, purely and simply, their moral duty and one that did not call for any further justification, as it is natural, self-evident, and elementary. One of the most remarkable findings of this research is that the most selfless among the helpers found it difficult to understand the unique heroism of their actions. Despite transcending personal concerns through a care and concern for others, they play down the courage such conduct required and the moral virtue it demonstrated.

Relations in Gift and Exchange

Returning to the two kinds of treatment which we discussed at the beginning of this chapter, as a first approximation, we may call the relationship with the relative *personal* and the relationship with the representative of the credit agency *impersonal*. What happens in the framework of a personal relationship tends to depend on the quality of the partners to the interaction and not on their performance. In an impersonal relationship, this tendency is not so evident. It is only performance which counts, not the quality. It does not matter who the people are, only what they are likely to do. The partner who is positioned to make the loan will be interested in past records as a basis on which to judge the likelihood of future behavior; all of which takes place under the rubric of satisfying the terms and conditions of a formal agreement.

Talcott Parsons considered the opposition between quality and performance as one of the major oppositions among conceivable patterns of human relationship that he gave the name "pattern variables." Among these is that between "universalism" and "particularism." Under the gift situation, people are not seen as part of a category, but a particular individual in need. With the official representing the credit agency, on the other hand, an individual client is part of a larger category of past, current, and prospective borrowers. Having dealt with many "like-others" before, they will assess the person on the basis of criteria that are applied to other cases. The outcome then depends on the application of general rules to particular cases. The relationship with the family member is "diffuse," while the relationship with the official is "specific." The generosity of the relative was not just a one-off whim; it was not an attitude taken specifically for the distress that was reported during a conversation. There is a willingness to assist in this particular case because they are generally well disposed towards the person in need and interested in all aspects of their life. The official's conduct is not geared to the specific application and their reactions to the application and their final decision are based upon a construction of the case, not other aspects of the person's life. According to the logic of the situation, those things important to the applicant are, from the point of view of an official who dispenses loans, irrelevant to the application and so ruled out of consideration.

Talcott Parsons wrote of the relationship between "affectivity" and "affective neutrality." Some interactions are infused with emotions – compassion, sympathy, or love – while others are detached and unemotional. Impersonal relations are not normally expected to arouse in the actors any feelings other than a passionate urge to achieve a successful transaction. The actors themselves are not objects of emotions in terms of being either liked or disliked. If they strike a hard bargain, try to cheat, prevaricate, or avoid commitments, some of the impatience with the unduly slow progress of the transaction may rub off on the attitude towards them, or they may be regarded as someone with whom it was "a pleasure to do business." By and large, emotions tend not to be regarded as central to impersonal interactions, while they are the very factors which make personal interaction plausible. In terms of the loan by a close relative, however, there is a probability that the parties empathize with each other and share a sense of belonging in which each person imagines themselves in the other's position in order to understand their needs and predicaments.

Carole Gilligan identified what she called a tendency for women to adopt an "ethic of care" (she did not rule out men having such a predisposition) in which concern is given over to others and a concern for oneself is considered "selfish." Such an ethic concerns a relational responsibility in which the parties do not see themselves as autonomous in terms of being governed by abstract rules, but as "connected" with others in relationships. If we see ourselves existing in isolation then to provide consideration, recognition, or even gifts to others would seem an offense to our authenticity. On the other hand, it is within our significant relations with others that we generate meanings, senses of value, and our moral compass. Such fundamental features of our lives are to be bracketed in the case of seeking a loan based on impersonal relations. A person seeking a loan might seek to avoid making an official angry and even flatter them, but otherwise concerns that arise in significant relations would be judged as interfering and detracting from the calculation of risk in terms of profit and loss.

An important distinction between personal and impersonal contexts of interaction lies in the factors on which the actors rely for the success of their actions. We all depend on the actions of others about whom we are likely to know very little, and the gaps in our understanding are frequently filled by stereotypical assumptions. We rely upon them in complex environments to meet our needs and navigate our ways through the world; given their number, routine interactions would be impossible and instead we relate in an impersonal manner. Under conditions of limited personal knowledge, appealing to rules seems to be the only way to make it possible. Imagine what an incredibly large, unwieldy volume of knowledge you would need to amass if all your transactions with others were based solely on your properly researched estimate of their personal qualities. The more realistic alternative is to get hold of the few general rules that guide the interchange. This is one of the justifications for the existence of the market mechanism that governs so much of our lives. Implied is a *trust* that the partners will observe the same rules in the transaction.

Many things in life are organized so as to enable partners to interact without any or with little personal information about each other. It would be quite impossible for many of us, for example, to assess, in advance, the healing ability and dedication of the medical practitioners to whom we might turn in times of illness. Such professionalism is not only about knowledge and competence as certified by professional bodies after lengthy periods of training and examinations, but also about trust. We often have no choice but to submit ourselves to their care and hope that, in exchange, we receive the care that our case warrants and requires. In this and similar cases people, personally unknown to us, took it upon themselves to endorse the competency of people whose credentials they then endorsed. By so doing and through upholding standards in terms of a set of professional ethics, they have made it possible for us to accept the services of such people on trust.

Anthony Giddens, along with the German sociologists Ulrich Beck and Niklas Luhmann, have all examined the relations between trust and risk. Niklas Luhmann makes a useful distinction between confidence and trust. As societies have become more complex and impersonal, the latter increasingly becomes more commonplace and cannot be conceived of without a sense of risk. As risk increases, so impersonal systems step in. Risk, after all, can be covered by insurance should it be affordable. Paradoxically, that itself can increase a sense of confidence that undermines the sense of risk that operates to prevent accidents through adopting more cautious behavior. The examples Luhmann uses include safety technologies in industry and the introduction of safer roads. In respect to the latter we can see this in the use of new technologies for traffic calming, as well as the placing of relations between trust and risk in driverless cars that are expected to take away "human error" and thus apparently offer us a safer future.

It is precisely because so many of our transactions are performed in an impersonal context that the need for personal relationships becomes so poignant and acute. Trust is a social relationship that, if overly subjected to the impersonality and the process of commodification associated with the market, will be transformed and even undermined. Therefore, it is not surprising that in their different ways the German philosopher and sociologist Jürgen Habermas, the American social commentator Francis Fukuyama, and the Hungarian financier and philanthropist George Soros have all noted how the success of such a mechanism is dependent upon a cultural basis of community and commitment. If permitted to reign unchecked, therefore, they argue that the market will undermine the basis upon which its existence relies. The realm of the economic cannot be reduced to the operation of an instrumental morality. Indeed, the very realm of the economic, as Ralph Fevre argues in *The New Sociology of Economic Behaviour*, needs to be expanded beyond this to include such things as dignity at work, well-being, and payment according to worth.

We have noted on numerous occasions that the more we depend on people of whom we have but vague and superficial knowledge and the more perfunctory and fleeting our encounters are, the stronger the tendency to expand the realm of personal relations. The result of this is to force the expectations that fit only personal transactions onto interactions that are best performed in an impersonal fashion. Thus, resentment of the indifference of an impersonal world is likely to be felt most strongly by those who move, in an abrupt fashion, between two worlds. Young people, for instance, who are just about to leave what may be the relatively caring world of the family and youthful friendships, find themselves entering the emotionally cool world of employment and occupational practice. Those retiring may find themselves without the structure, rhythm, and perhaps even fulfillment offered by work. For such reasons we witness attempts to opt out of a callous and heartless world where people appear to serve only as the means to some ends which bear little relation to their own needs and happiness. Some escapees try to establish commune-like, self-enclosed, and self-contained enclaves, inside which only relations of a personal type are allowed. Such attempts, however, may lead to disenchantment and even bitterness. It transpires that the unrelenting effort needed to maintain a high intensity of feelings over a long period of time and to absorb frustrations arising from the constant clashes between affections and the considerations of effectiveness, may generate more misery than that experienced by the indifference of the alternative.

Love, Intimacy, Caring, and Commodities

If the personal context cannot accommodate the whole business of life, it remains an indispensable ingredient. Our craving for "deep and wholesome" personal relationships and the importance of affect and emotion in our lives can grow in intensity the wider and less penetrable the network of impersonal dependencies in which we find ourselves entangled. If we have jobs, we find ourselves being employees at one moment and then at another moment one of the following: a customer in a shop; a passenger on a bus or train; a spectator at sporting events or in a cinema or theater; a voter for political parties; a patient in doctors' and dentists' surgeries, and numerous other activities in different places and various times in our lives. Everywhere we may feel that only a small section of our selves is present. In each context we may have to remind ourselves about appropriate forms of behavior and so judge those that are acceptable and unacceptable accordingly. Nowhere do we feel at home in terms of being truly "ourselves." So, who in the end is the real "I"?

Most of us would fall shy of settling for an image of ourselves as a mere patch-work of different roles. Nevertheless, sooner or later we grow to reconcile ourselves to a plurality of "Me's" and even to some lack of coordination between them. As the unity is evidently missing in the world "out there," split as it is into a multitude of partial transactions, it must be supplied instead by a quest for cohesion within ourselves through our actions. As Georg Simmel observed in the early twentieth century, in the densely populated, variegated world we inhabit, individuals tend to fall back upon themselves in the never-ending search for sense and unity. Once focused on us rather than on the world outside, this overwhelming thirst for unity and coherence is articulated as the search for self-identity. A resulting tension between adjustment and autonomy is a recurrent feature of the human condition and is demonstrated by the popularity of books that pick up on these very themes: for example, David Reisman's post-Second World War study on the changing nature of the American character entitled *The Lonely Crowd* to Robert Putnam's *Bowling Alone,* through to Sherry Turkle's *Alone Together*; a book charting how we seem to expect more of technology and less of each other as we appear willing participants in a social experiment that has consequence for our privacy, isolation, and togetherness.

None of the many impersonal exchanges in which we are involved will suffice to supply the identity we seek because it lies beyond any of those exchanges. In each single context we are, so to speak, displaced: our real selves, we feel, are located somewhere outside the context of the interaction taking place. Perhaps only in a personal context, with its diffuseness, particularity, emphasis on quality, and the mutual affection which saturates it, can we hope to find more of what we are looking for and, even then, we may be frustrated in our attempts. It is in the actions that we perform in its pursuit that our self lies, rather than some end-state in which autonomy and unity may be presupposed without question. If the self that seeks is the self that is sought, then no context can fully accommodate it.

We can place our restless searches in the domain of love. Being loved means being treated by the other person as unique, as unlike any other; it means that the loving person accepts that the loved ones need not invoke universal rules in order to justify the images they hold of themselves or their demands; it means that the loving person accepts and confirms the sovereignty of their partner and their right to decide for themselves and to choose on their own authority. Being loved also means being understood in the sense in which we use it whenever we say: "I want you to understand me!" Or, when asked with anguish: "Do you understand me? Do you *really* understand me?" This craving for being understood is a desperate call for someone to put themselves in our shoes, to see things from our point of view and to accept without further proof that we have a point of view that ought to be respected for the simple reason that it is ours. What we are pursuing in these situations is a confirmation of our private experiences: that is, our inner motives, images of ideal life, and of ourselves and our miseries and joys. It concerns the *validation* of our self-portrayal. Validation is sought through a partner's willingness to listen seriously and with sympathy and empathy when talking about ourselves. Denigration of that expectation in intimate relations can lead to misunderstanding, resentment, and hostility.

There is a paradox at work here. We find a desire for the unique whole of the self as opposed to a collection of roles. There is an assertion and desire for uniqueness and not to be just a cog in the impersonal machine of life. On the other hand, we are aware that nothing exists just because it is imagined to be so. The difference between fantasy and reality is thereby necessary and so whatever truly exists must exist for others in the way it does for us. Thus, the more that people feel they succeed in developing a truly unique self – in making their experiences unique – the more they require social confirmation of those experiences. It seems, at first sight, that such confirmation is possible only through love. As societies become more complex, most human needs are attended to in an impersonal way and the need we have for a loving relationship appears deeper than at any other time. The resulting expectation that love carries in our existence becomes heightened: if we seek validation in those relations and yet we are changing with new experiences, we do not wish just to be loved for being the person we were when romance first flourished, but the one we are now and even becoming. We expect consistency and depth in the face of dynamism, fluctuation, and change. The private consequences of our public troubles, as feminist researchers have long argued, lead to ever greater pressures, tensions, and obstacles that lovers must encounter and seek to overcome with differing degrees of success.

What makes a love relationship both special and fragile is the need for reciprocity. If we seek love then, in all probability, our partners will ask us to reciprocate – to respond with love. We act in such a way as to confirm the reality of our partner's experience: to seek to understand as we are seeking to be understood. Ideally, each partner will strive to find meaning in the other partner's world. The realities, however, will not be identical. When two people meet for the first time, they have experiences and biographies that are not shared and, for the relationship to flourish, they must be recognized, validated, and perhaps even renegotiated. It is improbable that both partners will regard each of their experiences as authentic and without the need for the effort of understanding which itself makes the relationship unique. They may even have to abandon elements of their past to produce a lasting relationship. Yet this can defy the very purpose of love and the need which it is expected to satisfy. If successful renegotiations do take place, the rewards can be great. The road to its realization requires much patience, understanding, and effort to travel it unscathed. Many succeed, but the gap between the ideal and the actual may lead to frustrations and tensions manifest in separation, divorce, and even domestic violence.

"Destructive Gemeinschaft" is a term for a relationship, coined by Richard Sennett, in which both partners obsessively pursue the right to intimacy. This is to open oneself up to a partner and share the whole, most private truth about one's inner life through absolutely sincerity. Nothing is hidden from view, however upsetting the disclosure may be for the partner. The result is to place an enormous burden on the latter's shoulders as the partner is asked to give agreement to things which do not necessarily arouse enthusiasm and to be equally sincere and honest in reply. Richard Sennett does not believe that a lasting relationship – particularly a lasting *loving* relationship – can be erected on such grounds. To be both singular and irreplaceable as a condition for love, but place the desire for total transparency upon a relationship, can lead to overwhelming odds that a partner will make demands of the other which they cannot meet. In the face of such pressures they will decide to call it a day by stopping the attempt and withdrawing. One or other of the partners will choose to opt out of such intensity and seek to satisfy their need for self-confirmation elsewhere.

The requirements of reciprocity in a loving relationship are thus double-edged. Strange as it may seem, the least vulnerable is love as a gift: a preparedness to accept a beloved's world, to put ourselves in that world and try to comprehend it from inside – without expecting a similar service in exchange. There is no need for negotiation, agreement, or contract. Once aimed in both directions, intimacy makes negotiation and compromise inevitable. At this point it is precisely the negotiation and compromise which one or both partners may be too impatient, or too self-concerned, to bear lightly. With love being such a difficult and costly achievement, it is no wonder one finds demand for its substitution: that is, for someone who would perform the function of love without the desire for reciprocity.

In the changing relations between the public and private worlds and the personal and impersonal we find varying social trends. What reason, for example, do we provide for the increasing popularity of psychoanalytic sessions, counseling, and marriage guidance? For the right to open oneself up, make one's innermost feelings known to another person? Is it to receive approval of one's identity, or to be prepared to enter into the uncharted territory of self exploration, with all the risks that this may entail, in the desire to become more self-aware? In respect to the analyst or the therapist performing care on the basis of being paid, it turns patients or clients into more impersonal relations. The patient may even think they are buying the illusion of being loved. However, as this relationship is in sharp disagreement with the socially accepted model of love, psychoanalytical sessions can be plagued with transference. This may be defined as the patient's tendency to mistake the "as if" conduct of the analyst for an expression of love and to respond with behavior that steps beyond the impersonal elements of the agreement.

One can be concerned with oneself and have the concerns shared, without giving a single thought to the people whose services have been bought and who may take on the obligation of care. Love and care, as Lynn Jamieson reminds us in her study of intimacy in modern society, are not necessarily the same. Here we find practices of intimacy varying according to gender. When it comes to care we see gender inequalities in both paid and unpaid work. Whilst this is a growing and vital area of work, the recognition and pay afforded to those who work in this sector does not represent that imperative. They meet practical needs and are not expected to love as such, but care for people. Equally, those who may express a deep connection and intimacy with another may not see caring for them as part of that relationship.

Identity and Commodification

The consumer market offers another, perhaps less vulnerable substitute, for love in putting on a wide range of "identities" from which a consumer can select. As culture and the economy have become increasingly intertwined, so the relations between affect and value alter. Commercial advertisements take pains to show the commodities they try to sell as a part of a particular lifestyle, so that prospective customers can consciously purchase symbols of such self-identity as they would wish to possess. Advertising is not a matter of representing, but creating markets through the constitution of new relations between consumption, identity, and goods. The market offers identity-making tools that can be used to produce results which differ somewhat from each other and are in this way personalized.

As a mechanism, the market enables those who can afford it to put together various elements of the complete identikit of a do-it-yourself (DIY) customized self. We can learn how to express ourselves through consumption in so many ways: as a modern and liberated person; a thoughtful, reasonable, caring person;

an aspiring and self-confident tycoon; as easy going and likeable; as oriented towards the outdoors and being physically fit; as a romantic, dreamy, and love hungry, or any mixture of all these! The advantage of market-promoted identities is that they come complete with elements of social approval – introduced as they are by using means of advertising that people seem to approve of – and so the agony of seeking confirmation is spared. Social approval does not need to be negotiated for it has been, so to speak, built into the marketed product from the start. It is, quite simply, big business, with estimates of total global spend on advertising being $600 billion per year.

For some, the pursuit of the authentic self in the market is nothing more than an illusion. Appearance is all we have. There is no deeper reality in terms of who we *really* are. Appearances are manufactured and taken on and off in the seduction that comes with continual consumption. With so many alternatives that are widely available and growing in popularity, the effort required by the drive to solve the self-identity problem through reciprocal love has a smaller chance of success. Asked in one interview about whether there was such a thing as love, Jean Baudrillard replied that there was "acting-out," but he does not have "a great deal to say about love." Nevertheless, if he is correct, the implications of his analysis seem to place ever greater burdens upon the need for reciprocity and recognition within loving relationships as people retreat to seek more authentic experiences.

As we have seen, negotiating approval is a tormenting experience for partners in love. Success is not possible without long and dedicated effort. It needs self-sacrifice on both sides. The effort and the sacrifice might be made more frequently and with greater zeal were it not for the availability of "easy" substitutes. With the substitutes being easy to obtain – the only sacrifice being to part with a quantity of money or use credit – and relentlessly offered by the sellers, there is less motivation for laborious, time-consuming, and frequently frustrating efforts. Resilience can wither when confronted with alluringly "foolproof" and less demanding marketed alternatives. Often the first hurdle, the first setback in the developing and vulnerable love partnership, would be enough for one or both partners to wish to slow down, or to leave the track altogether. The substitutes may be first sought with the intention to "complement" and hence to strengthen or resuscitate, the failing love relationship. They can also drain the energy from that relationship through externalizing desire and so moving attention away from the work of mutual understanding in intimate, loving relationships.

One of the manifestations of a devaluation of love, as Richard Sennett notes, is the tendency of *eroticism* to be ousted and supplanted by sexuality. Eroticism means the deployment of sexual desire and ultimately of sexual intercourse itself, as a hub around which a lasting love relationship is built and maintained: a social partnership of a stable kind, bearing all the features previously ascribed to multisided, personal relations. Sexuality means the reduction of sexual intercourse to one function only: the satisfaction of sexual desire. Such a reduction is often supplemented by special precautions aimed at preventing the sexual relationship from giving rise to mutual sympathy and obligation and thus from growing into a fully fledged personal partnership. Wrenched from love, sex is reduced to an unloading of tension, in which the partner is used as an essentially replaceable means to an end. Another consequence, however, is that the emancipation of sexuality from the context of eroticism leaves the love relationship considerably weakened. It now lacks (or has to share) one of the most powerful of its resources and finds its stability still more difficult to defend.

A loving relationship may collapse under the pressure of inner tensions, or it may retreat into a type of relationship that bears many or all the marks of an impersonal relationship – one of exchange. We have observed a typical form of exchange relationship when considering transactions with a credit agency. We have noted that the only thing which counted there was the passing of a particular object, or a service, from one side of the transaction to the other – an object was changing hands. The living persons involved in the transactions did not do much more than play the role of carriers or mediators in that they prompted and facilitated the circulation of goods. Although their gaze was fixed on their respective partners, they assigned relevance solely to the object of exchange, while granting the other party a secondary, derivative importance in terms of being holders or gatekeepers of the goods they wanted. They saw "through" their partners, straight into the goods themselves. The last thing the partners might consider would be the tender feelings or spiritual cravings of their counterparts. The supreme motive of their action was to give away as little as possible and to get as much as possible and so both pursued their own self-interest, concentrating their thought solely on the task at hand. We may say that in transactions of impersonal exchange, the interests of the actors are in conflict.

Nothing in an exchange transaction is done simply for the sake of the other. In this sense there is a tendency to experience an accompanying fear of being cheated and a need to remain wide awake, wary, and vigilant. They want protection against the selfishness of the other side. There is no reason to expect the other party to act selflessly, but there may be an insistence upon a fair deal. Hence the exchange relationship calls for a binding rule and an authority entrusted with the task of adjudicating the fairness of the transaction. This authority must be capable of imposing its decisions in cases of transgression. Various consumer associations, watchdogs, and ombudspersons are established out of this urge for protection. Such bodies are charged with the difficult task of monitoring the fairness of exchange and lobby the authorities for laws which would restrain the freedom of the stronger side to exploit the ignorance, or naivety, of the weaker one.

Seldom are the two counterparts of a transaction in a truly equal position. After all, those who produce or sell the goods know much more of the quality of their product than the buyers and users are ever likely to learn, regardless of the number of guarantees of quality that are made. They may well push the product to gullible customers under false pretenses, unless constrained by law. The more complex and technically sophisticated the goods, the less their buyers are able to judge their true quality and value. To avoid being deceived, the prospective buyers have to resort to the help of independent authorities. It is precisely because the partners enter exchange relationships only as functions of exchange, as conveyers of the goods and so remain "invisible" to each other, that they feel much less intimate than in the case of love relationships. They do not take upon themselves duties, or obligations, other than the promise to abide by the terms of the transaction. Aspects of their selves which are not relevant to the transaction at hand are unaffected and retain their autonomy – depending upon which side of the transaction they fall!

Is this really the case? There is a mode of thought, often taken for granted in economic and political reasoning, that human labor is a commodity, like others, and so can be treated as an object of exchange. Yet unlike exchangeable goods, labor cannot be detached from the laborer. Selling our labor means agreeing that our actions as a person can be subordinated to the will and decisions of others. The totality of the laborer's self and not just a detachable object in their possession, is parted with and transferred to somebody else's control. The apparently impersonal contract thereby reaches far beyond the normal boundaries constituting transactions of exchange. The promise to repay a debt, enforced by law, also involves an undertaking to work to make the repayments with, of course, handsome interest.

Summary

We have discussed love and exchange in this chapter. Here we find two extremes of a continuous line along which human relations can be plotted. We have discussed them in pure forms and most relationships are a recipe into which they are mixed in varying proportions. There are now ethical banks and investment funds whose purpose is to contribute to ends that are social and environmental and so not governed solely by calculations aimed at profitability for its own sake. We are also seeing the rise of the sharing economy, foundational and circular economy, de-growth, and steady state movements. Such values and varying forms of exchange may embody the elements of business-like bargaining that we find in loving relationships for the fair rate of exchange in the "I'll do this if you do that" style. Except for a chance encounter or one-off transaction, the actors in exchange relationships may not remain indifferent to each other for long and sooner or later may be involved in more than exchange around money and goods. Whilst we are routinely told that market transactions are impersonal, they are based upon networks of interdependencies in which norms, values, and evaluative judgments are routine features of interactions.

Each of our characterizations retains its relative identity even if submerged in a mixed relationship. Each has its own expectations and idealizations and hence orients the conduct of the actors in a particular direction. Much of the ambiguity of the relationships we enter into with others is accounted for by reference to the tensions and contradictions between the two extreme, complementary yet incompatible, sets of expectations. Pure relationships seldom appear in life, where ambivalence is the rule. That creates tensions within personal relationships as a response to an impersonal world. Our selves are part of that and may easily be played out upon others. As the impersonal and personal sphere mix in increasing ways and culture and the economy blend, it leads to other outlets, as well as the creation of new sets of services in response.

Our dreams and desires appear in tension between two needs that are difficult to satisfy when pursued separately. These are the needs of *belonging* and of *individuality*, to which we must add the capability to act in terms of being *positioned* in different ways within social relationships. Belonging prompts us to seek strong and secure ties with others. We express this need whenever we speak or think of togetherness or of community. Individuality sways us towards privacy as a state in which we are immune to pressures and free from demands to do whatever we think is worth doing. Yet what is worth doing for us is also that which is evaluated as worthy by others. Both needs are pressing and powerful. The nearer one comes to the satisfaction of one need, the more painful may be the neglect of the other. We find that community without privacy may feel more like oppression than belonging, while privacy without community can be more like loneliness than the desire to "be oneself." What we can say is that we are ourselves with others, in differing degrees, with all the accompanying joys, pleasures, hopes, wishes, frustrations, and constraints that accompany our states of being. To be a friend to ourselves means that we must have already entered into friendships with others.

6

Body, Sexuality, and Health

Sociological insight lies at the intersections between history, our biographies, and social reproduction. Each of us believe ourselves to be unique and yet we are part of social milieus that shape and influence our perceptions and actions, down to the deepest levels of what we take to be our individuality. Health and the wellbeing of our bodies are fundamental features of this process. After all, we are routinely subject to adverts about dieting, exercise, mindfulness, and holidays. In this process, concern with our bodies heightens, habits change, money is exchanged, and our skepticism concerning the expertise that informs the latest thinking about what is good for us may rise. We might reject the call to be healthy with binges of eating and drinking and allude to that which is apparently beyond the spheres of our responsibility in order to justify our actions. Holidays are advertised as a "break," but from what? As varying images and promises of possibility so routinely fill our everyday lives, we oscillate not only between the desire for intimacy and solitude, but in our relations between images of ourselves and our bodies.

Wellbeing, Security, and Shelter

We have seen how we come to know ourselves with and through others and how our relations can be both wonderful and vexing. Our interactions can send varying signals whose consequences require us to own a responsibility for our actions. When we refer to "I" we are performing in different ways: in terms of our bodies, our physical presence, and through taking a position in the world to others and to ourselves. We are surrounded, for example, by ideas of "wellbeing" whose characteristics include adopting a positive mental attitude and thereby remove from the scope of our experiences negative feelings. The growth in indicators of such a state can fall upon each individual whose internalization of those evaluations may lead them to ask if they exhibit sufficient evidence of such a state. That process can lead to further anxiety. No wonder, therefore, that many of us create strategies to avoid such situations. Finding confusion difficult to resolve, we may feel an urge to cut the strings and withdraw. Where do we go to find the secure shelter we seek?

Thinking Sociologically, Third Edition. Zygmunt Bauman and Tim May.
© 2019 John Wiley & Sons Ltd. Published 2019 by John Wiley & Sons Ltd.

Think of the world around us; about the places and people we know and believe we understand. We inhabit spaces and places that inform and are informed by the meaning we attach to them. The significance of such meaning is variable and can be characterized as a series of concentric circles exhibiting varying degrees of comprehension, each one being larger than the next. The circumference of the largest and most distant circle is blurred on our cognitive map. It is one with which we do not feel acquainted and much of the understanding we gain of it is mediated through varying sources: for example, social media, newspapers, and television news. The greater the distance the more unknown it seems. So we rely upon others to guide us through its terrain and characteristics, but without necessarily knowing about its accuracy. The smaller spheres in which we interact are more familiar because they exhibit rules and behavior we understand and we know how to respond to the routines of interaction.

Familiarity and trust lie in dynamic relations. The more time spent in a setting, in physical proximity, the more familiar it becomes. We come to better understand people and places by testing our knowledge against experiences that are informed by the past and present and even anticipations of the future. Proximity and our sense of vulnerability interact through regular patterns in which we may come to feel a part of a social scene and more secure. Knowing people's habits reduces the uncertainty that comes with unfamiliarity and so we come to know what we might expect from people. These are places where there is no need to prove anything, where we can show a "true face" and hide nothing. What we call "home" is often seen in these terms and regarded as a place of safety, warmth, and security, where we can be sure of our place and our rights without fighting or keeping watch. For this reason, the experience of homelessness is more than the absence of physical shelter for it is to be deprived of a home which Matthew Desmond characterizes in *Evicted* as a "wellspring of personhood."

As with all boundaries that demarcate spaces and places, familiarity and security within particular shelters are fine as long as they exist and exhibit continuity over time. As Alison Cavanagh notes in her *Sociology in the Age of the Internet,* people may feel a loss for community and seek solidarity in online communities. How that is created and reproduced is a focus for sociological understanding. In terms of the home itself, family break-ups, the struggles between generations over sexual orientation, marriage, and religious affiliations where we see clashes of tradition and belief, appear not to exist as long as the boundaries between the circles are assumed to be clearly demarcated and a homogenous world exists. We then know who we are, the expectations made of us, and where we stand in the order of things. We know what we may reasonably expect in each situation and which expectations would be illegitimate and presumptuous. Yet, what if the distinctions between the circles become blurred or even break down entirely? What if the rules which are in their right place in one circle leak into another, or are changing too fast, and different norms, expectations, and values enter the terrain of the familiar? Feelings of confusion and uncertainty, through to resentment and hostility, may result. Clarity and coherence give way to uncertainty. Anxiety might mix with a lack of willingness to engage and understand which leads to further divisions.

Nostalgia may come to play its role in the process of comprehension. A desire for a return to a past where harmony ruled and tradition operated so that people knew their place and the expectations correspondingly placed upon them. Whilst historical research has questioned the existence of these comfortable certitudes that often came with the cost of suppressing differences through oppression and intolerance, they persist as the popular imagination appropriates them as a relief from the response to contemporary conditions. Indeed, populist politicians may mobilize such rhetoric in order to attract support. We can be sure in the process that tolerance recedes and blame is the short circuit replacing the work of understanding which enables us to live together.

The speed of change now appears to govern the conditions in which we live, with people moving around quickly. As John Urry documents in *Mobilities,* our connected world can mean we appear to be both present and absent and can take our ability to move across boundaries for granted. Those who were once intimately known disappear from view and new people enter, of whom little is known. The feeling is that if we could have once defined who we were in terms of where we lived and in what era, those resources have evaporated, and if norms and rules seem to be changing rapidly and without notice, they no longer possess the legitimacy that must underpin their existence. Little can be taken for granted, with assumptions resting on shifting sands whose consequences are held at bay by constant refreshment through continuous efforts. Even in the innermost, most homely of circles, vigilance is required as precariousness governs more of our lives. Commodification penetrates the boundaries and can easily turn that home of security into an asset that is an object of exchange like any other.

We exaggerate somewhat to illustrate. However, we can easily assume that which affords our security that many do not possess, or have the means to acquire. We cannot move from the particularity of our experiences to generalization. In terms of the latter, there are processes that affect close relationships despite the prevalent belief that they are hermetically sealed off from social, political, and economic influences. Take, for example, the most intimate of relations: the family or love partnership. Anthony Giddens coined the term "confluent love" to describe the sentiments which hold the partnership together and "pure relationships" to characterize the kind of partnership that is built on this foundation. Confluent love simply means that at one particular moment partners love each other, are attracted to each other, and wish to stay together. For them, their partnership is pleasurable, satisfying, and desirable. Nevertheless, there is no promise or guarantee that this agreeable condition will last "till death us do part." Those things that flow together may also flow apart. Confluent love needs two, but to start drifting apart it is enough that the feelings of one begin to fade. A pure relationship, held together by confluent emotions, is a brittle and vulnerable construction. Neither of the partners can be really sure of the other, who may declare tomorrow that they do not feel like sharing lives and staying together. They need "more space" and would rather seek that elsewhere. Partnerships start to look like relations built on a "trial period," with a series of daily tests without end. They appear to offer freedom of maneuver as partners are not bound by timeless commitments, nor do they "mortgage the future" of either. The price to be paid, however, may seem high as such "freedom" is informed by perpetual uncertainty and lack of security.

All this cannot help but influence the status of the family – an institution regarded as a source of stability and security. After all, the family is seen as a bridge between the personal and impersonal and between the mortality of its individual members and its immortality. Sooner or later a member may die, but their family, kin, and lineage will outlive them; their legacy is to have perpetuated that lineage in some way. Families take many different forms and rearrange themselves in varying contexts, or simply dissolve into other relationships. As societal transformations take place, so the consistency, love, and support that we find in such circles also changes. Perhaps more things become tasks that have to be performed in order to sustain them. Lynn Jamieson called this process *disclosing intimacy* in which what was once assumed becomes something that needs to be rendered explicit in order that the bonds which unite are routinely sustained within relationships.

We could say that the places where we feel secure are shrinking. Only a few people may occupy it and, if they enter, they may or may not stay long enough to elicit trust and confidence. Nevertheless, there are numerous ways in which the circles we have suggested are sustained within everyday life, with differing consequences for those involved. The economies of time and gender, for example, have been examined by Pamela Odih in *Gender and Work in Capitalist Economies*. While paid work was a place assumed to be separate from the home, new technologies have opened up possibilities in terms of the domestic use of space and time, whilst also exhibiting patterns of flexible accumulation that rely upon female labor and the coexistence of informal and formal labor markets. That leads to new pressures within relationships in order that space and time within the home is demarcated to enable the work in the first place. If a partner in the relationship does not recognize that, adjust, and share the domestic division of labor, exploitation and conflict is heightened. We should, therefore, be cautious in our embrace of the supposed new-found freedoms that the technological and information revolution is supposed to provide: freedom for whom and at what cost?

Our Body, Ourselves: Satisfaction and the Pursuit of Perfection

As we have argued throughout this book, we know ourselves through others and so what is it to know ourselves and to what are we alluding when we make such a claim? A source of illumination lies in our *embodied selves*: that is, with reference to us as a "body." Let us pause here and reflect. This book is about what living in society means for our being, how we see ourselves, objects, and others and what happens as a result. Yet our bodies are something we have "inherited," fully made and thus apparently not a "product" of society. A belief in such immutability, however, is an error. Like anything else about us, the circumstance of living in society makes an enormous amount of difference to our bodies. Even if quite a lot in the size and form of our bodies and its other features has been determined by genes and so not by our own choices and intentional actions – by nature, not culture – societal pressures are such that we do all we can to bring our bodies to a condition that is recognized as being right and proper.

This process is dependent on the kind of society in which we live and whether we are at peace with our body. We may view our bodies as a task – something to work on which requires daily care and attention. Once working on our body has been formed into a duty, society sets the standards for a desirable and so approved shape, for what every person ought to do in order to proximate those standards. Failure to comply can induce feelings of shame, while those not meeting such requirements may find themselves subjected to routine discrimination: for example, prejudicial attitudes towards disabled people as manifest in the very design of buildings, or against those who are transgender because it questions what are assumed to be fixed sexual boundaries between opposites. Our bodies are the objects of social conditioning and thus also of resistance to the categories to which society wishes to consign them.

Michel Foucault's studies on the "technologies of the self" concerned how relations to ourselves and our bodies have changed over time. How we act upon our bodies and care for ourselves is not, of course, a matter that takes place within a social vacuum. His historical studies examined, for example, how sexuality is "the set of effects produced in bodies, behaviors, and social relations" and as far as care for the body is concerned, societies can be particularly demanding in terms of producing and regulating what is acceptable. Given the large volume of risk and uncertainty in the "world out there," the body emerges as what we hope to be the last line in a set of defensible trenches. The body can become a trustworthy shelter because it is a site that we can control and so feel secure, unvexed, and unharassed. Given the habit of the allegedly most stable and durable parts of the world "out there" to hold all sorts of surprises in store – to vanish without trace or change beyond recognition – the body seems the least transient, the longest-living component of our lives. While all else may change, our bodies will always be with us! If investment, effort, and expenditure carry a risk, it may be repaid in our bodies and, similarly, it will be punished through our carelessness and negligence. A great deal hangs on the body as a result and sometimes more than bodies can bear.

Fixing intense attention on the body has its advantages. Here is a site of activity that can produce real and tangible results by watching and then measuring the results. There is no shortage of health equipment to assist in this process: blood pressure and heart monitors, plus a wealth of dietary information, to name but a few. There is no need to be a sitting target for the card that fate may deal the body, for it can become the object of desire. Doing nothing feels worse – harrowing and humiliating – than doing something, even if that proves, in the long run, not to be as effective as you wished. Yet however much care and attention are devoted to the body, when are they sufficient? There appears an excess: when we are healthy the body may not feel the same and when we feel unhealthy the body may be fine. Whatever is required, as Mark Greif writes on exercise in *Against Everything*, we become obsessed with numbers in a process of constant self-testing in which the dream work of the gym is immortality. The sources of the anxiety that drive us towards such concerns will not go away for they derive from something external to the relationships with our bodies – the societies in which we live. People drive to the gym in their cars to exercise and turn to shelters from the pressures of the world with an appetite that perhaps can never be fully satisfied.

This leaves us with several possibilities. Those feelings of satisfaction we may derive from the success of one or other effort at improvement may be momentary and evaporate rapidly, to be replaced by self-criticism and self-reprobation. Instead of healing the wounds left by the fickle and uncertain world "out there," our body can become a site of insecurity and fear. Once the body is turned into a defensive stockade, all the territory surrounding it and the roads leading to it tend to become the object of intense vigilance. We must be constantly on watch: the body is on the attack or may come under assault at any moment, even if the enemy stays as yet hidden. You need to surround the fortress with moats, turrets, and drawbridges and it must fall under our gaze 24 hours a day. Some of the infiltrators "settle in" and pretend to be part of the body, while in fact they are not – they remain the aliens "inside." For instance, fat, which we see as being "in the body" but not "of the body," is a good example of such a process. These crafty and deceitful traitors-in-waiting must be spied out, so that they may be "taken out of the system" and "removed from circulation." There is no shortage of services offering to round up, clean, deport, and squeeze it out. Never, though, are lifestyles in general the subject of sustained public reflection, debate, and even transformation, for the entire project is based on the individualization and hence internalization, of social issues. Summer camps for overweight children appear, but the relations between the diets, lifestyles, and consumption patterns of whole groups of people, the sources of our foods, how they are packaged, and the ingredients of the products that companies sell in the pursuit of profitability, are occasional visitors to public debate, let alone change.

The "interface" between the body and the rest of the world "out there" is a vulnerable frontline to be defended, turned into a subject of concern and perfection and objectified in a never-ending fight for security and safety. The border checkpoints – the orifices of the body, the passageways leading "inside the system" – are precarious places. We should wish to watch closely what we eat, drink, and breathe, and government regulations vary according to the latest scientific insights and lobbying from business interests. Any food or air may do harm to the body or prove downright poisonous. It is not surprising, therefore, that we find a whole industry and set of marketing techniques that are part of the discourses of the body: for example, foods that are "good" for us and others that are "bad" for us. "Superfoods" become a marketed solution promising benefits that cannot be derived from other sources, or packaged as convenient for the busy lifestyle. We should select the right kind of diet with many offering to meet our desires at a price.

The process is not easy. Self-sacrifice, commitment, money, and time may be required. In the process we learn that the kinds of nourishment that were thought to be innocuous or even beneficial to the body have been found to have unpleasant side-effects, or are even contributory factors in disease. Such discoveries cannot but come as shocks since more often than not they are retrospective and so appear after the harm has already been done and cannot be repaired.

Food labels may be consulted, but then revealed to contain harmful ingredients. Lasting wounds may be left on our confidence inducing skepticism: who knows which one of the foods now recommended by the experts will be in the future condemned as damaging? No "healthy meal" can be consumed without some degree of apprehension. No wonder that "new and improved" diets run hard on the heels of those once favored and that allergy, anorexia, and bulimia, all arising on the interface between the body and the "world out there," have been described as disorders specific to our age. Allergy, as Jean Baudrillard observed, has wandering "points of attachment" and is difficult to pinpoint and this reflects a condition of diffuse and undefined anxiety which lies at the foundation of concerns with the maintenance and defense of the body.

If the care for the wellbeing of our bodies – understood as a vigilant prevention of contamination and/or degeneration – were the only motive guiding our action, then extreme reticence that borders on fasting would be a reasonable strategy to pursue. In this way we would reduce the "border traffic" to a bare minimum by refraining from indulgence and refusing to consume those foods that are in excess of what is absolutely necessary to keep us alive. For many this is not a choice for they do not know whether they will obtain food on a daily basis. As a solution to those who enjoy such access, however, this is hardly acceptable, for it would strip the body of the major attraction it holds for its "owner." Quite simply, the body is a site not only of anxiety, but also of pleasure. Here, we find outlets promoting varying sensation: magazines, commercials, online sites and subscriptions, flashing displays in public places and shop windows tempt us into experiences whose absence is a dereliction from the pleasure principle. Eating and drinking are social occasions inducing pleasurable sensations and exciting experiences. To cut down on food and drink is to reduce the number of such occasions and thus the interactions that accompany them. Is it any wonder that on the list of the top-selling books, aside from those on perfecting oneself through self-help and becoming more successful, you will probably find those on slimming and dieting and cookbooks with recipes for the most refined, exotic, and sophisticated dishes?

We have a clash of signals that vary according to nation, gender, race, and class. With an ideology that so often assumes biology is destiny for women and men tending to emphasize control and performance, how does all that advertising draw and contribute to dominant views? The body is often thought to be closer to nature than culture and whole modes of thought have unfolded that view the body as a source of mistrust through its capacity for indulgence and "sin." Thus, the seeking of pleasure in the body is something to be confessed by submitting ourselves to a higher authority who can forgive a temporary relapse from a righteous path. In the process, part of what we are is placed to one side. These and other ways of thinking add to modes of inclusion and exclusion that surround what we may realistically hope for in our lives. The ability to enjoy food and reflect upon it is also the capability to purchase it and be removed from the necessity of seeking food in order to survive. Ideas of healthy eating assume the resources of both time and money are at our disposal, but that is not the same for all. Similarly, surrounding ourselves with one or more of the growing armies of technicians of the body – personal trainers and dietary advisers – is based upon the same capabilities. For others, the "solution" may come in a celebration of that which is commonly derided and they are determined to live with their bodies and resist turning them into objects of manipulation according to popular whim.

In Pursuit of Health and Fitness

Is all this healthy? If we are asked what we want to achieve when we take measures to protect our body, to train it and to exercise, we may well answer that we want to be more healthy and fit. Both aims are commendable. The problem is that they are different and sometimes at cross-purposes with each other. The idea of health, for instance, assumes that there is a *norm* that a human body should meet, with deviations being signs of imbalance, disease, or danger. Norms have their top and bottom limits and so we can say that going over the upper level is, in principle, as dangerous and undesirable as falling below the lower level; for example, too high and too low blood pressure. Both possibilities call for medical intervention: for example, doctors are worried when there are too many leucocytes in the blood, but they also may exhibit concern when there are too few of them.

We remain healthy if, and only if, we remain around a norm. The idea of health suggests the preservation of a "constant state," with allowances for small fluctuations over time. Since we know, by and large, what the normal state is and so can measure it with some degree of precision, we know what to strive for as an "end state." Taking care of our health may be quite time-consuming and aggravating and it often generates a good deal of anxiety. However, there are guidelines in terms of what we can know and how far we need to go and so there may be a degree of contentment in our labor. Once we are back within an "acceptable norm," we can be reassured that this is indeed the case by comparing the indices of our body, its functions with the statistics of the "averages" for our age.

Fitness is another matter. Whilst patriarchal relations have rendered the body to be distrusted due to its proximity to nature that is apparently at odds with the rational world of men, fitness becomes a public spectacle. It is seen in such places as gyms, streets, pitches, courts, tracks, and stadiums and is big business. There might be a bottom line according to age, but the sky is the limit as far as the top line is concerned. It is about transgressing norms, not adhering to them. Gyms are full of mottos urging their members to excel. For Loïc Wacquant in his ethnography of boxing, *Body and Soul: Notebooks of an Apprentice Boxer*, it became a place of molding the body into both a shield and a weapon to be deployed against an opponent. Yet health, in general, is not oriented to such goals and is about keeping the body in a normal, functioning condition in order to work, earn a living, be mobile, engage in some kind of social life, communicate with other people, and use the facilities that the society provides to serve various life tasks. When it comes to fitness the question may not be what the body must do, but what the body is ultimately capable of doing if you are prepared to put the effort in. The starting point is what it can do in its present state, but more can always be achieved and should in the name of fitness and so there is, it seems, no end in sight to the care for the fitness of our bodies. Images of bodies honed through self-sacrifice adorn our various media to offer the devoted the idealizations to which to aspire.

The body is instrument; an object subject to calculation in terms of its capability to be worked on to reach the kind of experience that makes life thrilling, enjoyable, entertaining, exciting, and altogether "pleasant to live." It is a template whose progress towards the ideal end-state can be gazed upon, inspected, and tested for its ability to live up to a promise. Fitness stands for the capacity of the body to imbibe what the world has to offer now and what it may in the future. A flabby, tame, vapid body without vigor and appetite for adventure is unlikely to stand up to the challenges that life puts before us. Such a body would not be one that desires new experiences and this is what makes life thrilling. An old proverb suggests that it is better to travel hopefully than to arrive. We may say, therefore, that in consumer societies it is the desire that matters, not its satisfaction, for to reach such a state undermines the ethos that informs the journey. Quite simply, what desire desires is yet more desire.

A fit body is an adroit and versatile one, hungry for new sensations, capable of actively seeking and meeting new sensations by "living them to the full" when they appear. Fitness is an ideal by which the overall quality of the body is assessed. Since the body conveys a message, it is not enough for the body to be fit – it must be *seen* to be fit. To convince its viewers – self and others – it must be slim, trim, and agile and possess the look of a "sporting body" that is ready for all sorts of exercise and able to take any amount of strain that life may throw at it. Again, the suppliers of commercial goods are eager to help the body to assume such appearances and to convey the impression of fitness. So we find a wide and constantly growing choice of equipment for those who long for such ideals within a busy lifestyle: the right kind of jogging wear, gym equipment, tracksuits, and training shoes to document the body's love of exercise and its versatility and demonstrate that one is up to date in the latest adornments signifying belonging to a group of fitness seekers. What is left to owners of the body is to find suitable outlets with the right commodities and make the appropriate purchases.

It is not just what we do to our bodies to hone them, but what we put in them. Not all steps to a convincing presentation of bodily fitness are so simple and straightforward. There is a lot that the owners themselves must do: for example, weight training, jogging, and playing sports are the most prominent among such tasks. Even in these cases, commercial suppliers are keen to oblige desire. So we see a profusion of teach-yourself and do-it-yourself handbooks offering patented regimes and a huge variety of tinned, powdered, or pre-cooked food made specifically for weight-lifters and fitness-watchers, to assist them in what is a solitary struggle to attain an ideal. In this, as in other cases, the practice of actually undertaking activity towards this end can easily take second place to the art of shopping.

At this point we witness the pursuit of new sensations. The problem with all sensations, most prominently with sensual pleasures, is that they are known, so to speak, only from the "inside." Sensations, subjectively experienced, may not be "visible" to others and may be difficult to describe in a manner that allows others to understand them. There are visible signs of suffering such as sad expressions on the face, tears in the eyes, sorrowful sighs, or sulking silences, and happiness in smiling faces, bursts of laughter, gaiety, and sudden eloquence. It is possible for us to imagine these feelings by recalling our own "similar" experiences. Yet we cannot *feel* what others experience. Intimate friends, who wish to share all the experiences they go through separately, often ask each other, impatiently, and with a whiff of despair: "Do you *really* know what I feel?" They suspect, with good reason, that there is no way to find out whether the feelings of two different persons are "the same" or even "similar." Yet whilst these are seen as our "own" feelings, we cannot help but be in relations with the consciousness of others and understand ourselves as a result.

So we are caught between the feelings of the exceptionalism of our subjective experiences and their inevitable inter-subjective mediation through others. Yet whilst bodily sensations are subjectively experienced and not thought to be available to others in terms of them being able to experience the same feelings, these sensations vary according to history and culture. Thus, Carl Cederström and André Spicer argue in *The Wellness Syndrome* that wellness has become an ideology to the extent that a failure to conform leads to feelings of stigmatization. It is attached to a work ethic where the boundaries between life and work blur to an ever greater extent and even our private passions are infiltrated by corporate instruction. Feminist scholars, such as Judith Butler, have shown how the body itself is both "raced" and "gendered" in particular ways and medical sociologists have documented how interventions in terms of the healthy body are influenced by these factors. Graham Scambler, in *Health and Social Change*, charts how thinking about health, right down to the doctor–patient interaction, is structured by more general factors including organizational contexts and the deployment of typifications based on class, race, and gendered factors. It is for such reasons that Michael Marmot in *The Health Gap* argues that health and health inequity are good measures of how well a society is doing for the benefit of its citizens.

Our sensations are not simply the result of bodily stimulus, but expressions of judgments which are mediated through language which we make about our state of being. To that extent we have to learn ways to express such emotions and an understanding of their significance is available to others through local cultural displays and expressions. Thus, even the display of emotions is a social act that varies according to the repertoire of words and actions that are available within a given culture. Given this variation, we must also be sensitive to the cultures about which we speak in understanding the idea of "fitness."

We have noted that the ultimate indices of fitness, unlike those of health, cannot be measured. Therefore, the potential for interpersonal comparison becomes problematic. Again, there are a number of ways in which we can seek to measure our fitness via, for example, monitoring the heart rate during strenuous exercise. The comparison, however, may come in a running race or bodybuilding competition, but there is always room for improvement. The question that then arises with fitness, in terms of its differences with health, is "How far do we go?" Have we squeezed out of this or that experience everything that other people do and we could have done ourselves? In the pursuit of ever greater targets, these questions are bound to remain unanswered, but that does not mean we shall cease to stop looking for answers. Whether our preoccupation with the body takes the form of the care for health, or fitness training, the overall result may be similar: more anxiety rather than less, even though the prime motive to turn our attention and effort to the body was our craving for certainty and security so blatantly missing in the world "out there."

The Body and Desire

The body is site and tool of desire, but also its *object*. It is our body and at the same time, what other people see of our personhood. As the French philosopher Maurice Merleau-Ponty put it: "the body must become the thought or intention that it signifies for us. It is the body which points out, and which speaks." The body is the site of what it is to be "us," but it is inscribed in our identities and always on display and people tend to judge by what they can see. Even if we see our body as but a wrapping of what we take to be our "inner self," it is the attractiveness, beauty, elegance, and appearance of the wrapping that will entice others. The management of our bodies is learnt by us with and through others while, at the same time, how others see us is also the product of common expectations. Deviations may cause reflection, as well as reaction in others, leaving those who are identified as being different at a disadvantage, despite the skills, abilities, and contributions that they might otherwise make to society. The shape of the body, the way it is dressed and made up, and the way it does or does not move is a message to others.

Whether we find it easy or difficult to relate to other people and whether they are willing or not to relate to us, depends on many factors – the message written by our bodies being one among many. If other people avoid us, if we are not a "social success," if people with whom we would like to associate seem not to enjoy our company, or shun the prospect of lasting engagement, there might be something wrong with the messenger: our body. Perhaps, more to the point, there is something wrong with us as its owner, coach, and guardian. Is the wrong kind of message being displayed? Or the right message, but it is not salient enough or even unintelligible? We may have read the clues in our social milieu incorrectly. Even how we hold the implements with which we eat and our general bodily gestures during eating are infused with differing expectations.

So we have now come full circle. We may have deployed our bodies to facilitate the vexingly confusing and insecure relations with other people, but now find that bodily comportment has become a source of concern. With the body as a site of representation of ourselves, we may now have to consider another message to write, or find the way of making the message either more intelligible or socially acceptable. It is the message that matters and there is nothing to stop us from writing any message we think to be right and proper. In the available repertoire there is no shortage of pre-scripted messages on offer. Indeed, our consumer-oriented society offers a multitude of "presentation selves" to self-assemble.

Consider the film *Elizabeth*. It focused on the early years of the reign of Elizabeth I, who was queen of England and Ireland (1533–1603). Despite her evident abilities, she found it exceedingly difficult to convince the courtiers and other men of rank that, as a woman, she was the proper heir to the glory of her father, Henry VIII. She sought to convince them that she had all the skills and understanding needed to rule the country with wisdom. The powerful royal ministers refused to treat her seriously, for in their eyes she was just a bride-to-be, waiting for the right kind of husband who, once she married him, would be the true ruler of England. Significantly, Elizabeth dressed accordingly – the way the young women hoping to attract a "Prince Charming" were expected to dress. During a moment in the film there comes a wondrous reincarnation. A transformed Elizabeth enters the Great Hall of the royal palace and all the courtiers and barons fall on their knees and bow. In so doing they acknowledge the monarch whose heritage they no longer doubt and whose right to rule they no longer dispute.

Elizabeth changed her *appearance*. She had cut her long hair short and purchased huge jars of paint to cover her youthful face with a mask so thick that it disguised her emotions; she wore somber and sober dress and even managed to wipe the smile off her face. We, as the viewers of the film, do not know whether Elizabeth herself had changed, but are aware that she had not changed her "life-project": that is, a firm intention to rule England according to her own ideas and with the best of her abilities. The only thing we can be sure of is that the message sent to others by her appearance has altered. Elizabeth, it seems, sent the wrong messages and failed repeatedly. Yet, once the right message was transmitted via her appearance, she was more successful in her quest.

We are repeatedly told such stories by all kinds of authorities. Various authorities do not necessarily see eye-to-eye when it comes to the selection of the content, but they all agree that whatever the content may be, it is the message that makes the difference between success and failure. With the body being the prime, immediately visible message, the exhibit of the self displayed for public gaze and scrutiny, it tends to be loaded with enormous responsibility for the ups and downs of social life and this is informed by the dimensions of gender, race, and class. How aspects of our bodies are seen and endowed with particular significance effects how we see ourselves and how others see us. Our bodies, as objects of desire, are not simply tools for manipulation by some "inner-self" of the mind, but are part of how we are constituted as selves through the reaction of others to our actions and from there, our anticipation of those responses.

In this process no aspect of the body is allowed to escape our attention and left, so to speak, to its own devices. We are responsible for every part and function of our bodies, with everything, or almost everything, having the potential to be changed for the better. This may or may not be true, particularly if we think of the aging process, but even that is believed to be subject to change, or delay, via the application of the latest skin creams, particular interventions, and the latest technological and medical developments. Therefore, as long as the body is a focus of constant and acute concern, its owner does not appear to be affected by the truth or untruth of that belief. What matters is that if something in our bodies, and especially in the appearance of our bodies, stops short of the ideal, the repairing of the situation seems to remain within our power to alter depending on our capability to mobilize resources towards those ends. In this way our bodies fluctuate between being objects of love and pride to sources of annoyance and shame. At one moment we might award our bodies for loyal service and at another, punish it for letting us down.

The Body, Sexuality, and Gender

One aspect of our bodies that is calling for particular intense attention and care is sex. Our "sexual assignment," like anything else concerning our bodies, is not a quality that has been determined at birth. We live in times in which binaries of being either male or female are being questioned and people are living their lives in different ways. "Being a male" or "being a female" is a question of art which needs to be learned, practiced, and constantly perfected. Moreover, none of the two conditions bind us to a path we have to walk throughout our lives and neither offers clearly defined patterns of behavior. As far as sexual identity is concerned, the body – whatever its inherited biological traits – appears as a set of possibilities. This is not simply about being either male or female, but transgender. Recognition of the right to live one's life in a way that does not accord with dominant views is important in any society that claims to respect difference. With this comes the possibility of being open to experimentation. The original and apparent fixity of "sexual assignment" is not a verdict of fate. Our sexuality, like other aspects of our bodies, is a complex performance that includes not only sexual relations and practices, but language, speech, dress, and style.

Sexuality is not productively seen in terms of an "essence" and this implies a questioning of what is known as the "essentialist" approach to sexuality. The British sociologist Jeffrey Weeks defined that in terms of seeking to explain "the properties of a complex reality by reference to a supposed inner truth or essence." That sexuality is not a purely "natural," but cultural phenomenon is not, however, a novelty of our time. Over time there have been culturally patterned, taught, and learned habits and customs defining the meaning of being "male" or "female." Nevertheless, the fact that "maleness" and "femaleness" is assigned in this way and so possesses the potential for change was suppressed for the most part of human history and societies vary in expressions of intolerance and repression of difference.

Culture can appear as the mask of nature and cultural inventions were seen as being on the same level with "laws of nature." Men were made to be men, women to be women, and that was the end of any sense of interpretive flexibility. Gender identity is not left to human will, but to be obeyed and lived according to a "true" nature: what nature has decided, let no man (and particularly no woman) alter! Who spoke in the name of nature was rarely contested. Nevertheless, there were exceptions and the recognition of their contribution depends on who is writing the histories. In 1694, Mary Astell wrote *A Serious Proposal to the Ladies* and argued that differences between the sexes were not based on unexamined ideas of "nature," but on the power that men held over women in society.

In human history, hereditary distinctions in human bodies have been deployed as infrastructures of justification to sustain and reproduce social hierarchies of power. We can see this in the case in terms of "race" whenever the color of someone's skin is defined as a sign of superiority or inferiority and then used to explain and justify existing social inequalities. The same applies to sexual differences. Here we find biological distinctions between sexes forming the basis for gender inequality. "Gender" is a cultural category. It entails the totality of norms to which members of sexual categories are obligated to conform in their performance of appropriate behavior for their designated category. It is on the basis of such a history that women may be excluded from areas of social life that are reserved for men, or that barriers are placed in the way of their participation as, for example, in politics or business, where equal pay for the same work is still to be attained. At the same time, those activities that are fundamental to society, such as reproduction, household duties, and childcare, can be cast aside as exclusively feminine domains and devalued accordingly.

This is not a division of labor simply laid down by reproductive function; it stands for power relations. For instance, within organizations, as the Italian sociologist Silvia Gherardi notes, positions of subordination are reinforced in rituals surrounding the management of the body. The feminist movement has thus challenged social inequalities based on sexual characteristics of the body. This lengthy campaign has brought its results, but legislation alone cannot achieve equality. The most it can do is to reopen for negotiation those cases previously considered "unproblematic." The question as to which of these are eventually fulfilled is often left to individual ingenuity and persistence, with the resulting effects being carried by the individuals concerned. If the fight for acceptance is left to the individual, it can become another source of insecurity and fear, as opposed to a right to recognition through tolerance of diversity and a greater security and contentment for us all as we learn about what we are and might become.

Summary

As with those other topics we have considered, care of ourselves through our bodies, as well as bodies being the objects of desire and display to others, holds out the hope for security, but is also a site of insecurity. Our health and social policies tend to focus upon the individual. When it comes to issues of obesity, for example, there can be no doubt of the risks that this carries for individuals. Whilst not an issue that can be simply correlated with income it is, as Richard Wilkinson and Kate Pickett write in the *Spirit Level*, one associated with subjective measures of status. Focusing upon the individual does not tell us why such habits persists or how such behavior is seen to give comfort or status and what ingredients exist in our diets and for what reasons?

Our ideas of health, fitness, and the body are infused with meanings that are produced within cultures that are not simply separated from biological categories, but interact and construct what we are, have been, and possess the potential to become. With this comes the power to define which may be a source of comfort, but also something to resist in its invoking of norms that can stifle difference. Such differences are often translated as deviance, rather than being understood on their own terms and challenging for the dominant ways in which the body is considered, acted upon, and deployed as a form of communication and categorization. For these reasons sexual identity and relations become areas of negotiation and conflict with consequences that are often unpredictable. Surrounding all of this is a need to examine what we might take for granted, open ourselves to possibilities, and respect and recognize difference.

7

Space, Time, and Social Dynamics

In his *A Brief History of Time* the physicist Stephen Hawking referred to the "cosmological arrow of time." Here we find the universe expanding with distances between galaxies becoming greater. As we learn more about the universe we gain both a sense of our insignificance within a vast space and a wonder that feeds a thirst for exploration, discovery, and answers to the questions of our existence. In this chapter we are concerned with the sociological arrow of time and its relation to space. In the process we will ask how we experience and interpret the dimensions that inform and structure our lives, how they have changed over the course of history and in what ways they have transformed our understandings and with what consequences for how we live together?

Time and Space in the Dimension of Experience

To commence our journey we start from a completely different point from that of the cosmologist: time and space are shrinking. This seems to be an extraordinary statement at first glance. Time and space, surely, do not shrink? From a social point of view we think of events in terms of their occurrence within and through time, and similarly, of being located in space. We are able to make comparisons between ideas, attitudes, and actions by charting their historical variations within spaces that are both physical (urban and regional landscapes) and symbolic (how they are viewed and what significance is attached to relations and objects within those spaces as "places" of interaction). In his book *Spaces of Global Capitalism*, David Harvey refers to a tripartite division in which space can be understood: absolute, relative, and relational. The former is fixed, immovable, and subject to calculation. A lecture, for example, takes places within a room whose walls bound its words. The measurement of relative space depends, as Einstein observed, on the frame of reference of the observer themselves and we cannot understand space without time. To return to the example of the lecture, as Harvey notes, the words will be heard differently by people depending on their position in the room itself. Finally, in terms of a relational dimension, each person will bring ideas and experiences of their own into the room born of particular time–space trajectories.

Thinking Sociologically, Third Edition. Zygmunt Bauman and Tim May.
© 2019 John Wiley & Sons Ltd. Published 2019 by John Wiley & Sons Ltd.

Seen in these terms, time and space are not simply features of the "world out there," they are experienced relative to where we are located and how that informs our actions and perceptions. They are not independent dimensions in the planning, calculation, and execution of our actions. We tend to measure distance by the time needed to pass it, while our estimations of the remoteness or closeness of our destinations depends on the amount of time needed to reach them. The result of the measurement depends, therefore, on the speed at which we can move. That speed, in turn, depends on the tools or vehicles of mobility to which we have routine access. If using such tools needs to be paid for, the speed at which we move then depends on the amount of money we can afford. In terms of that speed, however, technologies have speeded up our communications and varying forms of media spread into all parts of the globe with effects upon our ideas and experience. To that extent we can say that space and time are shrinking. As Paul Virilio expresses it in his essay *Speed and Politics*, it is not in what period in time (chronological) we find ourselves, nor in what space (geographical), but in "*what* space–time?" This is changing rapidly in contemporary times.

During times (not so ancient, to be sure) when human or horses' legs were the only tools of traveling, the answer you would probably get to the question "how far it is from here to the next village?" would be "If you start now, you would get there about midday"; or "You won't get there before dusk, you had better stay in the inn for the night." Later, once the "artificial limbs" – human-made engines – had replaced human feet and horses, the answers ceased to be that straightforward. Distance then became a matter of which form of transport was used. It was not the same, and depended on whether you could afford to travel by train, coach, private car, or aircraft. We are now in a situation that John Urry, in *Mobilities*, characterizes as one in which some of us travel further and faster than ever before.

So we have means of transportation that carry and shift persons and/or things from one place to another. Means of communication, on the other hand, refer to the conveying and passing of information. We can say that for the greater part of human history there was not much to distinguish between transport and communication. Information could be carried by human carriers: for example, travelers, messengers, itinerant tradespeople and craft workers, or those who moved from one village to another in search of alms or casual work. There were a few exceptions to this general rule, such as the optical messages of the natives of the American plains or drum-telegraph in Africa. The ability to transmit information independently of human carriers, as long as it remained a rarity, gave tremendous advantage to those who had access to such means. There is a story that the pioneering use of mail-pigeons allowed Rothschild, the banker, to learn before anybody else of Napoleon's defeat at Waterloo and use that privileged information to multiply his wealth at the London Stock Exchange. Indeed, despite being illegal, the same kind of advantage still makes "insider-trading" seductive for those who seek to advance wealth on markets that move across time and national space without concern for boundaries.

The most impressive technical developments once served the needs of transportation. Thus, steam, electric, and internal combustion engines, rail networks, seafaring vessels, and motor cars were invented. Yet alongside those inventions a new "software" era was germinating in the discovery of things such as the telegraph and the radio. Here we find the means of transmitting pure information at long distances without a person, or any other physical body, moving from a place. In comparison, transport would never be "instantaneous." Except in science-fiction fantasies, it would always take time to shift humans and their belongings from one place to another and the more there was to shift and the longer the distance, the more cumbersome and costly the operation became. Now, some eight million people are estimated to fly by plane every day. Yet, in "hardware" terms, places mattered and this added value to space. It was cheaper and less trouble-some to be "in place." Owners of factories wished to produce every part of the final product under one roof and to keep all the machinery and labor necessary to produce them inside the same factory walls. This limited the need for trans-portation and the pursuit of economies of scale was seen to reduce costs.

Around these practices forms of discipline emerged whose target was the control of space and time. The closer the controllers were to the controlled, the more complete was their rule over everyday conduct. At the threshold of the nineteenth century, Jeremy Bentham, one of the most influential political scien-tists and philosophers of the time, proposed a solution to the issue of growing populations that was different from that of the economists and their concerns with poverty, food, and productivity. One suggestion he had was to design a huge building in which people were under surveillance for 24 hours a day, but would never be quite sure whether they were being watched.

The "Panopticon" served as the ideal pattern for all modern powers from the top level to the bottom. Exemplified in prison design with a central tower over-looking the cells of all the prisoners, as long as power is of the panoptical kind, the objects of constant surveillance might be obedient and refrain from insubor-dination, let alone acts of rebellion, because all deviation from the rule was too costly for them to be seriously considered. As a result, there was a move over the course of history, to paraphrase Michel Foucault, from the gaze of others to the interiorization of the gaze. How then do we understand the process in which companies sell the means to monitor emails and communications of staff to ensure they are conforming to expectations of proper organizational conduct? The means deployed might depend on the spatial arrangements of the condi-tions of work. In large, open call centers, supervisors can walk around listening to the operators and monitoring their calls, whilst the individuals themselves must meet performance targets. The form of gaze then varies according to the spatial arrangements in which work takes place, whilst interiorization is con-cerned with the ways to reach the correct training of staff and how they use their time in a "productive" manner.

Stretching and Compressing Across Time and Space

Information now moves separately from physical bodies. Given this, the speed of communications is no longer held down by the limits that are placed upon it by people and material objects. For all practical purposes, communication is now instantaneous and so distances do not matter because any corner of the globe can be reached at the same time. As far as the access and the spread of information are concerned, "being close" and "being remote" no longer have the importance they once commanded. Internet groups do not feel geographical distance to be an impediment to the selection of partners in a conversation or in gaming. If someone happens to live in Manhattan, communicating with someone in Melbourne or Kolkata takes them no more time than doing so with someone in the Bronx. Estimates are that we are approaching two billion digital images being uploaded to the Internet each day, Twitter has 330 million active users each month, and there are over 2.5 billion smartphone users (www.statista.com). All of this has to be stored somewhere and our use is not without consequence. Four percent of the world's electricity consumption goes into powering and cooling these giant servers and that is likely to increase threefold by 2030.

You may take all this for granted and assume it to be insignificant. It has become as much part of everyday life as sunrises and sunsets. You might have hardly noticed how profound has been this very recent *devaluation of space* through actions that have consequences; albeit at a distance from your relative position in space. Let us pause for a moment and think how the human condition changes once communication in this form takes over our lives and when the expedience and increasing urgency of information no longer depends on distance. What, for instance, happens to the idea of "community"? Sherry Turkle in her study *Alone Together*, talks about being at a close friend's memorial service. Those in the audience went off into corners to text, with one saying to her that she could not stand being away from her phone for too long.

Our willingness to be part of an experiment of such benefit to advertisers and industry seems to know no bounds. Bev Skeggs and Simon Yuill summarize their studies on values and value when it comes to this sort of activity: "Facebook represents a new form of capitalist capture, one based on monopolization and rent that shapes our current connectivity as it monetizes us and opens us up to forms of financialization, including increased indebtedness. This form of capitalist capture moves us into a new regime of accumulation, of profit without production, in which the command of surplus value is via the control of surplus information" (https://values.doc.gold.ac.uk). Information capture, transmission, and reception shape our practices in time and space. It is alleged the US election and the UK Brexit referendum were subject to tampering with "troll armies" spreading fake news. As Matthew D'Ancona expresses it in *Post Truth: The New War on Truth and How to Fight Back*, if anyone with a Twitter account is seen as a news source, then how do we distinguish between fact and falsehood? Everyone, it seems, is now an expert as we have knowledge ranging from that acquired in physical proximity to each other, to information by description using computers, laptops, and smartphones.

As we noted earlier, community can be seen as territorial or "local" because it is confined in a space that possesses boundaries drawn by the human capacity to move. The difference between the "inside" and the "outside" of a community is one between "the here and now" and the "there and far away." The backbone of any community was the web of communication between its members in a social network informed by territory. As such, the distance at which such daily "communicative interaction" could stretch drew the boundaries of community. Distant communication was awkward and costly and so a comparatively more rare event.

In this sense locality was an advantage over "far away," with ideas being born and discussed within the locality. Physical closeness and frequency of communication no longer need to exist in this manner as those who are party to interactions may be mapped in terms of dots around the globe according to their relative position to each other. It is no longer a territorial community in terms of belonging to a spatially defined network of people within a common place.

Communities of this type are brought together by communicational activities and it is these that bind them together. Yet those persons are not necessarily those from whom we derive our ideas about the world. Knowledge gained by description, in contrast to acquaintance with others in situations of "co-presence," may not come from those who are dots set relative to each other on a map. After all, we derive our knowledge from other sources. However, thanks to the electronically transmitted voices and images, it is the world which travels to us, while we remain in our place. This process of "embedding" and "disembedding" of knowledge means that there may be no mutuality or dialogue in our communications. We receive and process, but there is no meeting of points of view and, when that does happen, they can be drowned out by a tirade of criticism. What is a source of knowledge is also that which confirms our preconceptions and can easily lapse into a vehicle of prejudice.

Into this mix of isolation, interaction, and information, the public gaze on celebrities with their importance measured by the number of books written about them, the audience ratings of their shows, their Twitter followers, films made, or their position in the music charts. Celebrities become examples of success held up for public consumption whose fall from grace can be as rapid as their ascent. Yet in thinking about these images and their transmission and reception, while people remain in a locality the information that orients their experiences can be extra-territorial. Thus, we hear talk of information having become *global* in the sense that it has broken free from its *local* bonds. It travels freely between localities, states, and continents with the result that past boundaries are challenged and transgressed. Its speed is such that control is raised as a problem, but who can win the race when it comes to competing with electronic signals? All this has implications for the ways in which we lead our lives and the nature and distribution of power. To ignore these issues is not an option, while the questions that are raised are not easy to answer. That, however, is not a reason for inaction if we are to understand and act upon the consequences of the information age, as opposed to remaining passive through inactivity.

Juggernaut Wheels: Risk, Action, and Change

Given the issues raised by transformations in societies, Ulrich Beck proposes that we now live in a "society of risks." When we think of risk, we think of a danger or threat that relates to what we do or even refrain from doing. People often say "this is a risky step to take" in order to indicate that people are exposing themselves to an undesirable state of affairs. However, in a society of risks, these issues derive not so much from what each person does in isolation, but from the very fact that because they are in isolation the actions are dispersed and uncoordinated. There is a sense that despite all the knowledge we have, the risks compress into our sense of individual wellbeing, promoting not certainty, but concern. Outcomes and side-effects of varying courses of action are difficult to calculate and define and so have the potential to take us by surprise. How do we cope with this state of affairs when information is stretched across time and space and finds itself compressed at moments in time that call for decisive action that accompanies responsibility? In our saturated age, information easily runs free from its source of legitimation leaving the individual subject to misinformation.

As the barriers around time and space appear to become more permeable in the contemporary era, places start to matter. Globalization exerts a pull across space and moves across contexts. Under these forces places become the embodiment of distinction, rather than sameness, to which people can relate in an otherwise chaotic and uncertain universe. Localism ends up mixing with global forces, but what is the form through which the local is molded as images circulate with such intensity and speed in the contemporary era? The local may see itself as successful if it can attract the global in acts of time and space compression. High streets have similar shops, selling the same goods, but whose presence is seen to be indicative of economic growth and relevance. The distinction of the local competes in a mobile world and must demonstrate connectivity, as well as heritage manifest in a continuing cultural vibrancy that is attractive to those mobile workers who bring with them the skills, attributes, and knowledge that demonstrates the global excellence of a place.

As the compression of time and space finds itself expressed in the local we get a mixture of the relative in terms of distinction of place, with a sense of the relational in terms of judgments about its relevance to global development that appears to be absolute! In the face of such pressures it is suggested that a process of *detraditionalization* has taken place whereby the bonds that unite communities start to lose their grip on social dynamics as new technological innovations and information circulate ever faster. This can appear as both threat and opportunity. The opportunity is something always present to be molded in the image of a vibrant future that brings with it both constant potential and uncertainty. In the face of these pressures, a nostalgic yearning for a bygone age and a desire to return to consistency and certainty rears its head. Such desire is not for a utopian future, but one in which current efforts seek to produce particular memories as acts of binding communities to a past. Tensions play out between memory and forgetting as the bonds that unite find themselves questioned through forces of global capitalism whose search for profit through possibility seems an unquenchable thirst.

If we tried to prevent all undesirable consequences we would face a structural problem whose price would render our actions subject to impossible odds and, for some, this leads to resignation and inactivity. Yet such calculation of risk is not the result of ignorance or a lack of skills. In fact, the opposite is the case: risk grows out of ever greater efforts to be rational in the sense of defining and concentrating on *relevant* things that are deemed to be significant for one reason or another. As a popular saying puts it: "We will cross that bridge when we come to it." Of course, this presupposes the existence of a bridge and has little to say about what we do when we find out it is not there! Take the example of genetically modified (GM) food: that is, crops that are genetically modified in order that they grow more resistant to pests and diseases, or have larger yields or a longer shelf-life in the shops. Some suggest that the potential of these crops lies in the alleviation of poverty. That, however, may not be a matter of scientific advance, but the relative distribution of wealth between Western and majority world countries that are termed "developing." Others suspect that, judging by past experiences, there will be a price to pay for achieving these aims in terms of unintended consequences. They might point to the side-effects of manipulating genes in terms of the devastation of soil composition and long-term harm done to the health and life-expectations of the consumers. Therefore, the issue may be not so much one of increased production, but rather the distribution of existing resources and how crops are grown in the first place and with what effects on the environment. The debate revolves around uncertainty in terms of not knowing the price that will be paid in the future for current decisions, with views differing on the short-, medium-, and long-term consequences of present actions. The content of what we know, therefore, is not the same as its possible consequence, and when we enter into this terrain we also enter into the realm of desirability.

In the face of resistance to the promise of technological solutions to social problems, companies with an investment in such technologies may move elsewhere, or diversify into other areas that have the potential for profit. Transnational corporations move across time and space in this way, seeking advantage and potential in different places. As Barbara Adam puts it, when time becomes commodified, speed then becomes an economic value: "the faster goods move through the economy the better; speed increases profit and shows up positively in a country's GNP (gross national product)." The new volatility of information also frees up movement of money with foreign exchange speculation having reached over $5 trillion per day and global debt exceeding its GDP by nearly 300 percent. These are the factors that contribute to our chances of living decent lives and obtaining employment, education, and health-care opportunities, as well as the potential for sustainable environments.

When we see these sorts of figures of trading and debt across the globe, whilst gaze and proximity once mattered in the Panopticon, the technique of power now employed may be to threaten distance from those whose behavior is to be regulated or does not conform to expectations. If, for instance, a factory crew or an office staff are disaffected, unruly, or demand better conditions, one would expect the outfit to be closed down, "de-layered" or "sold off," rather than to anticipate more surveillance and the enforcement of stricter rules. The extraterritoriality of global powers does not bind them to any particular place and they are always ready to travel away at short notice in search of lower wages and greater profit. Such extra-territorial mobility is a freedom that few possess. After all, if the "locals" seek to follow the "globals," they would soon find out, as Richard Sennett warns in the *Corrosion of Character*, that the traits which allow for spontaneity become more destructive for those whose work is lower down the hierarchy of the "flexible regime."

Globalization is taken to be a process which moves across time and space, but without a locus of control. Göran Therborn, in his book *Cities of Power*, says there has been a shift of power, not from the national to the global, but from citizens to national and global capital. This is often invoked as a reason for inaction in the face of what are seen as overwhelming and abstract forces that shape time and place. Yet civil uprisings take place against the effects of such forces, and government policies can and do accelerate, mediate, dilute, and ameliorate them. In the process they offer the basis for resistance or simply reproduce these forces through embrace, passivity, and indifference. Globalization affects us at an individual level in varying degrees, for we can all experience anxiety and worry when we find it difficult to understand what is going on, let alone to influence the direction in which things seem to be moving around us. Agency that has the potential to take control of its worse effects, on the other hand, is something that lies beyond the individual. A willingness to act on this state of affairs requires that those who are its beneficiaries recognize they are positioned in this way only because others are excluded as a consequence.

Whilst we may have ideas about how to satisfy our needs, even if the means for such satisfaction is not equally distributed, the need to neutralize or cut down on risks is not like other needs. This is because risks are the kinds of dangers we do not see or hear coming and of which we may not be fully aware. We do not experience directly – see, hear, touch, and smell – the rising carbon dioxide in the air we breathe, or the slow yet relentless warming up of the planet, or those chemical substances used to fatten up the meat we eat, but which may be undermining the capability of our immune systems to deal with bacterial infection. These are real enough, but trends, or patterns over time, not simply things to be read off through events, and in coming to know these we often turn to "experts" in order to address what is our limited knowledge and experience. As they are discussing trends and patterns, there may be no way we can test their interpretations against our own experiences. One reaction is to celebrate our situatedness and constitute our understandings as relative to our time and place. In cutting off the relational, expertise is questioned, the particularities of our understandings are celebrated, and alternative explanations denied or subject to hostility. Risk, as Ulrich Beck put it, is "interpreted away" and rendered "non-existent" and so there will be no need for action. A reaction of this type is not unusual. It may be fueled by those who say they are protecting us, but are actually the spokespersons for those who do harm.

Order and Chaos in the Unfolding of the Social

How do we think of doing harm in these contexts? Leonidas Donskis, writing in *Moral Blindness*, argues that the "essence of contemporary culture and control is to excite desires, inflame them to the maximum, and then curb them with extreme forms of restraint." In the face of an oscillation between provocation and prohibition, how do we deal with the global forces? Hans Jonas, the German American ethical philosopher, examines the consequences of technological development on a global scale. Although our actions may affect those who live in other parts of the globe, of whom we know little, our moral outlook has not kept pace with these transformations. How often is it that people speak of events as being beyond their control? This begs questions about how we may have a global ethic that also respects and recognizes the differences between people. Without this, such forces are not tamed according to our needs, but unleashed by those with greater power whose actions have differing consequences. This is to relieve the human race of its moral responsibility towards others. As Karl-Otto Apel, a German philosopher argues, we have a responsibility for how institutions are shaped and reshaped because these are the places that facilitate the "social implementation of morality."

Even if we had a declaration of moral duties that is similar to the United Nations Declaration of Human Rights, it would require a great change in perception to be effective. If people do not see beyond the confines of their immediate neighborhoods they understandably tend to focus on things, events, and people close to home. Vague feelings of threat can then be anchored on visible, tangible targets that are within reach and characterizations and what is regarded as legitimate knowledge are then filtered accordingly. Thus, whilst the World Wide Web may be seen as a source of knowledge, it easily lapses into a self-fulfilling prophecy of seeking the like-minded and denigrating others in displays of bolstering prejudicial views. In such circumstances there often appears little we can do to hit distant, misty, and perhaps elusive targets. Locally, people can join a patrol of concerned and active citizens who target those who are perceived to be a threat to their way of life. Closed-circuit television cameras, burglar alarms, window locks, and security lights can all be installed to protect local space; explanations that seek understanding of these trends beyond those confines may be ruled out as irrelevant and even irresponsible for not "knowing" what it is like to live in a particular place.

A globally induced insecurity can find its outlet in a locally produced preoccupation with safety through an oscillation between threat and situated prevention. Perhaps we have fallen into the trap that Ulrich Beck warned against? That is, we have looked for the source of risks in the wrong place. A locally produced worry about safety exacerbates divisions that separate people – the very divisions that lead to misunderstanding and the ability to downplay the consequences of action upon others who are remote from our worlds. Those who can clearly afford to protect their properties may also be those who have something to protect that others desire, but lack the means to afford. Morally speaking, distances between people can enable them to bracket and ignore the consequences of their actions for others.

The consequences of globalization may be a threat, but also an opportunity. As Karl-Otto Apel argued, we could use our reason and our will to bring into being a truly global society that seeks to be inclusive and respectful of difference and seriously attempts to eradicate war. False interpretations and allocations of blame for risks may prevent us from acting and lead to further divisions, thus worsening and not addressing the problems. This is why it is so important to frame issues from a sociological perspective. Sociology cannot correct the shortcomings of the world, but it can help us to understand them in a more relational manner and, in so doing, enable us to act upon them for the purpose of human betterment. In this time of globalization we need the knowledge that sociology can provide more than ever before. After all, to understand ourselves in the present enables a hold upon current conditions and relations without which there is no hope of shaping the future. As Ruth Levitas expresses it in the final sentence of *The Concept of Utopia*, this concerns a search for an agency that is transformative, accompanied by the possibility of hope and "only if we find it will we see our dreams come true."

The source of such hope might lie in recognition of the reasons for chaos. At first glance this seems to be an extraordinary statement! Yet we have seen that order is enabled through boundaries and globalization itself has questioned those with differing consequences. A greater recognition of our dependence upon each other may then follow, but also an enhanced desire for separation. Which route to take depends upon a concerted effort that might start within neighborhoods in proximity or online communities seeking change, but the finishing will lie dynamically beyond them. The attempt to draw, mark, and guard boundaries becomes an object of ever growing concern in the search for consistency and coherence. At another level what were once regarded as "natural" divisions – well entrenched and resistant to change – dissolve, whilst those who were once separated now find themselves coming together across space and time through means of communication which were once unimaginable.

We could say that the effort that goes into maintaining and defending an established position varies according to its brittleness in the face of contemporary forces that question its existence. This situation is thought to have arisen with the type of society that established itself in the Western world approximately three centuries ago and in which we still live today. Before this time – what is often referred to as "premodern" – the maintenance of distinctions and divisions between categories was subject to different forces whose routine questioning of their existence were less apparent. Differences were often seen as self-evident and timeless because they were thought to be immune from human intervention. They were laid down by forces beyond human control, despite being sedimented in social tradition: for example, a "noble" from the moment of birth, with the same applying to peasant serfs. The human condition settled in the same manner as was assumed to be the case with the rest of the world and, if it did not conform, conquering was a consequence.

It was roughly towards the end of the sixteenth century that in parts of western Europe this picture of the world began to fall apart. As the number and visibility of people who did not fit neatly into any "divine chain of being" grew, the pace of legislative activity quickened in order to regulate areas of life that were originally left to take their natural course. Social distinctions, categorizations, and discriminations increasingly became a matter of examination, design, planning, and conscious, organized, and specialized efforts. Social orders were seen as human products and projects and therefore amenable to control over their direction. Human order became an object of attention of science and technology. We might therefore observe that whilst order was not born in modern times, a *concern* with order and a fear that without intervention it would descend into chaos was more apparent. In these circumstances chaos emerges as the perceived outcome of a failure to order things. What makes it so disorderly is the observers' inability to control the flow of events, to obtain the desired response from the environment and to prevent or eliminate happenings which were not planned. Chaos becomes *uncertainty* and only the vigilant technicians of human affairs appear to stand between it and the achievement of orderly conduct and affairs. Yet intervention can produce unintended outcomes and boundaries are porous and contentious. The management of order is uncertain and incomplete. It is like building upon shifting sands. What we end up with are islands of order that draw upon environmental resources for their solidity and their temporary relative autonomy is an achievement requiring vigilance.

We find ourselves in a situation that we have encountered on a number of occasions. The very effort to impose order leads to an uncertainty and ambivalence that keeps the fear of chaos alive. Efforts to construe an artificial order are bound to fall short of their ideal target. They conjure up islands of relative autonomy, but at the same time can transform adjacent territories into areas of ambivalence as a result. Questions then turn into matters of method for such achievement, rather than purpose: that is, how to make boundaries effective and so stop the tide of ambivalence washing over the islands of constancy. To build order is to wage war against ambiguity. However, at what cost? Lines may be drawn that physically demarcate those boundaries through which only the eligible may cross: for example, passport controls between different countries. There are also more subtle examples, such as receiving an invitation that classifies you as a guest at a party. If you cannot show a passport or invitation, you may well find yourself turned away at the gate or door. Even if you get inside without such means, there is the constant fear of being spotted and asked to leave. The relative autonomy of the enclave has been compromised and corroded by your presence and this has detracted from a state of expectation of predictability and order. During our life course, depending on our origins and the networks upon which we draw, we can find ourselves at different points over the course of time. Being on the inside is related to the outside; as a means of maintaining order through constructing difference comparisons can be more straightforward than the work which can go into ensuring obedience once located within the confines of the enclave. In this way, the relative is maintained by the relational and the latter is recognized only in particular ways to ensure the former is ordered.

Boundaries: Time, Space, and Consequence

Despite these social forces a person's character cannot be simply split into those parts that may be permitted inside and those that must remain outside (although, as the film *One Flew over the Cuckoo's Nest* demonstrated with great poignancy and Erving Goffman noted in his work on *Asylums*, total institutions go to great lengths to ensure obedience and conformity). Total loyalty to an organization, for instance, is notoriously difficult to achieve and usually inspires the application of most ingenious and imaginative expedients. Employees of a company or an office may be prohibited from belonging to trade unions or political movements and their time and use of organizational space may be subject to routine surveillance. At an individual level, psychological tests can be applied to detect affinity to role performance and potential resistance to the taking of orders, or even the propensity to discuss confidential matters with persons outside the organization, thereby potentially undermining competitive advantage.

One example is the British Official Secrets Act, which forbids particular state employees from divulging information and documents protected against disclosure. Indeed, that may be the case even if such disclosure serves the interests of those citizens whom the state is supposed to protect. Similarly, the desire for organizations to project a certain image to the public may lead to some practices within the organization that employees regard as being unethical. In the case of the British National Health Service, certain employees within hospitals adopted a practice known as "whistle-blowing" in order to bring to public attention what they regarded as dubious practices. In order to appear to be efficient and effective in the treating and discharging of patients as an apparent measure of the organization's performance, some patients were being released back into the community without being able to recover sufficiently, only to be readmitted at a later date. The quality of individual care was then said to be undermined by a measure of the quantity of patients treated and discharged through constituting boundaries between the health service in hospital and social-care provision in the community.

The desire to draw boundaries in this manner has an effect upon practices and perceptions, as well as on dependencies and bonds between people, in ways that are often unintended. What seems to be a proper, rational solution to the problem confronted from within one apparently autonomous unit, becomes a problem for another unit whose existence and practices are related to each other. As the units, contrary to their pretenses, are closely interdependent, the problem-solving activity rebounds eventually on the very agency which has undertaken it in the first place. It leads to an unplanned and unpredicted shift in the overall balance of the situation that makes the continuous resolution of the original problem more costly than expected or even altogether impossible. This may be compounded by calculations of efficiency that simply examine a unit on the basis of inputs and outputs without relational consideration. While apparently "rational," it has nothing to say concerning the effects of decisions of one unit upon the actions of another through particular constructions that bound concepts of efficiency, effectiveness, and economy.

The most notorious case of such effects is the destruction of the ecological and climatic equilibrium of the planet. The natural resources of the earth are depleted in the pursuit of profit, but there is nothing inherent in such pursuit that operates as a check upon such behavior. Large oil tankers may take short cuts in order to deliver their cargo on time, despite the risks involved, while the tankers themselves may not be designed with "skins" in order to prevent the cargo from spilling in the event of a collision. Such design, after all, is said to be costly to a company, but at what potential cost to the environment? Industrial organizations pollute air and water and so create enormous problems for those in charge of the space of human health and urban and regional development. In their efforts to improve the organization of their own activity, companies rationalize the use of labor, by the same token declaring many of their workers redundant and adding to the problems born of chronic unemployment, such as poverty and ill-health. The mushrooming of private cars and motorways, of airports and aircraft, once expected to resolve the problem of mobility and transportation, creates traffic jams, air and noise pollution, destroys whole areas of human settlement, and leads to such a centralization of cultural life and supply of services as renders many local settlements uninhabitable. In its turn, therefore, traveling becomes more necessary than ever before, while becoming more difficult and exhausting. Those things that once promised individual freedom, such as cars, contribute to a constraining of collective freedom of movement and the pollution of the atmosphere for current and future generations. Yet the solution sold to the problem is so often the building of more roads.

One solution to the problem is the increasing electrification of transport, including individual cars and motorcycles. The source of electricity itself, as well as accessibility and regularity of supply, then becomes an issue. Perhaps the roots of such issues lie in the apparent relative autonomy that is promised in wrenching a part of our lives from the whole in the promise of a particular idea of freedom. As we all inhabit the whole, such autonomy is at best partial and at worst purely imaginary. At some level our practices and sense of how we see and use time and space are delimited, yet this can also be achieved by being blinded to consequences or deliberately closing our eyes to the manifold and far-reaching connections between us and between everything we are each doing. The number of factors which are taken into account in the planning and implementation of solutions to problems is always smaller than the sum total of factors which influence, or depend on, the situation which gave rise to the problem in the first place. We may even say that power – the capacity to design, enforce, influence, and preserve order – consists precisely of the ability to disregard, neglect, and push aside factors which, if they were the subject of deliberation and action, would question the order itself. To have power means, among other things, to be able to decide what is not important and what should not be a matter of concern within domains of action. What can rebound upon it, however, is an inability to conjure what it has termed "irrelevant factors" out of existence.

Matters of relevance and irrelevance are contingent: that is, there is no timeless reason why the line of relevance should be drawn in any particular way for it could be drawn in many ways. Given this, the decision itself is open to dispute. History is full of such examples. For instance, at the threshold of the modern era one of the most seminal power struggles developed around the passage from *patronage* to the *cash nexus*. Faced with the callous indifference of factory owners to the fate of the "factory hands" (the name indicating that employers were interested only in the "hands" of the workers), the critics of the nascent factory system recalled the practices of artisan workshops, or even country manors, which behaved like "one big family" that included all people. The masters of the workshop and country squires could be ruthless, autocratic bosses, and unscrupulously exploit the drudgery of their workers. At the same time, the workers expected the boss to care about their needs and, if necessary, bail them out from impending disaster.

In sharp opposition to these older habits, no such expectations were accepted as legitimate by the owners of factories. They paid their employees for the labor performed in factory hours and other aspects of their lives were their own responsibility. The critics and the people speaking for the factory workers resented such "washing of hands." They pointed out that the protracted, stultifying, exhausting day-to-day effort demanded by factory discipline left the workers, to paraphrase Karl Marx, "mentally exhausted and physically debased." A demarcation between the physical space of the factory walls and the social space upon which it was dependent for its existence was separated. Workers became commodities that were disposable because, like the other parts of the factory product, they were considered useless from the point of view of the productive plan. The critics pointed out that the relationship between the factory owners and the factory hands was not actually limited to a simple exchange of labor for wages. Why? Because labor could not be cut out and isolated from the person of the worker in the same way as a cash sum was separated from the person of the employer. "To give away labour" means to subject the whole person, body and soul, to the task set by the employer for whom the worker becomes just the means towards the fulfillment of their ends. In this way, despite protestations to the contrary, workers were being asked to give in exchange for wages the whole of their character and freedom.

The power of the factory owners over the workers was thereby given in this asymmetry of power. It was for this reason that Karl Marx remarked that, at least in conditions of slavery in contrast to capitalism, the owners had some interest in the wellbeing of their slaves. What was substituted for this relationship was an abstract form of exchange in which employers had no interest in the physical and mental wellbeing of the workers. The employers defined the meaning of employment and reserved the right to decide what was and what was not a matter for their concern – a right denied to employees. By the same token, the workers' fight for better labor conditions and more say in the running of the productive process then had to turn into a struggle against the employer's right to define the limits and the contents of the workplace order.

The conflict between workers and factory owners about the definition of the boundaries of the factory system is just one example of the kind of contention that all definitions of order must necessarily trigger. After all, such definitions are contingent and in the last account rest solely on someone's power to enforce them. The factory provides a demarcation that enables management to organize conduct in space and time. Linear time enables calculation of tasks and routines that are seen to constitute efficient and effective working practices. As Pamela Odih writes in *Gender and Work in Capitalist Economies*, this has an effect upon the domestic sphere. In the history of the British textile industry, calculations of time, machinery, and labor bear witness to a restriction of the working hours of women by male-dominated trade unions, thereby enabling the factory system to exploit a domestic sphere and its divisions of labor in terms of time and effort. As women were paid less than men this cemented, rather than challenged, domestic divisions of labor. Those who relied upon home-working to supplement family incomes found themselves subject to the economies of scale associated with manufacturing as practices reached out of the factory into the private, domestic sphere.

These practices were, and are, open to challenge by those who fall victim to their damaging effects. Such debates can then enter the public arena as calls for action to ameliorate the effects of such boundaries upon which certain practices rely. Indeed, the reach of social media is such that it can move directly from global traffic to individuals in their homes. The narratives through which we convey and construct a sense of who we are and what our obligations are vary in accordance with our experience of time and space. In factory processes, such as just-in-time, there is immediacy: that is, production as instantaneity. Being subject to such processes means we experience time as alternative things all at once: the linearity of time measured according to the fitting of a component to a car and the social time in terms of who we consider ourselves to be in terms of our identity. Moves between "internal" and calendar time produce senses of continuity and discontinuity whose tensions can lead to the desire for more flexibility in order to have greater control over our lives.

As this occurs, and we seek to satisfy such desire, so forms of control in the process of accumulation see others, separated from us by thousands of miles, subjected to a 24-hour economy in which assembly lines in Asia may be seen to benefit from the "dexterity" associated with younger women paid low wages to produce the things we consume. The clash between an increasing feminization of the workforce and domestic divisions of labor repeats itself in the contemporary era. The economy is dependent upon the domestic sphere and this is an issue for all of our futures, but the negative consequences fall more upon some than others.

In terms of such consequences over time, whose responsibility is it to meet the costs of polluting the supplies of fresh water, disposing of toxic waste, or the damage caused to the landscape by mining or the building of motorways? One person's waste may well become an important element of someone else's life condition. The objects of dispute look different depending on the vantage point from which they are contemplated and their meanings derive from the place they occupy in those particular orders. Buffeted by what are often contradictory pressures, they can assume a shape that no one has planned in advance and no one finds acceptable. Affected by many partial orders, no one seems to assume responsibility for their existence and consequences.

Such issues have tended to become ever more acute as the power of technological instruments of human action has grown and with it the consequences of their application. As each island of order gets more streamlined, rationalized, better supervised, and more effective in its performance, the multitude of perfected partial orders can result in overall chaos. Distant outcomes of planned, purposeful, rationally designed, and tightly monitored actions may hit back as unpredictable, uncontrollable catastrophes. Think of the prospect of the greenhouse effect. This is the unanticipated product of numerous efforts to harness ever more energy in the name of increasing efficiency and production. Each effort, in isolation, may be hailed as a breakthrough and a technological advancement, justified according to short-term goals measured according to particular standards that demarcate the consequences of actions over time. Similarly, discharges of toxic substances into the atmosphere or rivers may be justified as rare events in otherwise safety-conscious processes that are hailed as beneficial to the public good. Each of these may be indicative of an earnest search for the best, most "rational" solution to a specific task faced by this or that relatively autonomous organization. Each newly engineered virus or bacteria has a clearly defined purpose and a concrete useful job to perform. Until, that is, it is found to have undesirable side-effects as a result of its application.

Much of the argument around such consequences falls into the domain of "ownership." While private enterprise is thought to be able to produce outcomes that are generally beneficial – judging, that is, by how few seem to challenge this assumption – such motivations may find themselves questioned by democratically elected governments. One such area is the mapping of human genes and their potential for manipulation in the name of progress. Large pharmaceutical companies claim that they are ultimately acting with the public good in mind, but who owns the patent to human genes? There are thousands of patents on DNA molecules. Are they something that can be "owned" in the sense that they are commodities to be bought and sold on the market place and manipulated according to the capability to pay? This is being challenged in a struggle that has fundamental consequences for us all as the boundaries between what it is to be human and the relation between the aging process and time itself are changing.

The results of such work may be aimed at what are seen as desirable, immediate targets: for example, vulnerability to a specific disease. Yet changes in "focus" cannot but affect those things that are left "out of focus" in targeted interventions. Artificial fertilizers used to enhance agricultural crops illustrate the issue very vividly. Nitrates fed into the soil may achieve their declared effect because they multiply the crops. Rainfall, however, washes away a good portion of the fertilizers into the underground supplies of water, thereby creating a new and no less sinister problem that requires rendering the water supply suitable for consumption. In these ways the struggle against chaos continues. There is no doubt that, given a willingness to think and act differently, there are ways to reduce future risks. Problem-solving activity can lead to the creation of new problems and thus inspire the search for new solutions. All too often this has taken the form of appointing a team charged with the task of finding the shortest, cheapest and "most reasonable" way of disposing of the current problem. The more uncomfortable and more searching questions are frequently left out of this process.

Summary

We started this journey with a focus on the sociological arrow of time and took our discussion into its relationship to space. We noted that struggles to replace chaos with order concern the control of space and time through making the parts of our world's rule abiding and predictable through the constitution of boundaries in particular ways. The attempt is never complete as the struggle for order is itself the most important obstacle to its own success because the disorderly phenomena arise precisely from narrowly focused, targeted, task-oriented, single-problem-solving actions. In this way the search for order appears as the cause of its deepest, most worrying ailments. Splitting the unmanageable totality of the human condition into a multitude of small, immediate tasks because they are small and confined in time which can then be fully scanned, monitored, and managed has, at one level, rendered human action more efficient than ever before. This way of doing things is strikingly superior to any that has existed before – as long as it is measured in terms of value for money and expressed in terms of particular definitions of costs and benefits. This is precisely what is often meant by "rational." It is an instrumental reason that measures the actual results against the intended end in terms of particular inputs and outputs over time and in a demarcated space.

These calculations appear oblivious, in their exercise of rationality, to those costs that scream out for attention whose effects are felt in other places and over time. Those that are borne by actors who are not party to its conception and those results that are not monitored in order to prove its efficiency, bear these costs, along with the environment as a whole. If, on the other hand, a more inclusive measure of losses and gains were taken into account, the superiority of the modern way of doing things would look less certain. It might well transpire that the ultimate outcome of the multitude of partial and separate rational actions is more, not less, irrationality. This is an irksome yet inescapable tension in the search for order, as it is with the struggle against ambivalence that has marked so much of human history in the modern era.

We are all trained to think of our lives as a collection of tasks to be performed and problems to be solved. Our identities are bound up with our memories over time and in different spatial contexts. Equally, we also find ourselves in conditions where forces – information technology and communications – know no bounds and move across time and space with regularity. Such forces are not restricted to small enclaves of order, as they affect our entire futures. What is now required is some understanding of the weaknesses, as well as strengths, of the ways in which we view each other, our ways of thinking, communicating, and acting, and the environments that we all inhabit. In this process of rethinking, established ways of viewing the world may find themselves questioned by new sets of circumstances that call for new ways of thinking. To some this may be a threat and to others an opportunity for indulgence. There is an urgency given by these conditions and this requires a willingness to change: no more, of course, than humankind has changed so many times before in the course of its history.

8

Culture, Nature, and Territory

In the last chapter we examined the constitution of boundaries that provide coherence and continuity to perspectives and practices in a fluid world permeated by global forces that move across time and space. We also saw how such boundaries, whilst seeking order, create issues through taking a relative, rather than relational, stand in the world. Such efforts create issues that radiate beyond their confines and return to the apparent impregnability of their walls with negative consequences. With sociological lenses in place we can see that the way in which we think about and examine a "problem" will itself give rise to what are seen as appropriate solutions. Thinking differently from a position that is not located within the particularities of a world view is not an indulgent activity. On the contrary, it can be the first step towards the construction of more practical and inclusive approaches to the issues that we all face in contemporary times. With that in mind, we continue our journey through an examination of nature, culture, and territory.

Nature and Culture: An Opposition in the Making

We have raised issues concerning a "modern" way of thinking about the differences between nature and culture. This image set nature and society sharply apart. One can say that nature and society were "discovered" simultaneously. Nevertheless, this was not a discovery of nature or society, but a *distinction* between them and especially between the practices that each one enabled or gave rise to. As the human condition increasingly became the product of legislation, management, and intervention in general, "nature" assumed the role of a huge depository for those things which human powers could mold, or had no ambition to alter. It was ruled by its own logic and that left human being and practices to be characterized through what Timothy Morton, in his book *Humankind: Solidarity with Nonhuman People*, calls a "severing" whose consequences are so apparent in contemporary times.

Changes in social thought occurred in the West during the seventeenth and eighteenth centuries. Philosophers began to talk about "laws of nature" as analogous to the laws promulgated by kings or parliaments, but also to distinguish them from the latter. "Natural laws" were like the laws of the kings, often working as the

Thinking Sociologically, Third Edition. Zygmunt Bauman and Tim May.
© 2019 John Wiley & Sons Ltd. Published 2019 by John Wiley & Sons Ltd.

agents of God and thus obligatory, but unlike the royal decrees they had no conceivable human author. Their force was "superhuman," whether they had been established by God's will and inscrutable purpose or were causally determined, with an unassailable necessity, directly by the way cosmic matters were arranged. The way to understand them was to exercise the human capacity of "reason" and such distinctions gave rise to a manner of boundary formation: for example, the assumption man is "rational" and so able to transcend the demands of nature, while women were "emotional" and subject to nature's impulsive forces. Similarly, there were developed countries that exhibited certain principles that distinguished them from those other countries that were "uncivilized" in their outlook.

These times of transformations in our ways of thinking, seeing, and doing were informed by a quest for certainty as a response to the ambiguity of the human condition. Over time and as societies became more complex and simple boundaries questioned, it was possible to stir a fear of ambiguity that comes with the "other" who represents difference and an apparent threat to constancy. In the process we employ distinctions between what is thought to be within "human power" to alter according to our desires, ideals, and aims. These are informed by the question of whether there is a standard, a norm, to which "something" or "someone" should submit. What are then brought within frames of consideration are those things that can be readily fashioned according to particular expectations. These are to be treated in a different manner from those things that are taken to be beyond human power to alter. The first we might call *culture* and the second *nature*. Thus, when we think of something as being a matter of culture, rather than nature, we are implying that the thing in question is subject to manipulation and our influence and, further, that there is a desirable, "proper" end-state from which to judge its effectiveness.

Culture concerns making things different from what they are and otherwise would be and about keeping them in this shape. It is characterized by a set of assumptions shared and developed by a group that demarcates a range of possibilities to produce order. Culture is about introducing, inculcating, resisting everything that departs from it as indicative of a descent into chaos. That can mean supplementing the "order of nature" (that is, the state of things as they are without human interference) with an artificial, designed one. Culture not only promotes and orders, but evaluates. Thus, the "solution" sold to many businesses in the name of productivity is an introduction of the "correct" culture into an organization that, in turn, permeates throughout the organization enabling each person to evaluate themselves according to their abilities to live up to its expectations. Culture, in this sense, becomes something to be acquired, rather than what we are as a result of being human. In the process, that which does not accord with the ideals that inform transformations, or even question them, are easily dismissed as "disorderly" impediments to the pursuits of ends such as "quality," "efficiency," and "effectiveness."

Drawing Demarcations

Where exactly is the dividing line between nature and culture? That depends on what skills, knowledge, and resources are available and whether there is an ambition to deploy them for previously untried purposes. In general, the development of science and technology widens the scope of possible manipulation and thus extends the realm of culture. Technology is often seen as a panacea for social problems. Consider our previous example: genetic engineering. That is, changing the idea of what it is to be a "normal" human being. Taking this one step further, if genetic control is applied to the regulation of what it is to be a normal and healthy human being, who will decide what this is and with what consequences for how we view ourselves and others? Such a culture may appear to the individual to be much the same way as the laws of nature: it is a fate against which one cannot rebel, or against which rebellion is, ultimately, a futile gesture. At one level nature determines us and, at another, it has the potential to be harnessed for human wellbeing and refinement. Who, after all, would not elect to be "healthy" and live a long life, but at what cost?

Let us take a close look at the "human-made elements" in our own lives. They may well enter into the space we occupy in two ways. First, they regulate and so render orderly the context in which our individual life-processes are conducted. Second, they shape the motives and purposes of our life-process itself. One enables us to rationalize our actions by rendering some more sensible and reasonable than others. The other orients us in terms of being able to select particular motives and purposes from innumerable others that may even lie beyond our imagination. These are not distinct from other environments that we come across, for each of our actions has effects upon other environments that we inhabit and interact with in our everyday lives. Thus, to take one example that many take for granted: the technological developments that gave us mobile phones are said to afford the phones' owners improved communication. At another level, there is now talk of the need to undertake a "digital detox" to improve health because they are stressful, antisocial, and damaging in their use.

We may distinguish the order that is enabled by cultural intervention from randomness or chaos by observing that in an orderly situation not everything may happen. Out of a virtually infinite set of conceivable events, only a finite number may take place. Different events thus carry different degrees of probability. That leaves us with a criterion of success being the establishment of order through the transformation of what was once improbable into the realm of the necessary or inevitable. In this sense, to design order is to manipulate the probability of events. It is a process in which preferences and priorities are selected according to particular values. These are then incorporated and stand behind those artificial orders which result from selection and manipulation. Once the order has become entrenched, solid, and secure, other ways of seeing may be forgotten and it becomes the only one imaginable.

As human beings, we all have a vested interest in creating and maintaining an orderly environment. This is because of the fact that most of what we do is learnt from the social environments in which we find ourselves and this learning accumulates over time thanks to interactions with others and memories passed on through narratives and documentary records. Our understanding is informed through prior judgments that are accumulated over time and passed down through the generations. The knowledge and the skills accompanying it remain beneficial as long as the contexts in which they were formed remain unchanged. Such alignment constitutes constancy in the world such that the actions that were successful before are likely to remain so if repeated today and tomorrow. Just imagine what havoc would occur if, for instance, the meaning of the colors of traffic lights were changed without warning. In a randomly mutable world, memory and learning would turn from a blessing that orientates and enables into a curse that confuses and paralyzes.

In alignment between order and our environment we find orderliness in our actions. We do not behave at a party in the same fashion as we do at a college seminar or business meeting. We conduct ourselves differently at our parental home during the holidays and at a formal visit among people whom we do not know. We use a different tone of voice and different words, depending on whether we are addressing a manager or colleague or chatting to our friends. There are words we deploy on one occasion and avoid on another. There are things we do in public, but also "private" activities which we do only when we are sure that we are not being watched. The remarkable thing is that while choosing a conduct "proper" for the occasion, we find ourselves in the company of others behaving exactly like us. As such, departures from what are apparently rules are lessened and this provides for a degree of *predictability* in the conduct of ourselves, others, and the institutions with which we deal and that inform our lives.

Culture, as the labor that makes up artificial order, requires distinctions: that is, setting things and people apart through acts of segregation and discrimination. In a desert, untouched by human activity and indifferent to human purpose, there are neither signposts nor fences making one stretch of land different from another. In other words, it is formless. In an environment subjected to the work of culture, on the other hand, a uniform, flat surface is divided into areas which draw in some people but repel others, or into strips fit only for vehicles and those that are suitable solely for walkers. The world thus acquires a *structure* that orients activity. People are divided into ranks, agents of authority, and lay-persons; those who speak and those who listen and are expected to take notice of what is said. Similarly, time occurs in a uniform flow via a division into designated activities: for example, breakfast-time, coffee break, lunchtime, afternoon tea, and dinner. Spatially, there is demarcation according to the "physical" composition and place of particular gatherings – being in a seminar, a conference, a beer festival, a dinner party, or a business meeting.

These distinctions are drawn on two planes. The first is the "shape of the world" in which the action takes place and the second is the action itself. Parts of the world are made different from each other, as well as different in themselves, depending on the periods distinguished in the flow of time (the same building may be a school in the morning and a badminton court in the evening). The actions within them are equally differentiated. Conduct at the table differs sharply depending on what has been put on the table, in what circumstances, and who is sitting around it. Even table manners differ according to the formality and informality of the meal, as well as the class location of the participants, as both Erving Goffman and Pierre Bourdieu have reminded us as a result of their sociological studies. There is a way of fitting into expectations given by cultures and a sense of belonging enabling a distinction between "us" and "them." It exerts a powerful pull until, that is, a yearning for something else starts to emerge, as is richly portrayed in Lynsey Hanley's *Respectable: Crossing the Class Divide*.

Such a setting apart provides for difference, but these things are not really independent from each other: there would be no formal dinner without people behaving in a formal manner. We can express these acts of coordination in another way: both the culturally organized social world and the actions of culturally trained individuals are structured in terms of being "articulated," with the help of oppositions, into separate social contexts. In turn, these contexts call for distinctive manifestations of conduct that are deemed suitable for each occasion. In addition, these articulations "correspond" to each other or, to employ a more technical term, they are isomorphic. The device that secures the "overlap" between structures of social reality and of culturally regulated actions is the cultural *code* which is, first and foremost, a system of oppositions. Indeed, what is opposed in this system are *signs* – visible, audible, tactile, olfactory objects or events like lights of different colors, elements of dress, inscriptions, oral statements, tones of voice, gestures, facial expressions, scents, and so on. These link actions and the social figuration sustained by them. The signs point in two directions at the same time: towards the intentions of the actors and towards the given segment of social reality in which they act. Neither of the two is just a reflection of the other, or is primary or secondary. Both exist together, grounded in the same facility of the cultural code.

Think of a "no entry" notice fixed to an office door. Such a notice might appear on one side of the door only and the door is usually unlocked (were the door impossible to open, there would hardly be a need for the notice). The notice is not, therefore, giving information on the "objective state" of the door itself. It is an instruction that is meant to create and sustain a situation which otherwise would not occur. What the words "no entry" do, in fact, is to distinguish between two sides of the door; between the kinds of people who approach the door from opposite sides and the type of conduct that those people are expected or permitted to engage in. The space behind the marked side of the door is barred to those who approach it from the side of the notice, but for the people on the other side of the door, no such restriction has been imposed. The sign stands for this distinction. Its achievement is to discriminate between people in an otherwise uniform space.

To know a code is to *understand* the meaning of signs and this, in turn, means knowing how to go on in a situation in which they appear, as well as how to use them to make such a situation appear. To understand is to be able to act effectively in context and thereby sustain coordination between the structures of the situation and our own actions. It is often said that to understand a sign is to grasp its meaning. However, this does not mean that a thought is then invoked as a mental image within our own mind. A thought, manifested in terms of a sort of "reading aloud" of the sign in our head, may indeed accompany the sight or the sound of the sign. However, to grasp meaning means no more and no less than to know how to go on. The meaning of a sign thereby resides in the difference its presence or absence makes. To express it another way: the meaning of a sign resides in its relation to other signs. Some, such as Jacques Derrida, take this one step further and argue that because meanings derive only from the relation between signs, they can never be fixed. We are left with an inability to decide based upon the idea of *différance*. Ultimate meaning can elude us due to the necessity for continual clarification and definition.

One sign does not usually carry enough information to fix a relation sufficiently to enable action. One sign may be read incorrectly and, if such an erroneous reading does happen, there will be nothing to correct the mistake. For instance, the sight of a military uniform tells us in unambiguous terms that the person in front of us is a member of the armed forces. For most civilians, this information would be quite sufficient to "structure" the encounter. Nevertheless, for members of the armed forces, with their complex hierarchy of power and division of duties, the information conveyed by the uniform might not be enough and so other rank-showing signs are "piled up" on the primary and general sign (the uniform) to provide further information. In certain instances such are the surplus of signs that they add little to the information already conveyed. Certain marketing tactics, for example, in their search for distinction between one product and another, merely replicate the information already conveyed by other signs, whilst private security companies may have uniforms whose appearance is not dissimilar from those of a public police force.

In these cases we may refer to the *redundancy* of signs. Here we find an insurance against mistakes through the elimination of potential ambivalence by misreading. Were it not for redundancy, the accidental distortion or overlooking of just one sign could prompt the wrong kind of behavior. We could even suggest that the more important the oppositions between signs for the maintenance and furtherance of the established order, the more redundancy we can expect. At one level this reduces the problems associated with mistaken readings and so seeks to reduce *mis*understanding via a surplus of signs. Yet, at the same time, this surplus can heighten ambiguity and render alternative meanings more likely. Thus, while pursuing the need for communication to coordinate activities, to push this venture too far can risk introducing ambiguity and, hence, distorted communications.

Such a feature is apparent in communications across time and space. The interpersonal interpretations, reminders, and enforcements of signs to coordinate activities appear to dissipate in the face of social media. The public and private realms blur in the individuated realms of typing, pressing buttons, and posting pictures of what one is eating or doing on a daily basis which can be seen and read by many. It becomes a public consumption of private life in which many are content to be a part, using platforms whose business models are concerned with advertising revenue. Seeking not only visibility, but perhaps validation, for one's lifestyle, viewpoints, and habits have consequences beyond self-presentation and affirmation. As subjects for advertising targets, such a culture informs how we see the world and transforms us into consumers for whom there is a competition for our attention in a process of circulations of signs. It can also transform us in other ways. The time spent online is free labor for the technology companies who have the resources to extract data. That, in turn, is sold on as a solution to problems of, say, market targeting through the promise of artificial intelligence (AI). Indeed, the possibilities are endless. Evgeny Morozov puts it in the following terms: "How did we end up in a world where tech firms build addictive services to grab our data – only to pitch AI solutions for the addiction problem they created?" (https://www.theguardian.com/technology/2018/jan/28/morozov-artificial-intelligence-data-technology-online).

We often consider such technology to be part of our freedom. Yet is it using us, or are we using it? To consider this, we demarcate differences in terms of attributes and characteristics: for example, in obtaining knowledge of natural phenomena we often refer to "signs" through which nature "informs" us of itself and which have to be read in order to extract the information they contain. Thus, we look at the drops of water flowing down the window pane and say: "it's raining." Or we observe a wet pavement and we conclude that it must have been raining, and so on. What is characteristic about signs like these is that unlike the cultural signs we discussed before, they are all *determined*: that is, they are effects of their respective causes. Rain sends drops of water down the window pane and leaves the roads wet; illness changes the temperature of the body and makes the head feel hot, leading us to conclude that someone has a fever. Once we know of such causal connections, we can reconstruct the "invisible" cause from the observed effects. To avoid confusion, it would perhaps be better to speak of *indices*, rather than signs, when referring to causally determined clues in our reasoning.

We have suggested that the natural causes noted in our above example place limitations on the interpretations that can then be made of the phenomenon in question. There is a separation between us and nature enabling a picture of natural reality to emerge. Two qualifying points need to be made here. First, social studies of the practice of science have suggested that much of what appears as the unproblematic interpretation of so-called natural events is, in fact, socially produced. Work conducted in scientific laboratories, for example, is a social activity in which social meanings play a large and important role, while much inference in the physical sciences concerns unobserved phenomena. In this latter instance there is not a placing of limitations, through observation, on possible interpretations. Second, while noting the arbitrary character of cultural signs, this does not suggest they are not real in their effects: that is, they place constraints upon our actions and the possibilities with which we are all faced in social life. To this extent they both enable and constrain our activities and the manner of their effects can vary according to the context and the power we may possess to alter their effects. Being defined as "poor" refers not simply to an arbitrary cultural category, but to the capability that people have, materially and socially speaking, of being able to have sufficient money and social standing to meet their everyday needs according to the basic standards of the society in which they find themselves.

The idea that cultural signs are arbitrary is not equal to complete freedom of choice. Language is a sign-system specialized in the function of communication. In language (and in language only), therefore, the arbitrariness of signs has no constraints. Those vocal sounds that humans are capable of producing can be modulated in an infinite number of utterly arbitrary ways, provided there are enough of them to produce the required oppositions. The same opposition, in various languages, may be construed with the help of pairs such as hot and cold, large and small, and so on. Language and power, as Pierre Bourdieu and critical linguists have all pointed out, go together in such a way as to limit what may be spoken. In his studies of the education system, Pierre Bourdieu examines how the construction of an official language authorizes not only what can and cannot be said, but also how to see and feel in particular ways. As we have noted throughout the book, those things that provide for the possibility for action are also those that may serve to constrain our potential and set limits on possibilities.

In terms of limits, we might say that culture is most effective when it is disguised as nature. What is artificial appears to be rooted in the very "nature of things" and so becomes something that no human decision or action may possibly change. Sharply distinct practices of the placement and treatment of men and women, inscribed from an early age, become truly well established and secure once it is accepted as beyond question that the relation between the sexes is somehow predetermined. Culturally produced, social differences between men and women appear as natural as the observed biological differences between the male and female sexual organs and procreative functions. Such processes occur as long as the character of the norms that culture propagates is not exposed. Culture looks and acts like nature as long as no alternative conventions are seen and known. Yet virtually every one of us knows that there are many different ways of life. We look around us at people who dress, talk, and behave differently from ourselves. We know that there are *cultures* rather than one single culture. Thus, culture is unable to hold the same firm grip on human conduct as if it were a universal condition free from alternative orders. In the process we may come across periods and times of doubt that require explanations and justifications for an existing state of affairs. These questions may be met through an open and inquiring culture, but may also prompt a forceful imposition of what is assumed to be the natural order of things.

Territory: State and Nation

As two responses in the sentence above, we see both an openness to explore justifications for particular courses of action and an imposition through the exercise of overt power around the idea that culture exhibits a fixed, natural order to be protected against the chaos that might arrive with greater permeability of its boundaries. The relief that apparently arrives through the maintenance of consistency avoids recognition of ambivalence. That may not be a pleasant condition and so attempts to escape from it are not uncommon. In this process, pressures to conform to norms promoted by cultural training can be accompanied by efforts to discredit and denigrate the norms of other cultures. The idea that nature is fixed is culturally appropriated through allusion to a "naturalness." We can see this in groups who deploy rhetorics of "purity" and "contamination" at one end of the spectrum and a right to live a culture, separately from others, at the other end. Even if other ways of life are acknowledged as viable cultures in their own right, they may be portrayed as bizarre and vaguely threatening. They may be acceptable for those who demand less of their people, but are not sufficient for those persons of distinction. What we witness here are varying degrees of *xenophobia* (dread of the alien) or *heterophobia* (dread of the different) as means for defending an order against ambivalence.

With the distinctions between "us" and "them," "here" and "there," "inside" and "outside," "native" and "foreign," we often see the drawing of a territory over which there is a claim for undivided rule and an intention to guard against all competition in the name of an established and unproblematic culture. Cultural tolerance is often exercised at a distance, which is not the same as recognition of difference as having equal worth. If tolerance at a distance is threatened through proximity of other cultures, a rhetoric of invasion and purity is often thinly disguised by another that proclaims the right of all people to live their life as they wish – as long as they do so within their "own country." So we have territory and culture mixing with the porosity of boundaries in an increasingly global world, all interacting with varying consequences. For Alain Touraine, in his study *Can We Live Together?* we have a process of "demodernization" in which the global economy turns us into consumers who merely exchange in the marketplace and that disassociates itself from culture and other forms of our identities. As nation-states have less control over the global flow of goods and services, so cultures may turn in on themselves in search of coherence in the face of these forces.

In the face of this we often find the phenomena of cultural *hegemony*. Antonio Gramsci wrote in the *Prison Notebooks* that national hegemonies could be seen as the terrain upon which both the exercise of coercion and the manufacture of consent interacted. What is indicated by this term is a subtle but effective process aimed at securing a monopoly of the norms and values upon which particular orders are erected. Hence, culture can become a proselytizing activity aiming at conversion by inducing its objects to abandon their old habits and beliefs and embrace others instead or, alternatively, by castigating other cultures based upon the assumed superiority of its own. On the other hand, in those situations where cultural designs coexist without clear demarcation lines separating their fields of influence, we find conditions of "cultural pluralism." Ideally, such situations are exemplified in recognition of the other side's worthiness and validity as an attitude necessary for constructive and peaceful coexistence.

Citizenship and the State

We are now dealing with issues that are linked to matters of identity and, in turn, to citizenship. Citizenship may be something to which a person is entitled by virtue of their place of birth. In addition, it may be conferred upon someone as a result of an application to a country, or by virtue of a past association and service to a country that is rewarded accordingly. In other instances, people may be refugees from persecution and so apply for political asylum and residence. In considering such issues, culture, nation, and beliefs concerning nationalism will inform the status conferred upon the person and the granting or refusal of their application. If granted, what may then occur is a link between personal identity and belonging in terms of being part of a nation.

Consider all the forms that we are routinely asked to complete when making particular applications. They ask details about us, our preferences, history, and affiliations and may often include a question about nationality. To this question a person may answer "American," "British," "German," "Indian," "French," "Kenyan," "Chinese," "Pakistani," "Portuguese", and so on. However, if answering "British," the person may also answer "English" (or "Welsh," or "Scottish," or "Greek") and be from different ethnic origins. As it happens, both answers are proper responses to the question of nationality, but refer to different things. When answering "British" they are indicating that they are a "British subject": that is, a citizen of the *state* called Great Britain or the United Kingdom. When answering "English" they are reporting the fact that they belong to the English *nation*. A question about nationality makes both answers possible and acceptable and demonstrates how the two memberships are not clearly distinguished from each other and thus may become confused. Yet while state and nation may overlap, they are quite different things and a person's membership of each involves them in very different kinds of relationships.

There is no state without a specific territory held together by a center of power. Every resident of the area over which the authority of the state extends belongs to the state. Belonging has a legal meaning. "Authority of the state" means the ability to declare and enforce the "law of the land." These are the rules that must be observed by all subjects of this authority (unless the state itself exempts them from such an obedience), including those persons who may not be its citizens but fall within its territory by virtue of their physical presence. If the laws are not observed and culprits apprehended and charged, consequences follow. They will be forced to obey, whether they like it or not. To paraphrase Max Weber, the state has a monopoly over the legitimate means of violence. The state claims the sole right to apply coercive force (to use weapons in defense of the law, to deprive the law-breaker of freedom through imprisonment, and ultimately to kill if the death penalty exists). In these instances when people are executed by the order of the state, the killing is regarded as legitimate punishment and not murder. However, that interpretation is open to considerable debate. The other side of the state monopoly of physical coercion is that any use of force which has not been authorized by the state, or committed by anyone other than its authorized agents, is condemned as an act of violence. Note, of course, that none of this is to suggest that those acting on behalf of the state may not engage in illegitimate acts of violence and terror. Indeed, whilst international law exists in regard to such matters as rendition and torture, states may deliberately send people to other places in order to carry out such acts.

The laws announced and guarded by the state determine the duties and the rights of the state subjects. One of the most important of these duties is the payment of taxes – giving away a proportion of our income to the state, which collects it and puts it to various uses. The rights, on the other hand, may be *personal*. Here we include the protection of our own body and possessions, unless ruled otherwise by the decision of authorized state organs, as well as the right to profess our own opinions and beliefs in such a way as not to subjugate the freedom of others. They may also be *political* in terms of influencing the composition and the policy of state organs: for example, by taking part in the election of the body of representatives who then become rulers or administrators of the state institutions. They may also include, as the sociologist T. H. Marshall argued, *social* rights: those that are guaranteed by the state in terms of a basic livelihood and essential needs such as cannot be attained by the efforts of given individuals.

As we have raised the issue of the relations between the economic and cultural, we have now introduced the role of state and being a citizen. How these balance out will vary between societies. Social rights may challenge property rights in that they are associated with, to employ the British philosopher Isaiah Berlin's famous distinction between two concepts of liberty, both "positive and negative liberty." "Negative liberty" denotes a freedom from interference based upon ownership of property. This is argued to grant a person entitlement to their land and possessions and a minimal state involvement in the means through which they dispose of their wealth. "Positive liberty," on the other hand, is about providing people with certain entitlements regardless of such ownership which may, of course, simply be an accident of birth. Charitable giving may be associated with the former whereby those with wealth choose to give a proportion of their income to worthy causes. However, for the recipients, this comes in the form of a "gift," rather than an "entitlement" as a result of their citizenship. Such issues inform the campaigning slogans that often surround the erosion or claim to rights: for example, "rights not charity" and "education is a right, not a privilege."

It is a combination of rights and duties that makes the individual a subject of the state. The first thing we know about being state subjects is that however much we might dislike it, we have to pay income tax, local tax, or value-added tax. Yet we can also complain to the authorities and seek their assistance if our bodies are assaulted or possessions stolen and have expectations concerning the infrastructures that enable our everyday lives. We can also, depending on the country in which we live, have access to primary and secondary education regardless of the ability to pay, as well as a health service. The British National Health Service, for example, is an institution that was set up precisely in order that all people could have access to health care and thus seek to ensure a more healthy population for both economic and social wellbeing.

Those conditions that we might take for granted until, that is, they are withdrawn and we see the consequences, are those that can be viewed as both enabling and constraining. In conditions where people celebrate an atomistic existence and deny a relational understanding, there is the potential for suspicion and threat. On the other hand, with collectivism often come ideas of the trampling of individual freedom. In both cases we may enjoy the relative peacefulness of life which we owe to the awesome force always waiting somewhere in the wings to be deployed against the breakers of peace. During the Cold War this balance was determined in our nuclear age by a process that came to be known as mutually assured destruction (MAD). As the state is the only power permitted to set apart the permissible from the impermissible and as law enforcement by the state organs is the only method of keeping this distinction permanent and secure, we believe that if the state withdrew its punishing fist, universal violence and disorder would rule instead. We believe that we owe our security and peace of mind to the power of the state and that there would be no security or peace of mind without it. On many occasions, however, we resent the obtrusive interference of the state into our private lives. If the *protective* care of the state enables us to do things – to plan our actions in the belief that the plans may be executed without obstacle – the *oppressive* function of the state feels more like disablement. Our experience of the state is, therefore, inherently ambiguous: we may like and need it and dislike and resent it at the same time.

How these two feelings are balanced depends upon our circumstances. If we are well off and money is not a problem, we might relish the prospect of securing for ourselves a better health service than that offered to the average person. We might regard the normal offer as insufficient precisely because it is available to all. In the British context, we might resent the fact that the state taxes us and runs the National Health Service. If our income, on the other hand, is too modest to buy exclusive health services, we might welcome the state as a device that protects us in times of ill-health. We may fail to see how, in general, the tax and benefit systems associated with the nation-state affect life-chances in different ways. UK expenditure on health care as a percentage of gross domestic product (GDP) might be lower than the USA, Germany, France, and Japan, but our focus is upon ourselves and how we are affected by our circumstances.

That is perfectly understandable. However, how would a person be able to afford private health care in the British context if it were not for the National Health Service training doctors and nurses and so providing the skills and knowledge that the private sector requires? Similarly, how would the economy be able to perform effectively if it were not for the state education sector furnishing the job market with skilled and knowledgeable individuals? We can see from this discussion that, depending on their position, some people may experience an increase in freedom as a result of state actions widening their choice, while others may consider such action as constraining and narrowing their range of choice. Some may be migrants or refugees fleeing countries in fear of their lives, or those seeking temporary work permits, or investing their wealth for various reasons. Once citizens, most would prefer as much enabling as possible and as little constraining as is truly necessary. What is perceived as enabling and constraining will differ, but the urge to control, or at least to influence the composition of the mixture, does not. The greater the part of our lives that depends on state activities, the more widespread and intense is likely to be this urge.

To be a citizen is twofold: first, as the bearer of rights and duties as the state defines and, second, having a voice in determining the policies that inform those rights and duties. In other words, citizenship refers to a capability to influence the activity of the state and thus to participate in the definition and management of "law and order." To exercise such influence in practice, the citizens must enjoy a degree of autonomy regarding state regulation. There must, in other words, be limits to the capability of the state to interfere with a subject's actions. Here, once again, we confront the tensions between the enabling and constraining aspects of state activity. For instance, citizens' rights cannot be exercised fully if the activities of the state are surrounded by secrecy and if the "ordinary people" have no insight into the intentions and the doings of their rulers. A government confusing its aims with those of the state can easily undermine those rights by denying them access to the facts which allow them to evaluate the real consequences of the state's action. In the absence of a public realm of deliberation and scrutiny for the justifications for such actions, the scales easily tilt from protection to oppression.

For such reasons the relations between the state and its subjects are often strained, as the subjects find themselves obliged to struggle to become citizens or to protect their status when it is threatened by the growing ambitions or inactions of the state. The main obstacles they encounter in this struggle are those related to the tutelage complex and therapeutic attitudes of the state, respectively. The first refers to a tendency to treat subjects as if they were unable to determine what is good for them and act in a manner that serves their best interests. The second refers to the inclination of state authorities to treat subjects in the same manner that doctors treat their patients. In this way they become individuals who are burdened with problems that they cannot resolve on their own. What is then assumed to be required is expert guidance, along with surveillance to resolve problems that, as it were, reside "inside" the patient. The treatment is then instruction and supervision in order that they work on their bodies in accordance with the doctor's orders. Here we can see a tendency, from the state's point of view, to see subjects as objects of regulation. The subjects' conduct may then be regarded as being in constant need of proscription and prescription. If the conduct is not what it should be, then there is something wrong with the subject themselves, as opposed to the context in which they find themselves. This tendency to individualize social problems takes place against a background of asymmetrical relations. Even if patients choose their doctors, once the doctor has been chosen, the patient is expected to defer to their expertise. This is what may be termed the exercise of *pastoral power* in order to protect the individual against their own inclinations.

In this process there may be justifications invoked concerning the need to withhold information for the good of the citizen. This practice of secrecy surrounds the detailed information that the state gathers and stores and processes. Much of this, of course, is information designed to assist in policy formulation and implementation. Yet, at the same time, data about the state's own actions may be classified as "official secrets," whose betrayal is prosecuted. As most subjects of the state are denied access to this type of information, or are required to make formal requests in order to access it, those few who are so permitted gain a distinct advantage over the rest. State freedom to collect information, coupled with the practice of secrecy can easily exacerbate the asymmetry of the mutual relations. Here we can think of *WikiLeaks*, set up as an anti-secrecy organization, which has published numerous documents classified as top secret in the name of public information. Yet it has been seen by governments and officials as irresponsible in its actions. Given this conflicting potential, citizenship carries a tendency to resist the commanding position aspired to by the state. These efforts may be manifest in two related, but different directions. The first is *regionalism* in which state power may be seen as an adversary of local autonomy. The specificity of local interests and issues become singled out as sufficient reasons for aspirations to the self-management of local affairs. Accompanying this is a demand for representative local institutions that will stand closer to the people in the area and be more sensitive and responsive to their regional concerns. The second manifestation is *de-territorialization*. Here we find the territorial basis of state power being open to challenge. Other traits are then promoted as being of more significance than mere place of residence. For instance, ethnicity, religion, and language may be singled out as attributes that possess a heavier bearing on the totality of human life. The right to autonomy, to separate management, is then demanded against the pressure for uniformity from the unitary territorial power.

As a result of these propensities and even under the best of circumstances, there remains a residue of tension and distrust between the state and its subjects. In the face of global forces, for example, the state may be "hollowed-out" by its inability to hold such power in check. Yet, equally, the regulatory regime of a state creates the external conditions that markets require for their operation. To return to our discussion on time and space, the state operates in such a way as to manage the relations between the global mobility of capital and how it alights in particular places for the benefit of nations. As Bob Jessop expresses it in *State Power*, such a role reflects a balance between "internal and external forces, with some states more willing and active participants in these processes than others." Internally, the state therefore needs to secure its *legitimacy* by convincing the subjects that there are valid reasons why they should obey the commands of the state. Legitimation is meant to secure the subjects' trust in that whatever comes from state authorities deserves to be obeyed, along with the conviction that it also must be obeyed. To this extent legitimation aims at developing an unconditional allegiance to the state in which security is apparent in belonging to a "homeland" in which the individual citizen can benefit from its wealth and might. With this we may see *patriotism* as a guide to actions seen in terms of a love of the homeland that generates feelings of belonging among its citizens. A combination of consensus and discipline are thought to make all citizens better off and concerted actions, rather than rifts, are held to be beneficial to all citizens.

If patriotic obedience is demanded in the name of reason, one may well be tempted to subject the argument to a test of reason on the basis that all calculation invites a counter-calculation. One may count the costs of obedience to an unpopular policy against the gains that an active resistance may bring. One may then find out, or convince oneself, that resistance is less costly and damaging than obedience. Civil disobedience cannot be simply written off as the distorted aspirations of those who are misled, for it takes place in those spaces created by efforts to legitimize state activities. As this process is hardly ever conclusive and without end, these kinds of actions can act as a barometer for the extent to which policies become too oppressive. This is an insight which Emile Durkheim was particularly concerned to emphasize when writing about such matters as the state, crime, and deviance. Indeed, one of his lasting legacies was to argue that society is an active moralizing force and this, of course, may be undermined or promoted by state activities and policies, as well as economic interests.

Nations and Nationalism

Unconditional loyalties to a nation, in contrast to the above, are free from the inner contradictions that burden discipline towards the state. *Nationalism* does not need to appeal to reason or calculation. While it may appeal to gains that can be afforded by obedience, it is normally characterized by obedience as a value in its own right. Membership of a nation is understood as a fate more powerful than any individual and, as such, is not a quality that cannot be put on or taken off at will. Nationalism implies that it is the nation which gives individual members their identity. Unlike the state, the nation is not an association entered into in order to promote and achieve common interests. On the contrary, the unity of the nation is a common fate that precedes all consideration of other interests and, further, gives the interests their meaning.

With that in place, the nation can lapse into nationalism. There is no need to legitimize itself by reference to a public sphere of deliberation concerning justification for actions and policies. Instead, it takes waves of emotion that block out consideration of the efficacy of actions and their effects on others and demands obedience on the grounds that it speaks in the name of the nation. This form of state discipline is a value that does not serve any objective other than pursuing its own purpose. In this situation, to question or disobey the state becomes something far worse than a breach of the law. It becomes an act of betrayal of cause – a heinous, immoral act that strips culprits of dignity and casts them outside the bounds of the human community. It is perhaps for the reasons of legitimation and, more generally, of securing the unity of conduct, that there is a sort of mutual attraction between the state and the nation. The state tends to enlist the authority of the nation to strengthen its own demand for discipline, while nations tend to constitute themselves into states to harness the enforcing potential of the state to the support of their claim to loyalty. Of course, not all states are national and not all nations have states of their own.

What is a nation? This is a difficult question, with no single answer being likely to satisfy everybody. The nation is not a "reality" in the same way in which the state may be defined. The state is "real" in the sense of having clearly drawn boundaries, both on the map and on the land. The boundaries are on the whole guarded by force, so that random passing from one state to another, entering and leaving the state, encounters real, tangible resistance which makes the state itself real through a set of bounded practices. Inside the boundaries of the state, a set of laws is binding which, again, is real in the sense that disregarding its presence, behaving as if it did not exist, may "bruise" and "hurt" the perpetrator in much the same way as disregarding walking into a material object might. However, the same cannot be said about the nation. A nation is an "imagined community" because it exists as an entity insofar as its members mentally and emotionally "identify themselves" with a collective body. True, nations usually occupy a continuous territory which, as they may credibly claim, may lend them a particular character. Seldom does this provide the territory with a uniformity that is comparable with that imposed by the unity of the state-sponsored "law of the land." Hardly ever can nations boast a monopoly of residence on any territory. Within virtually any territory we find people living side by side who define themselves as belonging to different nations and whose loyalty is thus claimed by varying traditions. In many territories no nation can really claim a majority, much less a position sufficiently dominant to define the "national character" of the land.

We might turn to a common language as a defining criterion. It is true that nations are usually distinguished and united by a common language. Yet what is deemed a common and distinct language is to a large extent a matter of a nationalist (and often contested) decision. Regional dialects may be as idiosyncratic in their vocabulary, syntax, and idioms to be almost mutually incomprehensible and yet their identities are denied or actively suppressed for fear of disrupting national unity. On the other hand, even comparatively minor local differences may well be exaggerated so that a dialect may be elevated to the rank of a separate language and of a distinctive feature of a separate nation. Groups of people may admit to sharing the same language and still regard themselves as occupying separate nations. Territory and language may also be insufficient as defining factors that make up the "reality" of the nation because people can move in and out of them. In principle, a person can declare a change of national allegiance. Depending on migration policies and conditions of residence, people move homes and acquire residence among a nation to which they do not belong and may then learn the language of another nation. If the territory of residence (remember, this is not a territory with guarded borders) and participation in a linguistic community (remember, one is not obliged to use a national language by the fact that no other languages are admitted by power-holders) were the only constituting features of the nation, the nation would be too "porous" and "under-defined" to claim the absolute, unconditional, and exclusive allegiance that all nationalisms demand.

As we have observed, this latter demand is at its most persuasive if the nation is conceived of as a fate, rather than a choice. It is then assumed to be so firmly established in the past that no human intervention can change it. As it is deemed to lie beyond what may be viewed as the arbitrary character of culture, nationalisms aim to achieve this belief with the *myth of origin* serving as the most potent instrument towards this end. This myth suggests that even if it were once a cultural creation, in the course of history the nation has become a truly "natural" phenomenon and so is something beyond human control. The present members of the nation – so the myth claims – are tied together by a common past from which they cannot escape. The national spirit is then regarded as a shared and exclusive property that not only unites people, but also sets them apart from all other nations and all individuals who may aspire to enter their community. As Craig Calhoun, the American sociologist and historian, puts it, the idea of nation then becomes established "both as a category of similar individuals and as a sort of 'supra-individual.'"

The myth of the origin, as well as the claim to "naturalness" of a nation and the ascribed and inherited nature of national membership, cannot but embroil nationalism in a contradictory situation. On the one hand, it is held that the nation is a verdict of history and a reality that is objective and solid as any natural phenomenon. On the other hand, it is precarious because its unity and coherence is constantly under threat by virtue of the existence of other nations whose members may become part of its ranks. The nation may then respond by defending its existence against the encroachments of the "other" and thus survives only through constant vigilance and effort. Therefore, nationalisms normally demand power – the right to use coercion – in order to secure the preservation and continuity of the nation. State power is then mobilized and that means monopoly over the instruments of coercion; only the state power is capable of enforcing uniform rules of conduct and promulgating laws to which its citizens must submit. As the state needs nationalism for its legitimation, nationalism needs the state for its effectiveness. The national state is the product of this mutual attraction.

When we find the state is identified with the nation, as the organ of self-government of the nation, the prospect of nationalist success increases. Nationalism no longer has to rely solely on the persuasiveness of its arguments as state power means the chance of enforcing the sole use of the national language in public offices, courts, and representative bodies. Public resources become mobilized in order to boost the competitive chances of the preferred national culture in general and national literature and arts in particular. It also means, above all, control over education to ensure consent. Universal education permits all inhabitants of the state territory to be trained in the values of the nation that dominates the state. With varying degrees of success, there is the seeking to accomplish in practice what has been claimed in theory, namely the "natural-ness" of nationality. The combined effect of education, of ubiquitous though diffuse cultural pressure and of the state-enforced rules of conduct, is the attachment to the way of life associated with the "national membership." This spiritual bond may find itself manifest in a conscious and explicit *ethnocentrism*. The characteristics of this attitude are the conviction that our own nation, and everything which relates to it, is right, morally praiseworthy, and beautiful. In terms of being constituted through contrast, this is also exemplified in the belief that it is vastly superior to anything that may be offered as an alternative and, further, that what is good for our own nation should be given precedence over the interests of anybody and anything else.

The reach of ethnocentrism can be pervasive for those who have been brought up in a specific environment and tend to feel at home in it. In such ways, by default, it may be perpetuated with deviations from the familiar inducing feelings of unease, resentment, and even overt hostility towards those who are deemed "aliens" and apparently responsible for the absence of coherence and certainty. It becomes "their ways" that require transformation. In such ways, nationalism can inspire cultural crusades through the efforts to change and convert alien ways and force submission to the authority of the dominant nation. The overall purpose is one of *assimilation*. The term itself originally came from biology in order to denote how, in order to feed itself, a living organism assimilates elements of the environment and so transforms "foreign" substances into its own body. In so doing it makes them "similar" to itself and so what used to be different becomes similar. All nationalism is always about assimilation, as the nation which the nationalism declares as having a "natural unity" has first to be created by rallying an often indifferent and diversified population around the myth and symbols of national distinctiveness. Assimilatory efforts are at their most conspicuous and fully expose their inner contradictions when a triumphant nationalism, which has achieved state domination over a certain territory, meets among the residents some "foreign" groups: that is, those who either declare their distinct national identity, or are treated as distinct and nationally alien by the population that has already gone through the process of cultural unification. In such cases assimilation can be presented as a proselytizing mission in much the same way as the heathen must be converted to a "true" religion.

Efforts at conversion can be half-hearted. After all, too much success can bear the mark of the inner contradiction always present in the nationalist vision. On the one hand, nationalism claims the superiority of its own nation, of its national culture and character. Therefore, the attractiveness of such a superior nation to the surrounding peoples is something to be expected and, in the case of a national state, it also mobilizes the popular support for state authority and undermines all other sources of authority resistant to the state-promoted uniformity. On the other hand, the influx of foreign elements into the nation, particularly when made easy by the "open arms," hospitable attitude of the host nation, casts doubt on the "naturalness" of national membership and thus saps the very foundation of national unity. People are seen to change places at will: "them" can turn into "us" under our very eyes. It looks, therefore, as if nationality were simply a matter of a choice which could, in principle, be different from what it was and even be revoked. Efforts at assimilation that are effective thereby bring into relief the precarious, voluntary character of the nation and national membership – a state of affairs that nationalism seeks to disguise.

Assimilation breeds resentment against the very people the cultural crusade aimed to attract and convert. In the process they are constructed as a threat to order and security for, by their existence, they challenge that which is believed to be outside human power and control. An allegedly natural boundary is exposed not only as artificial but, worse still, passable. Acts of assimilation are thus never complete for, in the eyes of those who seek their transformation, assimilated persons will appear as potential turncoats: they may pretend to be what they are not. Recognition and respect for difference do not then become an option for those with nationalist tendencies who, when faced with an absence of success, may retreat to a tougher, less vulnerable, and racist line of defense. Unlike the nation, *race* is perceived overtly and unambiguously as a thing of nature and so provides for distinctions that are neither human-made nor subject to change by human efforts. Race can thus be ascribed as having a purely biological meaning to the extent that individual character, ability, and inclination are closely related to observable, extrinsic characteristics that are genetically determined. Such characterizations can refer to those qualities that are seen to be hereditary and so, when confronted with race, education must surrender. What nature has decided, no human instruction may change. Unlike the nation, race cannot be assimilated and so among those who seek to maintain or construct boundaries upon such a basis, the language of "purity" and "pollution" is often apparent. To stave off such outcomes, segregation, isolation, and even removal to safe distances to make mixing impossible are means to protect one's own race from the effects of "others."

Whilst assimilation and racism appear to be radically opposed, they may be characterized as stemming from the same source: that is, the tendency to build boundaries that is inherent in nationalist preoccupations. Each one emphasizes one of the poles of the inner contradiction. Depending on circumstances, one or the other side can be deployed as tactics in the pursuit of nationalist objectives. Yet both are always potentially present in any nationalist campaign and so, rather than excluding, they may mutually boost and reinforce each other. Here also we find the strength of nationalism being derived from the connecting role it plays in the promotion and perpetuation of the social order as defined by the authority of the state. Nationalism "sequestrates" the diffuse heterophobia – the resentment of the different that we discussed earlier – and mobilizes this sentiment in the service of loyalty and support for the state and discipline towards state authority. In such ways, nationalism makes the state authority more effective. At the same time it deploys the resource of state power in shaping the social reality in such a way that new supplies of heterophobia, and hence new mobilizing opportunities, may be generated.

As the state guards its monopoly of coercion it prohibits, as a rule, all private settling of accounts, such as ethnic and racial violence. In most cases, it would also disallow and even punish private initiative in petty discrimination. Like all the rest of its resources, it would deploy nationalism as a vehicle of the one and only social order that it sustains and enforces, while simultaneously persecuting its diffuse, spontaneous, and thus potentially disorderly manifestations. The mobilizing potential of nationalism may then be harnessed to the appropriate state policy. Examples of such activity include inexpensive yet prestigious military, economic, or sporting victories, as well as restrictive immigration laws, enforced repatriation, and other measures that reflect, while certainly reinforcing, the popular heterophobia. In this space we can also see politicians deploying rhetoric aimed at the removal of ambiguity in the name of an imaginary of a bygone era of the whole and the one.

Summary

We have discussed various forms of boundaries, how they are constructed, with what effects, and mobilizing what resources. In each case they have tangible effects on how we view the social and natural worlds. The activity of cultural building is one aimed not only at achieving a unity among a population, but also at control of environments. These, however, have a way of reminding us of their force via floods, earthquakes, volcanic eruptions, and famines. Such a reminder breaks down the apparent separation of the two spheres. Anthropogenic climate change is the result of human activity producing greenhouse gases and their effects on the climate. Whilst a scientific consensus exists regarding the causes and effects of this process, cultures inform not only actions, but also reactions.

Those denying climate change may have a vested interest in the continued exploitation of finite resources. Into these relations and how we should proceed come questions concerning appropriate, just, and sustainable ways of living together informed by socioeconomic issues. In examining these kinds of issues we find extraordinary variations in national uses of energy, as well as having access to things that many cannot take for granted, such as the availability of clean drinking water. These raise questions about the effects of cultures upon environments and the distribution of resources between nations. Issues such as these refer to the need to recognize different cultures *and* the distribution of resources between them. It is no surprise that how much we have to change is a hotly disputed matter as it threatens those countries that have enjoyed a relationship to the environment that is not sustainable.

When it comes to nations, the state and nation historically merged in large parts of the world. In this way the states have been using national sentiments to reinforce their hold over society and strengthen the order they promote. Each was self-congratulatory regarding the order it had created by alluding to a unity that was allegedly natural. Enforcement, therefore, was not required in such situations. Let us note, however, the fact that the merger of state and nation did occur historically is not proof of its inevitability. Ethnic loyalty and an attachment to particular languages and customs are not reducible to the political function to which they have been put by their alliance with state power. The marriage between state and nation is not in any way preordained – it is one of convenience. As a result, its fragility can be manifested in both covert and overt acts of violence with what are disastrous consequences. However, as this relationship has changed in the past, so it may in the future, and judgments as to the beneficial and detrimental effects of any new configurations will be made in times to come.

We can look back to colonialism to understand some of these dynamics, but neocolonialism refers to the deployment of forces beyond those of political control and overt military coercion. In our discussions on citizenship we noted that global economic forces have a problematic relation to public deliberation and democratic culture. A fragmentation may result that is apparent in resurgences of nationalist sentiments as attempts to regain control. Here we can think of the role of civil society, as well as legal and political governance, to withstand the effects of global changes. Here we can consider the role of the state and human rights, not as a reflection of some universal human nature, but something to be achieved whilst realizing the frailty and incompleteness of the human condition.

In the understanding of rights we often refer to freedom as the absence of constraint in the pursuit of goods in the marketplace. Such a concept relies upon the reduction of freedom for others for its realization. It is for such reasons that, over time, policies came into being to regulate the dominance of the marketplace in recognition that it creates injustices which themselves undermine the freedom that comes with cultural belonging in a society. When the balance tilts, societies feel the effects.

9

Consumption, Technology, and Lifestyle

In our everyday lives we demonstrate an ability to get on with our tasks and interact and communicate with one another. That process requires an understanding and knowledge without which the fabric of our lives would not be possible. They become part of the background assumptions enabling us to navigate through the social world. Until, that is, we encounter resistance or times of crisis which lead us to consider, or question, how we get on in the world and perhaps the values, hopes, fears, aspirations, and desires that inform our ways of being. These acts of questioning may be temporary aberrations leading us back into the routines of life, or have more profound effects with one outcome being an alteration in the trajectories of our life-courses. Whatever the results, when we reflect upon our actions we may consider ourselves to be self-determined: that is, autonomous beings possessing the ability to act according to the ends we seek. Yet this presumes it is we who manipulate our environments. However, what if our environments manipulate us, or we are the product of the interaction between ourselves, others, and the environments we inhabit? In this chapter we examine these questions and the issues informing our daily lives.

Shaping in Action: Technology, Use, and Expertise

Each of us exhibits, in the daily routines of our lives, extraordinary abilities and varying characteristics. We eat, drink, communicate, move through time and space utilizing our bodies in various ways, experience times of happiness and sadness, stress and relaxation, engage in working activities that utilize various skills and, finally, rest and sleep. How we do so and the ways we see the world, when viewed through sociological lenses, enable us to see ourselves not only in relation to others, but also in relation to the objects and social settings that inform our actions. Such a process is fundamental to the ways in which we organize our lives and what we may realistically hope for not only for ourselves, but others.

In these processes our question concerning the relations to our environments and the objects in them and how they inform our perceptions and actions becomes of central concern. Take, for example, the numerous information technologies that surround people living in countries where they are now taken

Thinking Sociologically, Third Edition. Zygmunt Bauman and Tim May.
© 2019 John Wiley & Sons Ltd. Published 2019 by John Wiley & Sons Ltd.

for granted. Do we utilize and manipulate those technologies to our advantage, or do they have the effect of making us increasingly reliant upon them, with the result that they structure our relations with others thereby diluting our independence? After all, in their design, purchase, and maintenance they make us reliant upon shops, electricity plants, and companies who distribute the electricity for profit and on the experts and designers who built them. Mobile phones, smart TVs, and computers are purchased, but are immediately rendered obsolete as new, updated features are introduced and processor speeds and memory increase. Can or should we live with these changes, or is our focus solely upon whether we can afford to live without them?

A dependence on technologies may easily grow over time. Bombarded with advertising that links use to the apparent freedom that comes with a particular lifestyle and brand, the seduction is clear. If they are misplaced it can lead to anxiety as a result of detachment from what has become an essential and indispensable connection, rather than a desirable part of life. If they go wrong and possess faults, for example, a short battery life, they do not accord with expectation which can rapidly exceed what might actually be technically possible. Here we find a gap between expectation and use in which companies may not admit to limitations for fear of losing competitive advantage, and consumers seek more in the insatiable realm of desire, with questions of need viewed as curtailments to the realization of freedom. It is not just having, but being seen to have the latest on offer that becomes woven into the fabrics of social identity. New models that enter the marketplace represent not only new features, but the outdated ways of older models for which parts may not be available for repairs and they may even be manufactured in ways that render such possibilities difficult, if not impossible.

What is the cost of this activity? Once posed, the process itself is questioned and issues are raised concerning what interests are fulfilled by its continuation. There are costs to the environment in terms of the extraction and use of finite materials and the disposal of what becomes "rubbish" as a result of these forms of consumption. These can become externalities in a twofold sense: they are not part of the consideration of the person making the purchase and are factors that are consequences of manufacture that affect other environments and habitats, but are not necessarily reflected in the idea of "cost." Thus, we are locked into a cycle of purchasing goods if we regard them as essential to our lifestyles. Such choices can be sold as those designed to enhance our freedom, which is assumed to occur independently from the industry of seduction that has grown up around the marketing of goods and services. As Andrew Sayer notes in *Why Things Matter to People*, capitalism links us to others more than any other economy, but also gives us the means for living without consideration for them, or the consequences our choices have for their lives.

If we consider what is real in terms of our ability to exchange goods, it is an act at a moment in time. The values of the thing we seek and acquire in the economic sphere of the market place are assumed to be separate from the other values that inform our lives. Exchange and consumption in our everyday lives is framed in such ways and binds what we do into particular spheres of action. Over time, however, we have witnessed a merging of economic value and affect.

Here we find studies of market branding that seek to produce particular feelings when engaged in certain activities. These are not simply online collections of numerous preferences that are aggregated and sold on to those who seek to influence the market, but studies such as the relationship between background music played in supermarkets and patterns of consumer purchasing. Nothing, in the desire to influence consumers, is left to chance and the sphere of exchange and consumption is now enlarged to take in values beyond narrow, instrumental calculation. In *Weapons of Math Destruction*, Cathy O'Neil described how she was recruited to design an algorithm that distinguished between those just browsing Internet sites from those who would make purchases on the same travel sites. Her experiences demonstrated a statistical transferability from hedge fund models to those in e-commerce. In both sectors she saw the same process at work for those who participated in designing the models: their wealth moved from becoming a means to get by, to becoming a measure of judging their worth as a person.

If these trends are informing an evaluation of our worth that moves beyond the confines of the economic sphere, we should also note that technology is not simply something that we use in a one-way relation. With development, new skills are required and these may enhance our general abilities. Yet just how many functions does a machine require? New software comes on to the market and machines require regular software updates. Is learning how to interact with new technologies a means to an end, or an end in itself? Two people may have different systems and need to respond to varying demands on their time. They may choose to remain with an older machine because the focus is on what it affords in terms of its production, not on the desire to be up to date. Yet the machine can become obsolete and parts difficult to acquire and software no longer available. The choice is constrained by what remains to support the hardware. Moving to a new job, on the other hand, may require becoming familiar with new calendar systems for appointments that organizational personnel use to coordinate activities. Without becoming familiar with that use, the rhythms of everyday coordination and communication become impossible. Our actions are thereby modified and constrained in different ways by our relations with technologies and the situations in which we find ourselves working.

With each change we may need to acquire new skills; how and why they impact upon our lives depends upon the social conditions in which we find ourselves. We may deploy these technologies with little understanding of their inner workings. As a result, in their construction and use there is a division of knowledge and as that grows wider we become less able to resolve the problems that may arise in their use. Our dependency grows as more sophisticated knowledge and tools are required for their repair and maintenance. As we acquire new ways of interacting with these technologies, they render our old skills outdated, thus making us more dependent on a need to change in order to keep up with developments, and our places of work may evaluate us accordingly. Our past abilities are rendered obsolete as we become absorbed into new technologies. An apparent growth in our autonomy easily lapses into an increase in dependence.

A growth in expertise now appears to fill the gap between expectation and actuality in the service of the promises that come with the age of information technology. Everyday skills that were once assumed to be fairly widespread, or at least within the grasp of people, given time, are now subjected to careful scientific study. Tasks are split into elementary parts and each one examined in detail and represented as an issue with its own intrinsic requirements. To every problem, there is now a solution available given time, effective and efficient design, and experimentation through comparison. New products are the culmination of the effort of specialists who participate in the production of the ultimate goods whose design encapsulates a model driver who seeks not only particular functions, but a symbolic representation of a lifestyle. Cars become replete with various gadgets designed to maximize the comfort of the driver and passengers and something in which the driver wishes to be seen as the core component.

In the face of the continued improvements made to the technology and comfort of vehicles, when it comes to car maintenance the increase in computer-controlled engine-management systems leads to a need for more complicated diagnostic equipment – to say nothing of the increasing expense of repairs. Mechanics, who once performed diagnostic work and made repairs accordingly, can then find themselves replaced by "fitters" who change entire components because their repair is not possible given their complicated functioning and/or the fact that they are "sealed units." Digital displays may indicate that an engine service is needed, but the means to prevent that appearing may only be technology available to specific garages that are recognized by the manufacturers.

Lives have transformed in what are often termed "advanced" industrial societies in so many spheres of everyday activities: for example, sweeping the floor, mowing the lawn, cutting the hedge, cooking a meal, washing the dishes, and having remote access to control of heating in the home for the purposes of comfort. Technology offers a means to navigate through our lives. Diagnostic apps exist to detect medical conditions; facial recognition software can assist those with dementia; smart technologies in the home enable those with varying disabilities to continue to live independently. These technologies have enormous applications. Even an activity like shopping is changing: it is possible to shop without any human interaction: for example, by using self-service tills to become both the customer and cashier and going online to make purchases whose convenience is constituted through home delivery.

So we have enabling and constraining applications of technology which share a characteristic: expertise is locked in gadgets whose continual advancement polishes and sharpens everyday control. In the process we perform new skills to replace the old, obsolete, and forgotten ones and deploy our time to develop the skills to find and operate the right technological instruments. However, the promise of technology does not simply lie in replication, but addition. Things become central to people's lives that would never be possible without the technology itself. After all, mobile phones and computing opened up new possibilities that did not previously exist. Internet platforms provide customized viewing options through collecting information on preferences and then using key words for customers to inform and attract them to particular genres. They generate revenue through subscription which then provides for production of new media and a need develops where previously it did not exist. These developments do not simply replace older ways of doing things; they induce people to do things they did not before.

Technology does not simply respond to need, it creates and molds it. It is often the case that those who offer us their expertise and products must first go to great lengths to persuade us that we actually have a need for the goods they sell. However, even in cases where new products are addressed to well-established needs they could continue to be satisfied were we not tempted by the allure of a new gadget. Thus, new technologies are not simply a response to a need: in no way has its appearance been determined by popular demand. It is rather the demand that has been determined by the availability of new technology. Whether the need did or did not exist before, the demand for new products comes after their introduction. In this way the presumption that demand creates supply is reversed by the suppliers actively creating demand via their marketing strategies. Affect and value merge in displays that embody the capability to purchase, the wish to be seen with a particular product, and a set of justifications that provide for its consumption and use.

Purchase, Product, and Persuasion

So what causes ever new, deeper, more focused, and specialized expertise and sophisticated technologies to appear? The probable answer is that the development of expertise and technology is a self-propelling, self-reinforcing process which does not need any extra causes. Given a team of experts supplied with research facilities and equipment, we can be pretty sure that they will come up with new products and propositions, guided simply by the logic of activity in an organization. This logic is characterized by a need to excel, to prove superiority over competitors, or just the all-too-human interest and excitement in the performance of our work. Products may become scientifically or technologically feasible before their use has even been ascertained: they have an attributed value expressed in potentiality. It is this potential that propels the efforts and when the technology is produced, attention turns to application. After all, if we have it, it would be unforgivable not to deploy it.

With such potential, solutions go in search of problems to solve. To put it in a different way: an aspect of life is frequently not perceived as a problem, as something that cries for a solution, until expert advice or technological objects appear claiming to be the solution. The very lure of technology becomes something that is an instrumental solution to a practical problem that is separated from the realm of value aside from instrumental use and a difference between people that is assumed to be beyond political contestation. Technology and politics are apparently separate fields of activity. Yet as we have seen, the human and technological are not simply separate. In our discussion above we need to separate, as Andrew Barry suggests in *Political Machines: Governing and Technological Society*, a technical device as a machine or apparatus, from a technology in which knowledge, skills, energy, interpretations, and calculations all emerge to make it work. Technology, whilst not reducible to politics, is bound up with the social elements of our lives and thus open to contestation and challenge in terms of its production, value, consumption, and use.

Into this space of possible contestation arrive the many projects of persuasion. Prospective buyers need to be reached and informed that the object to be sold has a value for everyday use. If they are not persuaded, they will not part with their money. If money is an issue, payments over time may be possible, with goods targeted at particular groups, accompanied by allusion to lifestyle choices and tactics of distinction in order to clearly demarcate the product from others. If that is not enough, "free" goods with purchases made by a particular date and advertising at certain times of year when gift-giving is prevalent are just some of the means of persuasion mobilized in the process. We become consumers whose choices are embodied in our powers of discernment and of course, income and wealth. At one level, identities are mobilized for the purpose of enhancing lifestyle choices and yet goods also need to be sold in a global mass market. Difference is deployed in the art of persuasion, whilst homogeneity across contexts in the sale of the same product, is the enhancer of profit.

Depending on the purchase, there are variable implications for how we then use them. Some may have verbal instructions but an expertise is also locked inside others with technologies being a clear example. As we have said, there are variable consequences for our knowledge and skills. Even those with particular expertise may succumb to this when venturing outside the fields of their own specialism, with much of the expertise entering our lives doing so without being invited or seeking permission. Think, for instance, of the increasingly sophisticated technology that is deployed for the purposes of routine surveillance which is often justified according to safety and comfort. At one level, its presence is said to accord a greater freedom of movement. Yet that may also mean the power to exclude certain persons who are considered "undesirable" and increase anxiety and restrictions over freedom of movement. In extreme cases, they may even make us helpless victims of someone else's arbitrary decisions. Nevertheless, much of the technology that is used in everyday life is meant to enhance, not limit, our range of choices. It is sold to us on the basis of providing more freedom and security through exercising more control over our lives. It is often not a matter of consideration and is provided on the basis that new technology offers us a liberating or enriching experience. When visible in the realm of public discussion, these developments are frequently justified in terms of the enhancement of human capability. We might need to be persuaded of this potential. So many experts, armed with numerous tactics and sums of money, are routinely deployed in order to convey the belief that we can trust what happens and what we hear and see. After all, what other ways of knowing are available to us?

In the gap between publicly available new products and their potential to create and satisfy needs, marketing steps in to induce a process in which need melts into desire which, if not met, will lead potential consumers to be unfulfilled in their aspirations. We may not even know what need the latest product on offer is meant to satisfy. Take, for example, the idea of something being a threat, but whose existence is beyond our senses to comprehend. Washing ourselves with "ordinary" soap may not remove the "deep dirt" which can apparently be extracted by using specialized applications. What about those invisible bacteria that accumulate in our mouths which ordinary brushing of the teeth cannot remove? They require special brushes and liquids for their eradication. Perhaps we did not know that our camera is absurdly primitive and unable to respond to the "normal" demands which we place on it. Images of disappointment saturate the results and so we require a new phone or camera in order to capture those moments that are fleeting in order that the memorable is not obliterated by the inferiority of our technological choices.

Once told all those things, perhaps we might wish to obtain the products in order to satisfy our needs, and once those are identified, to fail to act seems wrong. When opportunities are presented, doing nothing will be evidence of our negligence and will somehow detract from our self-esteem and the respect we might command from others. These objects become indicative of what we are and offer something in terms of what we might become. Think of this relationship in terms of a scale. At one end we may view objects as things to be utilized in the service of our ends. In the middle of the scale this relationship is modified as we interact with objects such that they co-construct our identities and our skills and characteristics are modified as a result. At the other end of the scale things are very different. This position was expressed by Marshall McLuhan, a leading analyst and commentator on the growth of electronic media and communications, when he observed that we cannot escape the embrace of new technology unless we escape from society itself and so "by consistently embracing all these technologies, we inevitably relate ourselves to them as servomechanisms."

The flows and flux of consumer preferences are part of the Big Data captured routinely by large corporations concerning our habits, desires, and patterns of behavior. They are aggregated through a techno-informational system that does not recognize subjectivity except as a consumer as part of a category. This is what the artist Warren Neidich calls the "Statisticon": this does not simply monitor and predict consumer behavior, but seeks to mold the consumer in a particular image. It yields not just a practice, but frames the potential in which information technology seeks to become the answer to any current malaise.

Those wonderful, skillful, and powerful things arrive as commodities marketed, sold, and paid for with income or greater debt. Someone wants to sell them to us in order to make a profit. To achieve this, they first have to convince us that parting with our money is worth our while. This requires that the commodity has the *use value* that justifies its *exchange value*. Use value relates to the utility that a commodity has in relation to satisfying human need and exchange value refers to its ability to be exchanged for other goods or services. People who want to sell their products must therefore seek a distinction for their commodities by making the old products seem out of date, obsolete, and inferior. Now, as we have indicated, a desire for the product must be created whereby any sacrifice that is incurred in its purchase is sidelined by the desire to possess the commodity. Advertising is central to this system of cognitive capitalism in which the values of creativity are assumed to be embodied. Whilst monies spent on global advertising are variable, one estimate of annual expenditure by 2020 is $724 billion dollars (www.statista.com).

Advertising may seek to achieve several effects. Our own understanding of our needs and the skills that satisfy them should be rendered in either some doubt or reinforced by our active choices. It is then either reinforced that we are good judges when it comes to the purchase of the product the advertisers seek to amplify, or we are led down avenues of doubt concerning what we truly need and therefore there is an introduction of recognition of lack. Reinforcement and recognition of lack and hence desire are then linked to dependable, reliable products that address need. In these processes there is a fine line between the dissemination of information to address what are assumed to be pre-existing, individual preferences and the numerous techniques of persuasion that create desire and are routinely employed to target particular consumers. In being persuaded of the wonders of application, we might be invited into a world in which we ridicule those who seek to achieve their tasks by employing "old-fashioned" methods. The product on offer is sold as a means of saving time and perhaps even realizing the desire for control over our lives.

Forms of advertising may employ a trustworthy authority who testifies to the reliability of the product on offer. Such an authority may be embodied in a number of ways: for example, the dispassionate scientist who makes a judgment on the quality of a product apparently free from the influence of the fee they are paid for such a purpose; a dependable expert in car technology who was once a racing driver; testimony from an avuncular, well-wishing character who speaks about the wonders that some banking or insurance package offers the normal "person in the street"; the trust in a product that comes from the endorsement of a caring and experienced mother; the use of an acknowledged, seasoned expert in the kind of job the product is meant to serve; a famous person who the viewer knows is also known to millions of other people and, finally, in the striving for distinction in order to capture attention, the juxtaposition of unlikely pairs such as a bishop or nun driving a fast car in order to show that the product can unleash a part of people that was hitherto repressed. These are just some of the myriad ways in which advertisers, as technicians of persuasion, seek to seduce audiences into the need for their products and an enormous amount of time and money is devoted to this effort.

Advertising copy and commercials are meant to encourage us and prompt us to buy a specific product. Between them, however, they promote our interest in marketplaces and the convenience of consumption. We may not even leave our homes if purchasing online, whilst there are also department stores and shopping malls where a number of commodities may be found in one place surrounded by car parks for ease of access. A single message would not have much effect if our interests were not already well entrenched. In other words, the "persuading efforts" of advertising agencies appeal to what is assumed to be an already established consumer attitude and thereby reinforce it. To endorse such an attitude means seeing everyday life as a series of problems which can be specified and clearly defined in advance and thus singled out and acted upon.

Nothing appears beyond control and even when such a situation might arise, there are ways of ameliorating or even rectifying its effects. This induces a sense of responsibility in that dealing with actual or potential problems is one's duty, which ought not to be neglected without incurring guilt or shame. For every problem, therefore, there is a solution that is prepared for the needs of the individual consumer who needs only to go shopping and exchange money for goods and services. If they cannot afford it now, they can always pay later through various schemes that can be tailored to their income. Aside from gaining the power to possess them once found, the main focus is upon translating the task of learning the art of living as the effort to acquire the skill of finding such objects and recipes. Links are established in such an attitude between identity, shopping skills, and purchasing power. Through advertising, a person's identity may become bound up with the ability to locate the best products to meet the needs of those who are close to them. Other needs and forms of recognition of worth are bracketed in the process of making connections between identity, need, product, fulfillment, and satisfaction through purchase and use.

Lifestyles, Flux, and Social Standing in the Marketplace of Possibility

The consumer attitude concerns the apparently inextricable relationship which exists between life and the marketplace. It orients desire and each effort in the search for a tool or an expertise one can buy. The problem of control over the wider setting of life – something which most of us will never achieve – is subsumed into a multitude of acts that are, in principle, within the reach of most and, if not, there are means to further debt. In these acts issues that are *public* – shared and social – are *privatized* and *individualized*. It becomes the duty of each person to improve themselves and their lives, to overcome their short-comings, *as if* all had equal access to the means for this purpose and our relations with others and the environments which we inhabit were not of fundamental significance in this process. Thus, as we move from a holistic-relational view to an individualized-atomistic one, the unbearable din of heavy traffic is translated into the urge to install double-glazing and polluted urban air is dealt with by the purchase of eye drops, facemasks, and domes over school playgrounds that filter the air. The oppressed conditions of overwork and stress are ameliorated by a massive quantity of prescribed anti-depressants, while the dilapidation of public transport is responded to by purchasing a car and thereby adding to noise, pollution, congestion, and stress, with complaints concerning there being too much traffic. Each of these situations can be responded to via the freedom to choose that underpins the sovereignty of the individual consumer in the marketplace.

Our lives are forged into individual affairs and to call attention to extra-individual factors is believed to deny responsibility for the choices and situations in which we find ourselves. The activity of being a consumer makes us into an individual, yet almost always what we create and produce takes place in the company of others. Here we are concerned with production, but reproduction is the most important thing that occurs in a society: without this, there would be no future generations and the economy would perish. What recognition does the economy afford to motherhood and parenthood in general? Forms of support and welfare for such purpose are often taken up by governments creating the conditions for economic survival and growth. For the market the process of becoming a parent is translated into an attitude whereby parenting comes with the purchase of the latest baby products. The vulnerability of infants is matched to the characteristics of what it is to be a responsible parent. It seems in the end that the message is that we are made up of the things that we buy and own. Tell us what you buy, why you buy it, and in what places you make your purchases and we can tell who you are, what you do and desire to become. Thus, as our problems are increasingly privatized, so is the shaping of our personal identities. Our self-assertion, self-esteem, and the task of forging ourselves into concrete persons are for us alone. It is we who stand as testimonies to intention, diligence, persistence, ambition, and success and we who are accountable for whatever is the result of our actions.

Where do we find inspiration for this purpose? We are ably assisted by plenty of models from which we can choose and many more that will arrive into our everyday lives tomorrow through many means of communication. They come complete with all that is required to assemble them: genuine DIY "identikits." Even when the technicians of persuasion, through carefully crafted advertising underpinned by enormous sums of money, offer us single, specific products ostensibly addressed to a specific need, they are frequently portrayed according to the characteristics of a lifestyle to which they "naturally" belong. The dress, language, pastimes, and even physical shapes of the people in adverts are all subject to careful calculation whatever the advert seeks to convey: encouraging us to drink a given brand of beer or spirit; using an exquisite brand of perfume or aftershave; driving a luxury car; and even the sort of owner who really cares about the cat and dog food they purchase. What is being sold is not simply the value of a product, but a symbolic significance forming part of the building blocks of particular lifestyles.

The models fluctuate according to *fashion*. When it comes to fashion, complacency is the enemy of constant innovation and that keeps the wheels moving forward to ensure the consumer thirst is unquenchable in its desire. Selling goods on the mass market which meet needs over long periods of time would bring sales spiraling down. Fashion embodies and reinforces values and even becomes a vehicle in socialization and belonging in particular groups or a sign of liberation. It is part of a material culture in which things are discarded and replaced not because they have lost their usefulness, but because they went out of fashion. Products become easily recognizable, from their looks, as goods chosen and obtained by consumers whose tastes are clearly outdated, and so their presence casts doubt on the status of their owners as respectable and responsible consumers. To retain this status, one must keep up with the changing offers of the market and in obtaining them reconfirm a social capacity – unless, that is, many other consumers do the same, for the distinction may then evaporate. At that point the fashionable item which bestowed a particular identity then becomes "common" or "vulgar" and calls for its eager replacement in the name of what is, noticeably, unique.

As the market seeks a mass outlet for economies of scale, so too do niches develop to meet the desire for distinction. Thus, models vary in the degree of popularity that they enjoy in particular social circles and the amount of respect that they are likely to bestow upon their owners. Each possesses differential rates of attraction according to the social position which consumers hold. By selecting a given model, purchasing all its necessary accoutrements, and diligently performing its attributes, an image is portrayed as being a member of a group that approves of the model and adopts it as its trademark. In this way it becomes a visible sign of belonging. To render oneself a visible member of a group is to wear and own the right signs: dress in the appropriate way, listen to certain music, go to particular bars and cafes, and watch and discuss certain films and theater productions. Homes may even become embellished with group-specific adornments and evenings are spent at specific places that exhibit particular patterns of language and action.

The groups we join in the search for and reinforcement of our identities are unlike those that explorers are said to have discovered in "distant lands." What makes the tribes we join by purchasing their symbols superficially similar to these is that both set themselves apart from other groups and seek to underline their separate identity and avoid confusion; they both cede their own identity to their members – define them by proxy. Here the similarity ends. A decisive difference emerges for these consumer-oriented *neo-tribes* have no councils of elders or boards or admission committees to decide who has the right to be in and who ought to be kept out. There are no overt gatekeepers, border guards, or institutions of authority – no court adjudicating on and sanctioning various courses of action. The form of control is dissimilar and they do not undertake to monitor degrees of conformity at a collective level. It thereby seems that one can wander freely from one neo-tribe to another by changing one's dress, refurbishing one's dwelling, and spending leisure time at different places.

These differences can appear as a result of a casual glance. If the neo-tribes do not guard entry in a formal manner, there is something else which will: the market. Such affiliations are lifestyles and these relate to styles of consumption. Access to consumption leads, through the market, to acts of purchasing commodities. There are few things one can consume without first buying them and these products are often deployed as the building blocks of recognizable lifestyles. If some of them do contribute to a specific lifestyle, they may be looked down on, deprived of glamour and prestige, disdained, considered unattractive, and even degrading. Indeed, wearing the wrong type of training shoe has been linked to bullying in school playgrounds and the wrong type of clothes from anything from ridicule to ostracization. What of those who lack the means to exercise the choices that are apparently open to all? If they cannot afford to be choosy, their acts of consumption are limited. The silence surrounding those who find themselves in conditions of poverty in a consumer-oriented society can become deafening. As Lynsey Hanley puts it in her book *Respectable*, it is both too hopeful and dangerous to believe you can move out of a world from which "no one you know has managed to climb."

The availability of a wide and growing range of lifestyles has a powerful yet ambiguous effect on our lives. On the one hand, we experience it as the dismantling of all limitations to our freedom. We are apparently free to move from one quality to another, choose what we want to be and what we want to make of ourselves. No force seems to hold us back and no dream is one to which we are not routinely exposed – even if it is at total odds with our existing social position. Liberation from the constraints of reality is everywhere; exhilarating experiences in which everything, in principle, is within our reach and no condition is final and irrevocable. Nevertheless, each new point of arrival, no matter how lasting or temporary, appears as a result of the way in which we have exercised our freedom in the past. Thus, it is us and us alone who can be blamed for where we stand, or praised depending on the degrees of satisfaction we derive by recognition mediated through the objects we possess.

The idea of being "self-made" is part of common characterizations in which individuals are held up as icons of enterprise who seemingly achieved success through their hard work exercised separately from social contexts and the efforts of others. We are all self-made persons and, if not, we have the potential to become those we should aspire to be. Repeatedly we find ourselves reminded that there is no justification for cutting our ambitions short and that the only constraints we face are those that reside within us as individuals – in *isolation* from one another. We face challenges in which the only impediment to achievement is the matter of our individual attitudes. Every lifestyle is a challenge. If we find it attractive, if it is more vaunted than ours is, proclaimed more enjoyable or respectable than our own, we can feel *deprived*. We feel seduced by it, drawn to it, prompted to do our best in order to become part of it. Our current lifestyle begins to lose its allure and no longer brings us the satisfaction it once provided.

As the wheels of consumption and the production which feeds it are lubricated by frenetic activities that stand guard against complacency, there is no halt to efforts directed at finding suitable lifestyles. At what point can we say "We have arrived, achieved all we wanted, and so can now relax and take it easy"? Just when this may be possible, a new attraction will appear on the horizon and celebration feels like an indulgence that derives from an unjustified contentment. The result of this freedom to choose in pursuit of the unattainable appears to be condemned to remain forever in a state of deprivation. The sheer availability of ever new temptations and their apparent accessibility detract from any achievement. When the sky is the limit, no earthly destination seems pleasant enough to satisfy us. Publicly flaunted lifestyles are not only numerous and varied, but also are represented as differing in value and so in the distinctions that they bestow on their practitioners. When we settle for less than the best in the pursuit of cultivating ourselves, we may then believe that our not very prestigious social standing is a natural effect of a half-hearted self-cultivating diligence.

The story does not end at potential accessibility, but the temptations which derive from visibility. What makes other lifestyles so temptingly close and within reach is that they are on display. They appear so seductively open and inviting because neo-tribes do not live within fortresses guarded by impregnable walls and thus may be reached and entered. That said, despite appearances to the contrary, entry is not free for the gatekeepers are invisible. What are referred to as part of everyday parlance as "market forces" do not wear uniforms and they deny all responsibility for the final success or failure of the whole escapade. The effects of global market forces, for instance, are not only a description for a state of affairs, but are often referred to as having consequences for which no one has responsibility, or to which a response is demanded that necessitates transformations among recipients in both attitude and organization. In contrast, state regulation of such forces in terms of meeting the needs of citizens, which cannot but stay visible, are more vulnerable to public protest and an easier target for collective efforts aimed at reform.

Exceptions do occur, as is evident from protests in different countries against the effects of globalization and a desire to take back control from its forces and beneficiaries. In the absence of effective collective resistance and change, however, the hapless walker must believe that their inability to achieve their desires was their own fault, pure and simple. The stakes are high for the individual and for the society of which they are a part, for they risk losing faith in themselves, in the strength of their character, intelligence, talents, motivation, and stamina. Internalization of blame is manifest in self-questioning and if they can afford the cost and/or have access to such a service, they might seek an expert to repair their faulty personality. What might result from this process?

Suspicions are likely to be confirmed during the consultations. After all, the identification of any cause beyond that which an individual can act upon may be considered an indulgence, for it is not within the power of the individual to alter. An inner flaw, something hidden in the broken selves of the defeated that prevented them from availing themselves of the opportunities which were undoubtedly there all along, will be revealed. Anger born of frustration is not likely to spill over and be directed at the outside world. The invisible gatekeepers barring the intended way will remain invisible and more secure than ever. By default, the dream-states that they so alluringly paint will not be discredited as a result. The unsuccessful are thus also denied the tempting consolation of decrying in retrospect the value of the lifestyles they sought to adopt in vain. It has been noted that the failure to reach the goals that are advertised as superior and richly satisfying results in feelings of resentment that are aimed not simply against the goals themselves, but spread to those people who boast of having attained them, or stand as symbols of their achievement. However, that too can be constructed as the response of an individual who, when abstracted from the social conditions of which they are a part, is held fully responsible for their actions.

If they are to be successfully marketed, even the most elaborate lifestyles must be represented as universally available, despite their allure being distance from possibility. What fills the gap is their alleged accessibility as a condition of their seductiveness. They inspire the shopping motivation and interest of the consumers because the prospective buyers believe that the models they seek are attainable. In addition they must be admired in order that the models are legitimate objects of practical action and not merely of respectful contemplation. These forms of presentation, which the market can ill afford to abandon in its claims, imply an *equality* of consumers in terms of their capacity to freely to determine their social standing. In the light of such assumed equality, the failure to obtain goods that others enjoy is bound to create feelings of frustration and resentment.

The failure seems unavoidable. The genuine accessibility of the alternative lifestyles is determined by the prospective practitioners' ability to pay. Quite simply, we live in times of extraordinary inequality of income and wealth and so some people have more money than others and thus more freedom of choice. In particular, those with the largest amount of money, who possess the true passports to the wonders of the market, can afford the most lauded, coveted, and hence most prestigious and admired styles. Yet this is a tautology: that is, a statement which defines the things it speaks about while pretending to explain them. This occurs because the styles which can be obtained by relatively few people with particularly large stocks of wealth are by the same token seen as the most distinguished and worthy of marvel. It is their rarity that is admired and practical inaccessibility that makes them wonderful. Therefore, once acquired they are worn with pride, as distinctive marks of exclusive, exceptional social position. They are the signs of the "best people" as occupants of the "best lifestyles." Both the commodities and the people who use them – display being one of the main uses – derive the high esteem they enjoy precisely from this "marriage" to each other. The result is that the reference group becomes those who have similar amounts of wealth and even the total length of a super yacht a matter of significance in overall social standing.

All commodities have a price tag. These tags select the pool of potential customers. They draw boundaries between the realistic, unrealistic, and feasible which a given consumer cannot overstep. Behind the ostensible equality of chances the market promotes and advertises lies the practical *inequality* of consumers in terms of sharply differentiated degrees of practical freedom of choice. This inequality is felt as oppression and a stimulus at the same time. It generates the painful experience of deprivation, with all the morbid consequences for self-esteem which we have surveyed before. It also triggers off zealous efforts to enhance one's consumer capacity – efforts that secure a demand for what the market offers. Its championship of equality notwithstanding, the market thereby produces and reinstates inequality in a society made of consumers. The typically market-induced or market-serviced kind of inequality is kept alive and perpetually reproduced through the price mechanism.

Marketed lifestyles bestow a sought-after distinction because their price tags put them out of reach of the less well-off consumers. In turn, this distinction-bestowing function adds to their attraction and supports the high price attached to them. At the end of the day, it transpires that with all the alleged freedom of consumer choice, the marketed lifestyles are not distributed evenly or randomly; they tend to concentrate in a particular part of society and acquire the signs of social standing. Therefore, lifestyles tend to become class-specific. The fact that they are assembled from items that are all available in shops does not make them vehicles of equality. However, that makes them less bearable, more difficult to endure for the relatively poor and deprived, than it was when possessions were overtly ascribed to the already occupied, often inherited and immutable, social ranks. Beneath the claim that suggests achievement is within the reach of all lies the reality of ascription that is set according to an unequal distribution of the ability to pay. The struggle for recognition, in this sense, is only likely to arrive with redistribution.

The market thrives on the inequality of income and wealth, but it does not appear to recognize ranks. All vehicles of inequality are denied but those of the price tag. Goods must be accessible to everybody who can afford to pay their price. A purchasing ability is the only entitlement that the market can recognize. It is for this reason that in a market-dominated consumer society the resistance to all other, ascribed inequality grows to unprecedented proportion. Exclusive clubs that do not accept members from certain ethnic groups and/or women, restaurants or hotels that bar access to customers because they have the "wrong color of skin," estate developers who will not sell properties to particular types of people, all find themselves under attack. The overwhelming power of market-supported criteria of social differentiation seemingly invalidates all its competitors. Quite simply, there should be no goods that money cannot buy and the market is not assumed to be the embodiment of particular values and prejudices, but a universal and value-free force that all reasonable people ought to accept.

Despite claims to the contrary, market-oriented and ethnicity-grounded deprivations overlap. The groups that are held in an inferior position by "ascriptive" restrictions are usually also employed in poorly paid jobs, so that they cannot afford the lifestyles destined for those who benefit from their labors. In this case, the ascriptive character of the deprivation remains hidden. Visible inequalities are explained away as the results of the lesser talents, industry, or acumen of the members of the deprived group; were it not for their innate faults, they would succeed like everyone else. To become like those who they should envy and wish to imitate would seemingly be within their reach if they acted on their wishes. The inequality upon which the market relies is thereby enabled by the barriers to entry that such groups routinely encounter, thus giving further rise to explanations that are targeted not at the conditions in which such groups find themselves and the prejudices they encounter, but at the characteristics assumed to be peculiar to "their" group.

Members of the otherwise depressed category who might succeed in market terms still find the gates to certain styles of life firmly shut. They have the financial power to afford the high fees of the club or hotel, but are barred entry. The ascriptive character of their deprivation is thereby exposed and they learn that, contrary to promise, money cannot buy everything and so there is more to human placement in society, to wellbeing and dignity, than earning money and spending it. As far as we know, people may differ in their abilities to buy tickets, but should anyone be refused a ticket if they can afford one? Given the claim in a market society that goods and services are open to those who can afford them, ascriptive differentiation of opportunities is unjustifiable. The era of "self-made persons," of the proliferation of lifestyle "tribes," of differentiation through styles of consumption is also an era of resistance to racial, ethnic, religious, and gender discrimination. Here we find struggles for *human rights* expressed in terms of the removal of any restrictions except those which may be overcome by the effort of any human being as an individual.

Summary

Our identities are being transformed in various ways not only through the introduction of new technologies which transform our skills and knowledge and even question what it is to be "human," but also through the increasing role that markets play in our everyday lives. For those who can afford and have access to them, new technologies require a constant updating of skills. Nevertheless, there is a question over whether we use such means towards our ends, or the means becomes an end in itself. As we orient ourselves towards the future, some science-fiction writings seem to become more pertinent as strict demarcations between humans and machines increasingly blur. The implantation of mechanical valves, the fitting of artificial limbs to the human body, may be more than just the recovery of "natural" functioning, but have the potential to serve as enhancements to human-mechanical capabilities. Technological innovations may permit greater control, but with what consequences and for whom? These matters require an understanding that is derived from outside of a process that recognizes nothing other than its own rationalizations.

Important ethical issues are raised by such questions. Yet in societies driven by the logic of consumerism, where do the resources lie from which to draw for this purpose? Apparently, the only thing that is recognized here is the ability to pay, and technology can make that easier through smart cards and readers enabling rapid transactions. We have also seen that a supposed equality in the pursuit of commodities on the market is met by the prejudices that exist within societies. Equality of opportunity and outcome are differentially distributed, so not only do people bring different capacities to choose to the marketplace, but also it rewards them according to their acceptability within the order of things. The market reflects those forces and adapts to their reproduction. Thus even the possession of money may not be sufficient to benefit from such arrangements and protests against such inequity are far from unusual. In the meantime, we are continually encouraged to consume in the pursuit of the unattainable – the perfect lifestyle in which contentment reigns supreme. The effects of this on wellbeing, social justice, and the overall sustainability of our planet is a vital issue now and for the generations to come.

Part III

Retrospect and Prospect

10

Sociological Lenses

Retrospect and Prospect

Our journey has taken us through a world of interactions, relations between ourselves and objects, as well as experiences and interpretations of the issues that inform our lives. With sociological lenses as our guide, the task was to illuminate what we see and do as a result. As with any guided tour, it was hoped not to miss anything of importance, as well as bring to attention those things which, if left to ourselves, we might pass by unnoticed. In the process, dynamics and relations have been explained that might only be known superficially and, perhaps, perspectives have been provided that had not hitherto been considered. Within this journey it is hoped you have reached a point where you know more and have improved your understanding. In this final chapter, there is a reflection on this understanding and a consideration of the place of sociological knowledge in social life now and in the future.

Sociological Lenses: Relational and Contextual

Societies are sites of changes and they have varying effects on the individual and groups who comprise them. Therefore, they are also sites of contestation due to the consequences of those transformations. As we have seen, science has increasingly become a factor in determining the forms of contemporary societies and the content of political, social, economic, civic, and moral debates. In the process there has been an increasing blurring of boundaries between scientific and political knowledge; the latter attempting to justify itself as if it could be confused with the former, or it denigrates the former through the exercise of doubt, denial, and denunciation because it does not conform to the beliefs being promulgated. That adds to uncertainty and renders public skepticism more amenable to forces that seek to shrink the world into unproblematic boundaries which, as we have seen, have a tendency to exhibit a desire to eradicate ambiguity.

Governments and their policies at international, national, and sub-national levels attribute great value to particular forms of science under the idea that knowledge is a driver for economic growth. Science is increasingly looked to in response to public policy dilemmas, such as climate change, and it is to scientific advances that we turn for medical cures, genetic fixes, advances in green transportation, colonization of other planets, physical alterations to our bodies, and longevity.

Thinking Sociologically, Third Edition. Zygmunt Bauman and Tim May.
© 2019 John Wiley & Sons Ltd. Published 2019 by John Wiley & Sons Ltd.

Science is a transformational agent not only in the competitive fortunes of nations, but the very reshaping of the human form leading to ideas on being post-human. We also see a questioning of science being deployed in particular ways and the emergence of alternative ways of living that take scientific understanding in varying directions for the promotion of sustainability and social justice. In the process we learn that we ask too much of science if we assume it can provide solutions without raising further problems in the process.

Scientific understanding is part of what comes under the general forms of understanding that lie at the core of our lives. We have seen how such factors as our backgrounds, social positions, reference groups, and techno-economic changes shape how we see the world, but also how we act in the world. As we move from our action to explanations we shift through different types of understanding. In our everyday lives we deploy knowledge of our environments that enables us to practice and navigate our ways within them. We routinely draw upon an understanding without which we could not accomplish and orientate our lives. The order of things appear to us as given and their ebbs and flows may require a change in our orientations, but their existence stands before us as indomitable and a reminder of our impotence. Such understanding is rich, contextual, and routinely performed. Part of this is sometimes referred to as tacit knowledge: that is, we know more than we can tell.

As we have also seen in our journey, there are events and practices that are often taken to be alien and threatening. For this reason, seeking to understand those may well prove challenging to existing ways of seeing from particular points of view. In these cases the attempt to understand may be subject to denunciation because it not only brings recognition to something that is a threat, but can also appear as a critique through its potential to question that which has been taken for granted. This is a form of understanding that is context-sensitive and relational which is not content to simply provide a reflection upon what is known, but situates people in terms of how their lives are bound up with others. In so doing, it draws upon both forms of understanding: that is, not only how our lives are formed of achievements of interpretation and action, but also how these are informed by events and processes that are not normally part of everyday understandings.

Both dimensions of understanding have informed this journey. How we get on with others and how that relates to us as people, as well as the role that social conditions and relations in general play in our shaping our lives, better enables us to cope with the issues we face in everyday life. Our attempts to solve them will not automatically be more successful as a result, but we may then know how to frame problems in ways that can provide more long-lasting solutions. Thinking sociologically, therefore, is central to that task, but its success is dependent upon factors that lie outside of the influence of any discipline. Framing problems that require action and finding appropriate solutions is an ongoing task and this requires a willingness to listen and act, as well as the capability to bring about change.

The role of sociology as a disciplined way of thinking is to inform this process. To this extent, it offers something that is fundamental to social life in general: that is, an interpretation of experiences through the processes of understanding and explanation. For this task, it has acquitted itself very well and its insights fall between the existential and the analytic. As a commentary on our lives it provides explanatory footnotes to our experiences and in so doing raises implications for how we conduct our lives and what informs our actions. In this way it acts as a means for adding to our knowledge by bringing into focus our achievements, but refining and reformulating our understandings by bringing into view the constraints and possibilities we face by connecting our actions to the positions and conditions in which we find ourselves. Sociology is a disciplined set of lenses that examines "how" we get on in our daily lives and locates those and additional factors onto a "map" that extends beyond them. It provides both proximate and intensive studies and extensive examinations of what might appear to be abstract in our life situations. Taking both qualitative and quantitative dimensions enables us to see how the territories we inhabit fit into and relate to a world that we may have no opportunity to explore ourselves but which, nevertheless, inform and structure our lives.

When lying on a continuum between the existential and analytic, sociology may correct our impressions and challenge our opinions, but perhaps is not helpfully seen in terms of simply producing truth and error. After all, our actions can be described and explained at different dimensions of experience and this is exactly what happens when we move between varying contexts: for example, when working, being at home, online chats, shopping, or with friends at a party. Therefore, to say that there is one explanation that will suffice for all time and place is not only inaccurate, but forecloses differences within both the present and the possibilities for the future. On the existential plane, people do act contrary to expectations and that is part of what it is to exercise freedom. Sociology explains the reasons for this, but because of its modes of study it is also an inducement to go on searching in the quest for understanding. As societies, issues, and dynamics change, there is no final point of absolute truth because to remain vibrant and insightful it must also continue to be relevant and responsive, without succumbing to fashion. Sociological knowledge, as in all spheres of science, improves through its adequacy to explain those things that were previously undiscovered or little understood.

Such knowledge illuminates the means through which we conduct our lives, but also has the effect of questioning such adequacy through the production of studies and works that prod and challenge the imagination. This may be a demanding process in that it views what are familiar things from unexpected and unexplored angles. Feelings of confusion can then arise because of the beliefs that we carry about forms of knowledge and what we can expect of them. We often expect them to justify our existing ideas, or provide new knowledge which does not disturb our understandings, but adds to them in significant ways. Of course, sociological knowledge may meet both of these expectations. However, it may question these by its refusal to close down that which is open or ambivalent in our lives and thereby moves from the familiar to defamiliar. Because of this it raises possibilities for thinking differently by including those aspects of our lives that are normally bracketed from consideration and raises issues about our own actions in relation to the conditions of others. This makes it a very practical discipline, but perhaps not in the ways that this term is often invoked by those who seek to turn their visions of society into certitudes. As noted earlier, efforts then move into denial and denunciation, or seeking to prevent such knowledge from entering the public domain.

Knowledge, Expectation, and Desire

There are tensions between the above forms of understanding and the expectations that are often made of scientific knowledge. These are then manifest in what is expected of sociological research. For instance, it is questioned whether it is a "science." The revolution that the philosopher René Descartes ("I think, therefore I am") brought to our understandings was to place our experiences within the realm of science. Prior to that time, experience tended to belong to common sense, and science to its manifestation in an active individual who takes the pathway to knowledge through the application of method. Whereas the divine captured that which we did not know, it was science, given time, which would render all we did not know finally explicable. With these expectations in place, science became the single repository of all experience that was to be admissible and judged as knowledge.

Although it has been shown that the actual practice of science does not live up to the criteria often invoked for this purpose and many physical scientists recognize the non-linear nature of their enterprise, the above frequently still takes the following form: science is a collection of practices that provides for a clear and unproblematic superiority over forms of knowledge through the production of reliable and valid knowledge pursued in the name of the "Truth." Using this as a basis to judge knowledge, sociologists can then be placed and judged alongside other experts who can tell us what our problems are and what we must do about them.

These expectations are born of a belief in "scientism." As Jürgen Habermas puts it, this is "the conviction that we can no longer understand science as one form of possible knowledge, but rather must identify knowledge with science." Sociology may then be viewed as a form of DIY briefing, with its textbooks containing foolproof information about how to succeed in life, where success is measured in terms of how to get what we want and how to jump over or bypass anything that may stand in our way. The provision of "toolkits" is one manifestation of these expectations, as if knowledge can be unproblematically transferred across contexts, with learning between them being a secondary consideration. This is informed by the belief that the value of knowledge comes from the ability to control a situation and thereby subordinate it to our purposes. The promise of knowledge is then taken to be its ability to tell us, beyond any doubt, what will happen and that this, in turn, will enable one to act freely and rationally in the pursuit of particular ends. Armed with this knowledge, the only moves that will be made are those guaranteed to bring about the desired results. We cannot doubt the value attributed to knowledge in this way. After all, the bookshelves seem full of works by gurus peddling their panaceas to whatever are the latest ills of society.

Such an orientation means, in one way or another, luring, forcing, or otherwise causing other people, who are always part of the social conditions, to behave in a way that seeks to obtain what is desired. Control over a situation cannot but mean control over other people. Such expectations translate into the belief that the art of life involves how to win friends and control people. That, in turn, produces contestation and conflict and in these spaces sociology can find its services being enlisted in the efforts to create order and eliminate chaos. As we have noted in our journey, this is a distinctive mark of modern times. By exploring the hopes, wishes, desires, and motivations that inform human action, sociologists may be expected to provide information about the way things need to be organized in order to provide for the actions people ought to exhibit.

Such a course of action requires the eradication of forms of conduct that the designed model of order deems unsuitable. That leads directly into political and ethical terrains: for example, managers of call centers and factories may enlist the help of sociologists in order to extract more productivity from their employees; online companies may want to know about consumer habits and profiles in order to sell them yet more goods and services; army commanders may commission surveys and observation studies that enable greater discipline within the ranks or reveal information concerning enemy targets; police forces may commission proposals on how to disperse crowds and deploy methods of covert surveillance effectively; supermarkets may send their security officers on courses designed to detect and reduce shoplifting via proactive offending profiling and public relations officers may want to know the best methods for rendering politicians more popular and electable by appearing to be "in touch" with the people through rhetorical tactics and targeting social media.

Practices and even demands of this type require that sociologists should offer advice on how to combat those things that are already defined as problems by particular groups in ways that ignore, or find "irrelevant," alternative explanations, solutions, and possibilities. Intentionally, and perhaps even unintentionally, outcomes may reduce the freedom of some people so that their choices are confined and their conduct controlled according to the desires of those who commission the studies. Knowledge is required on how to transform the people in question from *subjects* of their own action into *objects* of intervention or manipulation. Understanding in terms of the relations that exist between a person and their environment is subordinated to the wishes and images of those who seek control in the first place. Deviations from those expectations are likely to demand ever greater forms of control, rather than a questioning of the whole enterprise itself. Indeed, the latter may be considered an indulgent attitude that is deemed a luxury in the face of what are framed as "necessities."

Expectations of knowledge along these lines amounts to the demand that research produce recipes for the control of human interaction. What we see here is the desire to possess control over the objects of study. As we saw in relation to the interactions between culture and nature, this has a long history whereby the latter was to become an object of intervention so that it could be subordinated to the will and purpose of those who sought to utilize resources for satisfaction of their own desires. A language, purified of intent and embroiled in technicalities that appeared to be distanced from emotional content, then emerged in which the objects of intervention received, but did not generate or question, actions. Spheres of action appear that are devoid of being related, via separation and compartmentalization, are then manipulated in order to fulfill particular ends. As culture and nature became part of this process, the latter was conceived as a "free for all": a virgin territory waiting to be tilled and transformed into a purposefully designed plot better suited to human habitation. Questions of our relations with the planet and its resources and matters of balance were not raised until, that is, study after study concluded it was near to exhaustion due to the results of interventions and extractions. Despite that, those whose interests are not served by such recognition prefer denial to action and whilst we see the rise of alternative energy sources and concerns with sustainability, the history of the emergence of such sources and how they remained subordinated to the pursuit of particular ends is still being written.

As nature and culture cannot be simply separated, nor can environment and society. So, whilst sociology sees the importance of sustainability, it is bound to link that to matters of social context and justice. Respect for the environment varies within and between societies with differences between communities and types of climate, whilst some societies are more extractive than others and power differentials and inequalities are apparent within all. Any knowledge that moves into this relational terrain will meet expectations that not only seek explanation, but also justification. Yet that is a responsibility that lies beyond any discipline. In the meantime, doubts about embarking upon such a process can be turned into the questioning of this vital need due to its apparent complexity or the belief that technology separate from the social sphere is the solution. Matters of complexity have not stopped humanity in its history before. The process may yet again lead to attacks based on the assumed neutrality of particular ideas of knowledge which are devoid of the very issues that render human life purposeful and meaningful: that is, the ethical dimension to our existence.

Knowledge and Being

A separation between knowledge and our being in the world produces a difference between knowledge and action. Knowledge is taken to be that which informs action prior to it being undertaken. Any discipline seeking legitimacy in such a context must seek to anticipate this model of knowledge production. Any kind of knowledge that aspires to obtain public recognition through a place in the academic world and a share in public resources needs to prove that it can deliver on this basis. Thus, we find that even if the role of architects or builders of the social order did not cross the minds of the early sociologists – it certainly did for some – and even if the only thing they wanted was to comprehend the human condition more fully, when they sought to construct the discipline they could hardly avoid the dominant conceptions of what was held to be "good knowledge." At some point, a demonstration was needed that human life and activity could be studied under these conditions. A need emerged to prove that sociology could elevate itself to a status whereby it would be recognized as a legitimate activity as given in particular terms.

In the institutions of research where the struggle for disciplinary recognition took place, we find sociological discourse taking a particular shape, with the effort to make sociology accord to the discourse of scientism becoming a task that took pride of place among the participants. Varying strategies emerged as a result of the interpretations; one of which was concerned with the *replication* of the scientific enterprise as given by dominant assumptions. In this respect, it was Émile Durkheim who sought nothing less than a basis for sociology within a united set of social disciplines aimed at providing a rational, systematic, and empirical basis for society's civil religion. In the process he pursued a model of science which was characterized first and foremost by its ability to treat the object of study as strictly separate from the studying subject. The subject thus gazes upon an object "out there" that can be observed and described in a neutral and detached language. From this point of view scientific disciplines do not differ in method, but in their attention to distinct areas of reality. The world is thereby partitioned into plots, with each being researched by a scientific discipline that draws boundaries around its object of curiosity. A scientific gaze is cast upon those things that are separate from their activities and simply await observation, description, and explanation. What demarcates scientific disciplines is solely the division of the territory of investigation, with each taking care of its own "collection of things."

The generation of sociological knowledge, according to this model, is like a seafaring explorer, seeking to discover a terrain over which no one has claimed sovereignty. Durkheim found this in *social facts*. These are collective phenomena that are irreducible to any one individual. As shared beliefs and patterns of behavior, they can be treated as things to be studied in an objective, detached fashion. These things appear to individuals as a reality that is tough, stubborn, and independent of their will. They cannot necessarily be recognized, nor wished away. To that extent, they replicate the characteristics of the physical world in much the same way as a table or chair might occupy a room. To ignore them is akin to assuming that one can ignore gravity. In this sense, to transgress a social norm can result in punitive sanctions as a reminder not to transgress that which no person may alter. Thus, social phenomena, though obviously not existing without human beings, do not reside *inside* human beings as individuals, but *outside* them. There would be no point in learning about those social phenomena by simply asking those people who are subjected to their force. The information would be hazy, partial, and misleading. They might, instead, be asked about their reactions to the environment in order to see how changes in those situations might improve behavior, or be indicative of those forces that reside within the environment itself.

In one important respect, as Durkheim agreed, social facts differ from the facts of nature. The connection between violating a law of nature and the damage that follows it is automatic: it has not been introduced by human design (or, for that matter, by anyone's design). The connection between violating the norm of society and the sufferings of norm-breakers is, on the contrary, "human-made." Certain conduct is punished because society condemns it and not because the conduct itself causes harm to its perpetrator (thus, stealing does no harm to the thief and may even be beneficial to them; if the thief suffers as a consequence of their actions, it is because social sentiments prohibit thieving because they have done harm to their victim). This difference, however, does not detract from the "thing-like" character of social norms or from the feasibility of their objective study. A researcher is thereby entitled (and exhorted) to bypass the individual psyche, intentions, and private meanings that only the individuals themselves can tell us about and concentrate instead on studying phenomena which can be observed from outside and would, in all probability, look the same to any observer watching them.

We can take a second direction through recognition that human reality is different from the natural world because human actions are meaningful and relate to our active being-in-the-world. People possess motives and act in order to reach the ends they set for themselves and these ends explain their actions. For this reason, human actions, unlike the spatial movements of physical bodies, need to be understood rather than explained. More precisely, to explain human actions means to understand them in the sense of grasping the meanings invested in them by actors. That human actions are meaningful is the foundation of *hermeneutics*. This refers to the theory and practice of a "recovery of meaning" that is embedded in literary texts, paintings, or any other product of a human creative spirit. In order to understand its meaning, the interpreters of the text must put themselves in the author's "place": that is, to see the text through the author's eyes and think the author's thoughts. They should then link the author's actions to the historical situation in which they find themselves. The hermeneutic circle – from the particularity of the author's experiences and their writings to the general historical context in which they wrote – is a matter for the effort of interpretation.

Not all human actions may be interpreted in this manner. As we have seen, much of our activity is either traditional or affective in the sense it is guided by habits or emotions. In both cases it can appear as *unreflective*. When, for example, we act out of anger or follow a routine, we do not calculate our actions, nor pursue particular ends. Traditional and affective actions are determined by factors outside of our direct control and may be best comprehended when their cause is pointed out. On the other hand, *rational* actions are calculated, controlled, and oriented towards consciously considered ends (the "in order to" actions). Thus, while traditions are manifold and emotions are viewed as thoroughly personal and idiosyncratic, the reasons we deploy to measure our ends against the means we select in order to achieve them is common to all human beings. We can then wrest meaning out of observed action not by guessing what has been going on in the actors' heads, but by matching the action to a reason that makes sense and thus renders the action intelligible. Thus, we find both causal explanation and the importance of meaning in our lives. Fused in this manner, Max Weber considered sociological knowledge to be scientific, but with a clear advantage over the physical sciences: it not only describes, but also understands, the topics of its inquiries.

Sociological knowledge can also pursue not replication, or reflection and modification, but studies of action in context. In contrast to the ideas of Descartes, pragmatism was developed from the basis that it was actions, not consciousness, that formed the foundations of knowledge. We do not take consciousness into action, but it emerges and develops within our interactions. The result is an adjustive relationship to our environments, and consciousness comes to the fore when seeking to solve issues and it is this that should be the focus of study. We see this tendency most clearly in the development of North American sociology. As the pragmatist philosopher William James put it, "It is quite evident that our obligation to acknowledge truth, so far from being unconditional, is tremendously conditioned." With that in mind, sociology is given a practical edge through an ethos expressed in diagnosis because it also has an adaptive relationship to changing societal conditions and issues. Over the course of the history of pragmatist-inspired research, insights were sharpened in the study of criminality, juvenile delinquency and gang culture, alcoholism, prostitution, homelessness, race relations, the changing dynamics of family ties, and so on. As a discipline, its bid for recognition was grounded in engagement with topical issues in order to inform social progress.

Each of these strategies mixes with societal changes and those ingredients constitute sociological knowledge which accumulates various insights over time. Whilst important for understanding in terms of historical contexts, we can take each of the above and see elements in contemporary practice. Durkheim was strongly critical of utilitarian views and felt that societies that promote individualism offer little peace and happiness for their citizens. With social norms breaking down and leading to atomization and distance between people, it is easy to see how the financial crisis and the cultures of the banking sector approximated what he called anomie. Weber saw a forward march of an instrumental attitude that increasingly saturated the realm of meaning that gave life its purpose and subordinated it to calculation. That is prevalent in the development of forms of working practices in organizations that treat people as a means to an end. We can see this in advertising practices and the potential for "malicious development" in artificial intelligence and machine learning (see: https://maliciousaireport. godaddysites.com). With the advent of the generation of data by large corporations from online activities, we will also see more of the tensions between our numerated and narrated selves as we seek the desire for authenticity whilst drowning in the abstraction of algorithms.

In the face of such contemporary developments and pronounced inequalities within and between societies, sociology cannot simply place itself in the service of the construction and maintenance of social order in order to be seen as relevant to those whose task is to manage human conduct. Seeking to generate knowledge to control rather understand, sees a blending of truth with usefulness, information with control, and knowledge with power. Sociology cannot simply provide solutions to the problems that are seen and articulated by the technicians of order. Society can then be viewed from the top, as an object of manipulation that throws up resistant material whose inner qualities must be known better in order to be made more pliable and receptive to the final shape that is desired. In resisting that call, sociology will turn its attention to issues in ways that are often not seen as acceptable from that point of view and bring into view other ways of being and thus possibilities for how circumstances may be different.

Tensions, Targets, and Transformations

By raising alternatives in the generation of its understanding of societal transformations, perhaps via the study of marginalized populations who are subject to particular perceptions, or by bringing to attention the problematic elements of what is assumed to be reasonable, mundane, and normal, the status of sociology can find itself questioned. However, for a discipline to define its success in terms of servicing the requirements of the powerful or through regurgitating popular belief is, by default, to ignore its responsibilities as a discipline, along with alternative values, as well as to set limits to its investigations within narrowly defined boundaries. What is foreclosed is an analysis of the causes and consequences of change and bringing voice and recognition to those who may not be its beneficiaries. In addition, as a society, we then lack an understanding of alternatives within the possibilities that are pregnant within all contemporary arrangements.

Because of these and other factors, sociology can be a site of controversy which is not of its making. It becomes a target for struggles within society due to the presence of different values and ways of life and its work may become subject to pressures that are not within its power to reconcile. What one side may ask sociology to achieve, the other side may view as an abomination and is determined to resist. Along with relevance and insight come conflicting expectations that inform its practice, regardless of the rigors of its methods and the refinement of its theories. It can fall victim to real social conflicts that are part of the tensions, ambivalence, and contradictions within society at large. Sociology, in its raising of social issues through systematic investigation, may find itself used as a convenient target that displaces the need for serious debate and action. That, in turn, may simply reveal what is the absence of spaces for public deliberation and listening to those experiences and voices that are frequently unheard.

Consider this in terms of the ways in which rationality in society is a two-edged sword. On the one hand, it clearly assists in the process of obtaining more control over actions. Rational calculation informs actions in a manner that is better suited to selected ends and thus increases its effectiveness and efficiency according to meeting particular criteria. On the whole, it seems that rational individuals are more likely to achieve their ends in comparison to those who do not plan, calculate, and monitor their actions. Placed in the service of the individual, rationality may increase the scope of freedom. There is also another side to rationality. Once applied to the environment of individual action – to the organization of the society at large – rational analysis can serve to limit choices or diminish the range of means from which individuals may draw in order to pursue their ends. Thus, it constrains individual freedom. Sociological analysis reflects this tension: it can provide the means to enhance such rationality and draw attention to its limits and consequences. As Marshall McLuhan wrote in relation to new technologies, if we understand the ways in which they are transforming our lives then "we can anticipate and control them; but if we continue in our self-induced subliminal trance, we will be their slaves."

The replacement of human energies, work, and livelihood by technology is evident now and in the ways in which its promise is continually rehearsed for the future. Take one scenario. Classrooms may find themselves with teachers behind a computer tracking progress of students on mobile devices with less verbal interactions and discussion. Will such techniques educate the mind to be liberated by removing more discretion from teachers in order that each pupil is subject to the same learning materials? Or will removing discretion from the teacher, which of course has variations, also remove the very creativity that can bring learning alive? The technology can be mobile, enabling learning beyond the school into all spheres of life, which also allows the teacher to track the dedication of pupils to their learning. The result can reduce staff costs as fewer teachers are need to teach, or track, the progress of more students using the technology. Potentially, they could even reduce the cost of having a school to attend. In the process, is there an alignment of interests between teachers, pupils, and their carers, the tech companies selling the hardware, the software engineers, the broadband and electricity companies providing the connections and energy to make it all happen? How do all of those interests then align with the educational values that a society wishes to see in practice, along with its aspirations and hopes for future generations?

Underlying human relations in all forms are issues associated with trust, but that mixes uneasily with the type of calculations that are routinely made in global businesses. Some of them command power and wealth that is equivalent to that of nations, but are democratically unaccountable for their actions. We have witnessed protests against the consequences of their actions and the austerity politics that accompanied the bailing out of banks with public funds after the financial crash of 2008. For global business this may be nothing more than manifestations of local impediments to the realization of their global goals, whilst the austerity politics continues with regimes that believe the realm of finance and economics is somehow separate from the realms of the social and political. In the process we hear about community values and their importance for social solidarity. Yet, as we have seen in our journey, this often translates into a defensive attitude towards the "other." As Richard Sennett has written, important aspects of community architecture are frequently manifested as walls standing against a "hostile economic order." The situation easily becomes that politics, to paraphrase Paul Virilio, is seen in terms of a freedom from fear and social security is only associated with the right to consume.

In these cases we see the deployment of varied resources according to the realization of particular goals and the resulting boundary-making activities which are made according to responses to social conditions. Some of these are even to propose that there should be no boundaries at all on the basis that they are a curtailment to freedom. That, of course, begs the question as to what is meant by freedom, who would benefit from such arrangements, and whether the mobility and the opportunities it affords are actually available to all and with what consequences? In thinking through such issues, these developments are informed by frames of knowledge that are not just retrospective, but prospective in containing visions of how the world could and even should, be. Knowledge, in this sense, does not simply reflect things as they are, but it sorts, orders, and places into containers of categories, classes, and types. The more knowledge we possess, the more things we assume we see and the greater number of different things we discern. To study the art of painting, for example, leads us not to see "red" in a picture, but different forms of red such as Adrianople red, flame red, hellebore red, Indian red, Japanese red, carmine, crimson, ruby, scarlet, cardinal red, sanguine, vermilion, damask, Naples red, Pompeian red, Persian red, and so on.

The difference between the trained and untrained eye is manifest in the power to discern and explore in a methodical manner and to obtain a greater degree of certainty over the domain of inquiry. The acquisition of knowledge consists of learning how to make new discriminations. In the process the uniform is rendered discrete, distinctions made more specific, and large classes are split into smaller ones, so that the interpretation of experience gets richer and more detailed. We often hear of how educated people can be measured by the richness of the vocabulary they deploy in their discriminations and descriptions. Things may be described as "nice," but then elaborated upon in terms of being enjoyable, savory, kind, suitable, and tasteful, or "doing the right thing." Language, however, does not come into life from "outside" to report experiences and events that have already occurred. Language is in and thus constitutive of life, from the start. As Pierre Bourdieu charts in his numerous studies, the social uses of language owe their value to being "organized in systems of differences" and these, in turn, reproduce "the system of social differences." Sociological language is part of that process.

From this we may say that language is a *form of life* and every language – English, Chinese, Portuguese, working-, middle-, and upper-class language, gendered language, the argot of the underworld, the jargon of adolescent gangs, language of art critics, of sailors, of nuclear physicists, of surgeons, miners – is a form of life. Each brings together its map of the world and a code of behavior. Inside each form of life, the map and the code intertwine. We can think of them separately, but in practice we cannot pull them apart. Distinctions made between the names of things reflect our perception of the difference in their qualities. At the same time our recognition of the difference in quality reflects the discrimination we make in our actions towards them and the expectations from which our actions follow. Recalling an observation made earlier in our journey: to understand is to know how to go on and, if we know how to go on, we have understood. It is precisely this overlapping, this harmony between the two – the way we act and the way we see the world – that makes us suppose that the differences are in the things themselves.

In this mix we find both an ease and certitude. In our being in the world, the discriminations enable navigation and communication. They are part of the background upon which we rely in our exchanges and relations. There is an extraordinary richness in this form of understanding and sociologists have explored it with considerable insight. In the process, they render manifest what is latent and the taken for granted may be rendered strange and unfamiliar. To some degree, our everyday practices must be indifferent to the conditions of their possibility in the normal course of events. Without this in place, how could we act if we spent all of our time thinking about our actions and their relation with the conditions of which we are a part? To do this would be a recipe for uncertainty and inaction. Nevertheless, the forms of life that allow for this are not simply separate from one another. Sociological understanding is not simply about how we get on in life, but how our lives are informed by structures and bound up with others even if these are not apparent on a daily basis.

That form of relationalism is not confined to what we normally recognize as sociological thinking. This is exactly what the armies of those who market goods and services do in the name of consumption. Boundaries between forms of life then find themselves subject to images and possibilities that come from different media and, as we have seen during our guided tour, have varying effects depending on our social positions. The forms are intended to sell us things as confirming instances of desire or those to which we might aspire. Sociological understanding, however, cannot be interpreted as simply coming from "within" in the sense of adding to the local pool of knowledge in terms of how to get on in a form of life. These forms of understanding cannot simply be viewed as confirming instances of new knowledge that can be incorporated into our lives without reflection, but represent interpretations that can make demands upon us to accord them recognition in a way that, by default, we either do, or do not, view from our own point of view. Understanding in this way is recognizing that the distinctions we deploy in our forms of life are not the *only* ones that exist. We are not separated from each other by impermeable walls that, without question, take inventories of their contents, and their owners. Because of such effects, sociology can become an easy target for those who believe their ways of life are impervious and without consequence.

As noted, a reaction to this state of affairs can be denial and denunciation, as well as resorting to boundary enforcement with ever greater means employed to ensure the walls are impervious to outside influences. Yet whilst forms of life may be orderly and share patterns of action, they are often superimposed on each other, overlap, and vie for selected facets of the life experience. They are, so to speak, different selections and alternative arrangements of the portions of the total world and the same items drawn from the shared pool. In the course of one day we move through many forms of life, yet wherever we go we carry a piece of other forms of life with us. In every form of life through which we pass during our lives we share knowledge and behavioral codes with a different set of people and each of those possess a combination of the forms of life of which they partake. No form of life is "pure" and, as history has demonstrated on countless occasions, attempts at purification lead to catastrophic results.

Our point of entry into the forms of life we inhabit and move across is not a passive process. We are not simply twisted and then molded into a fixed identity, nor can the knowledge and skills we exhibit be read through reference to a set of constant and unyielding rules that underpin our actions and the contexts in which we find ourselves. Rules as orientation and structures that enable and constrain our actions exist, but we are also co-authors and actors in social life and as we enter various settings, we utilize and change them by bringing with us other forms of life. These, in turn, orient our actions and inform our understandings, judgments, and decisions, but may not necessarily be suited to these new settings. Each act of entry is creative *and* potentially transformational. Sociological understanding of this process then turns to such questions as at what levels, to what extent, for what reasons, and utilizing what resources and with what consequences?

In these dynamics and movements, issues of understanding constantly arise. With these come feelings of confusion, threat, and possible breakdowns in communication, as part of the human condition. To ignore that outcome in the name of imposing a social order is to remove a central aspect of the process of understanding in which meanings undergo subtle, yet steady and unavoidable alternations. Indeed, the very process of communication – action aimed at achieving joint understanding – checks against any form of life being static. Think of this in terms of whirls in a river. Each one looks as if it possesses a steady shape and so remains the same over a protracted period of time. Nevertheless, it cannot retain a single molecule of water for more than a few seconds and so its substance remains in a permanent state of flux. Just in case it is tempting to think that this is a weakness of the whirl and it would be better for its "survival" if the flow of water in the river were stopped, remember that this would mean the "death" of the whirl. It cannot keep its shape or its form as a separate and persistent identity without a constant influx and outflow of ever new quantities of water. Remember, too, that the water itself carries different ingredients.

Forms of life, like whirls, stay alive precisely because they are flexible, permanently in flux, and able to absorb new material and discard that which is no longer thought to be useful. Forms of life would die were they ever to become closed, static, and repellent to change. They would not survive final codification and that precision that prompts the attempts at codification. To express it another way, languages and knowledge in general need ambivalence to remain alive and to retain cohesion, to be of use. At the same time, those powers concerned with ordering reality are likely to view the same ambivalence as an obstacle to their aims. They tend to seek to freeze the whirl, to bar all unwelcome input into the knowledge they control and attempt to seal the "form of life" over which they wish to secure a monopoly. Concerns for order underpinned by limited views of social life lead to searches for unambiguous knowledge.

In this quest, the expectations of knowledge are that it should be exhaustive and serve as a justification for actions. Simple allusions to neutrality can then alleviate those who apply it of the burden of judgment, but it cannot live up to such ideals for the effects will be there for all to see. To want full control over a situation is to strive for a clear-cut map in which meaning is purified of ambiguity and links are binding upon all those who constitute the form of life. Over a given terrain different strategies will emerge according to the investment that people have in the order of things. On the one hand, we may find acceptance by virtue of existing practices remaining unquestioned. As noted, that enables a disposition which informs actions in everyday life. On the other hand, those who are unaccustomed to the accepted ways of thinking who enter such relations carrying other forms of life may find, by default, that their existence questions and may even disrupt, the accepted ways of being.

In the process such persons may question themselves, but their actions have effects on the form of life itself. Resulting efforts may be directed at the preservation of the status quo through preventing or eliminating what is viewed as heresy through the monitoring and control of interpretations. Power becomes the exclusive right to decide which interpretations ought to be chosen and made binding. The quest for a monopoly of power expresses itself in casting the proponents of alternatives in the role of dissidents and outcasts who do not understand the self-evidence of a given reality. It is accompanied by an intolerance that may be exemplified in persecution. Any discipline, from this point of view, that seeks something other than the production of knowledge to achieve such control, will be the target of attack from those who have an investment in a given order of things.

Sociology and Freedom

Sociology is an excavation of the conditions that inform actions and perceptions and an interpretive discipline that enables us to examine the meanings we deploy to make sense of the world. It possesses no magic solutions because that, as we have seen, is born of a particular disposition towards knowledge. It is practical because it provides lenses upon which to see ourselves, others, and society as a whole. Its insights generate understandings that move from the "in order to" to the "because of." For those who do not wish to enter that realm, it is troublesome. For those that do, it is reflexive and can be uncomfortable as it moves from the familiar to unfamiliar as our perceptions and the forms of life we inhabit are bound together in our being-in-the-world. As a vocation it requires, as Zygmunt put it, a "balanced blend of self-confidence and demureness. It also takes some courage: interpreting human experiences is not the kind of life I would recommend to weathercocks."

Sociology produces an interpretive–relational understanding. Understanding context is part of its distinction, but not to see things in isolation, because that is not how social life exists. It is ill suited to the demands of "closing down" that which is not, nor could be, hermetically sealed from outside influences. Sociology is an extended commentary on the experiences that arise in social relations and is an interpretation of those experiences in relation to others and the social conditions in which people find themselves. This is not to suggest that it possesses a monopoly of wisdom in respect to those experiences – even though it undoubtedly enriches them through helping us to understand ourselves better through and with others. If anything, thinking sociologically broadens horizons of understanding because it is not content with the exclusivity and completeness that comes with any one interpretation and it brings to attention the cost of attempts to bring about such situations in the first place. By enlarging the scope of our understanding it is capable of bringing into focus those things that might otherwise go unnoticed in the normal course of events. These include a plurality of experiences and forms of life and how each exhibits and deploys its forms of understanding, while also demonstrating how each cannot be a self-contained and self-sufficient unit. Thinking sociologically facilitates the flow and exchange of experiences.

Sociological knowledge is a route from the order of things to a revealing of the features of the world in order to expand the horizons of human freedom. No method or theory can exhaust such an excavation, nor short-circuit its potential. As an empirically informed discipline, it moves between the interpretive and explanatory, requiring both imaginative exploration to open up possibilities and rigor, relevance, and vitality to inform its excavations. It is not a weakness to oscillate between these views. On the contrary, between these lie its very strengths and where the best insights are generated. We over-extend the scope of a discipline if we grant it, or give over to it, the power to make choices. It can certainly contribute to informing those and rendering them both contextually and relationally intelligible to us. It can also inform, but never steer, a developmental ethic about what we might become in the future for in its analysis of the present, informed by the past, it opens up possibilities for us into the future. In *Gender on Planet Earth*, Ann Oakley wrote that such possibilities have become a need for "a new world order which values all human beings, the right to satisfy all basic human needs, ecological tolerance and a respect for the future."

The issues that exist now and for our futures are matters for collective action and cannot be simply passed on to techno-economic magical thinking. Surely knowledge must, in the right doses, lead us towards resolution of our problems. To attribute such things to any form of knowledge is to relieve ourselves of how we think, feel, and act. Despite that, a powerful few are seeking to forge futures based upon promises whose very utopian elements carry with them dystopian elements. In the face of this, if sociology refuses to freeze the flux in the pursuit of such ends, it leads some to conclude that it only adds to ambiguity. Approached in this way, it can be viewed as part of the problem, not the solution. However, if a society is serious about its wish to learn from the past and present to inform the future, sociological understanding better equips us for that task. The great service that sociology is well prepared to render to human life and human cohabitation is the promotion of mutual understanding and recognition of us with our environments as a paramount condition of shared freedom. Because of its forms of inquiry, sociological thinking cannot but promote the understanding that informs tolerance and the tolerance that makes understanding possible. Between our expectations for the future and experiences obtained from the past and present, lies a space that thinking sociologically illuminates and from which we can learn more about ourselves and the futures we seek. As a way of thinking and seeing ourselves and others, it is central to the journey towards more just and sustainable relations.

Questions for Reflection and Further Reading

The intention in this section is to provide you with a basis for further investigation into the rich and rewarding insights that sociology offers. Below you will find questions for discussions, reading groups, or for those of you who have read the book and wish to explore, in more depth, the issues and themes raised in this journey.

A series of questions is provided for each chapter, as well as suggestions for further reading. In addition, throughout the chapters you will find reference to particular scholars and studies so you may investigate their ideas and insights in more detail. Inevitably, these are selective, because particular areas of interest have often generated a considerable amount of research. Sociology is a growing and dynamic discipline that is adapting to new social phenomena and producing new studies all the time; many of which are often practiced in collaboration with other disciplines.

Immersing oneself in sociological knowledge is highly rewarding. As noted in the book, such immersion can feel both familiar and distant. Starting with our own perceptions and experiences, engagement with these texts requires us to constantly ask questions of ourselves, others, and the dynamics and trajectories of societies in general. It only remains to say that it is hoped you not only enjoy your continuing journey into thinking sociologically, but find the process rewarding and insightful.

Introduction

Questions for Reflection

1 Can there be a science of common sense?

2 What do you think is distinctive about sociology compared to other disciplines?

3 What are the advantages and disadvantages associated with the process of "defamiliarization"?

4 What are the differences between theoretical and practical reason?

Thinking Sociologically, Third Edition. Zygmunt Bauman and Tim May.
© 2019 John Wiley & Sons Ltd. Published 2019 by John Wiley & Sons Ltd.

Suggested Further Reading

Bauman, Z. (2014) *What Use Is Sociology? Conversations with Michael Hviid Jacobsen and Keith Tester* (Cambridge: Polity). A book of four conversations, one of which includes addressing the question "what is sociology?"

Giddens, A. and Sutton, P. (2017) *Sociology*, 8th ed. (Cambridge: Polity). A textbook of over a thousand pages providing a general overview of sociology with a glossary of terms and sources.

May, T. and Perry, B. (2019) *Social Research: Issues, Methods and Process*, 5th ed. (London: McGraw-Hill). Sociology, as part of the social sciences, is an empirical discipline and this book provides a tour of the perspectives and methods used in the practice of social research.

Scott, J. (2014) *A Dictionary of Sociology*, 4th ed. (Oxford: Oxford University Press). A reference work that is helpful for clarifying the meanings of key sociological terms.

Chapter 1

Questions for Reflection

1   What do you think are the social relations that inform your life plans?

2   What are the reference groups in your life and how do you think that affects your actions?

3   What is the relationship between individuals and society and how does that inform our understanding of ourselves and others?

4   How would you define freedom and what role does it have in how societies develop?

Suggested Further Reading

Bauman, Z. (1988) *Freedom* (Milton Keynes: Open University Press). The book examines some of the issues we have addressed in this chapter.

Hanley, L. (2016) *Respectable: Crossing the Class Divide* (London: Penguin). A rich and insightful account of aspirations and the realities that are faced in seeking to achieve them.

Lawler, S. (2014) *Identity: Sociological Perspectives* (Cambridge: Polity). The book examines identity in social life through an emphasis upon how it is accomplished in our actions.

May, T. and Powell, J. (2008) *Situating Social Theory*, 2nd ed. (Buckingham: Open University Press). Situating the development of social thought in cultural traditions, with an eye to the relations between structure and agency, this book discusses different approaches to understanding society and social dynamics and includes chapters on globalization and emotions.

Chapter 2

Questions for Reflection

1 Does humanity as a whole have a "togetherness" or "common bond" they share?

2 The boundaries between "us" and "them" provide for the maintenance, via distinction, of identity. Does this vary between interactions online and in physical presence?

3 What practices of segregation and entitlement do you see within the city?

4 What did Erving Goffman mean by "the interaction order" and how is it manifested?

Suggested Further Reading

Bauman, Z. (2004) *Identity: Conversation with Benedetto Vecchi* (Cambridge: Polity). A short book which considers the importance of identity and particular events and processes that inform our lives.

Cavanagh, A. (2007) *Sociology in the Age of the Internet* (Buckingham: Open University Press). How new communications technologies have shaped and organized social life, alongside their implications for the practice of sociology, are examined in this book.

Goffman, E. (1990) *The Presentation of Self in Everyday Life* (London: Penguin). A unique insight into social life through deploying Goffman's "dramaturgical" approach.

Hall, S. (2012) *City, Street and Citizen: The Measure of the Ordinary* (Oxford: Routledge). An account of the changing features of the urban landscape and its impact upon people's lives.

Chapter 3

Questions for Reflection

1 What did Raymond Williams mean by "the remarkable thing about community is that it always has been"?

2 In what ways do sects and organizations differ?

3 How are communities and self-identity linked?

4 Would you consider exposing practices in organizations that you consider unethical? If so, what sort of activities, why, and under what type of circumstances?

Suggested Further Reading

Aldridge, A. (2013) *Religion in the Contemporary World: A Sociological Introduction*, 3rd ed. (Cambridge: Polity). A book investigating the role of religion in social life that includes issues of choice and constraint and anxiety and certainty.

du Gay, P. (ed.) (2005) *The Values of Bureaucracy* (Oxford: Oxford University Press). An edited volume examining how bureaucracy has an important role to play in society.

Lyon, D. (2015) *Surveillance After Snowden* (Cambridge: Polity). The author examines the forms of surveillance deployed in the digital age, its political and ethical dimensions, and what that means for our attitudes, actions, and legal frameworks.

Tyler, I. (2013) *Revolting Subjects: Social Abjection and Resistance in Neoliberal Britain* (London: Zed Books). A study not only of how groups are configured and so viewed by society in particular ways, but also how they resist that process and in so doing show how things can therefore change.

Chapter 4

Questions for Reflection

1 What is the difference between coercion and choice and how would you know?

2 How far does your universe of obligation stretch towards others?

3 What does it mean to say that people are ends in themselves, rather than means towards the ends of another?

4 Traditionalist legitimations play an important role in our lives. Can you think of some examples and how they relate to your actions?

Suggested Further Reading

Bauman, Z. and Donskis, L. (2013) *Moral Blindness: The Loss of Sensitivity in Liquid Modernity* (Cambridge: Polity). Adiaphora, defined here as indifference, is seen as part of contemporary society. Why and with what consequences for societies, are examined by the authors.

de Beauvoir, S. (1994) *The Ethics of Ambiguity* (New York: Citadel). A highly insightful essay by a leading figure from the French existentialist movement that examines the choices we face in situations of ambiguity.

Putnam, R.D. (2000) *Bowling Alone: The Collapse and Revival of American Community* (New York: Simon and Schuster). A classic study of how, with the development of contemporary society, people are becoming more isolated.

Seidler, V.J. (2010) *Embodying Identities: Culture, Difference and Social Theory* (Bristol: Policy Press). Drawing on issues associated with class, race, gender, sexuality, ethnicity, and religion, the book examines the ways in which we can produce our own identities.

Chapter 5

Questions for Reflection

1   Does the idea of a "pure" gift in a social relationship make sense to you?

2   How do calculations of risk inform your everyday judgments?

3   Can we have an identity outside of the processes of commodification?

4   Is the impersonality of exchange underpinned by social relationships such as emotional attachment and trust? If so, in what ways do they manifest themselves?

Suggested Further Reading

Desmond, M. (2016) *Evicted: Poverty and Profit in the American City* (New York: Penguin). This is a rich, detailed, and moving account of the relations between poverty and housing in contemporary America.

Hochschild, A.E. (2012) *The Managed Heart: Commercialization of Human Feeling*, updated ed. (Berkeley: University of California Press). A study on the importance in our lives of emotional labor and the management of feelings.

Sennett, R. (2012) *Together: The Ritual, Pleasures and Politics of Cooperation* (New York: Allen Lane). This book looks at cooperation as a skill needed for the coordination of social life, but also as an ethical dimension that recognizes how we need each other.

Smart, C. (2007) *Personal Life: New Directions in Sociological Thinking* (Cambridge: Polity). The author examines the feelings and relations that inform our connectedness to significant others and explores beyond those boundaries to uncover the richness of social life.

Chapter 6

Questions for Reflection

1   In seeking security are we in search of the unattainable?

2   How are habits and bodily postures and mannerisms related?

3 In what ways are different bodies represented in the popular media and for what reasons?

4 Are health and fitness different because of the existence and absence of a "norm?"

Suggested Further Reading

Cregan, K. (2006) *The Sociology of the Body* (London: Sage). Embodiment and the rules of bodily probity vary across cultures. This book examines these differences and their importance in our interactions.

Nettleton, S. (2013) *The Sociology of Health and Illness*, 3rd ed. (Cambridge: Polity). The book provides an in-depth examination of medical knowledge, the body, care, inequality, and health.

Saha, A. (2018) *Race and the Cultural Industries* (Cambridge: Polity). A study of the cultural politics of representation and the role of the industries involved in the process.

Wharton, A.S. (2012) *The Sociology of Gender: An Introduction to Theory and Research*, 2nd ed. (Oxford: Wiley Blackwell). An examination of the history of understanding gender, along with how it relates to personhood and its manifestations in areas such as family life and the workplace.

Chapter 7

Questions for Reflection

1 What consequences do "hardware" and "software" times have for the ways in which we lead our lives?

2 Are communications freed from limits placed upon them by "people and material objects"?

3 How do you think of the relations between "internal" and "calendar" time in your life?

4 What are the relations between problem-solving activities and knowledge?

Suggested Further Reading

Bauman, Z. (2000) *Liquid Modernity* (Cambridge, MA: Polity). An examination of the fluidity of life, which we have discussed here, in relation to such topics as work, time and space, community, emancipation, and individuality.

May, T. and Perry, B. (2018) *Cities and the Knowledge Economy: Promise, Politics and Possibilities* (Oxford: Routledge). The study examines how knowledge is shaping urban development in the age of globalization and what alternatives exist for more inclusive, just, and sustainable futures.

Odih, P. (2007) *Gender and Work in Capitalist Economies* (Berkshire: Open University Press/Mc-Graw Hill). Where once there were textile factories, there are now call centers and global assembly lines. This book examines transformations at work and their gendered dynamics and consequences.

Urry, J. (2007) *Mobilities* (Cambridge: Polity). John Urry examines a world on the move, including transport and mobile technologies and their implications for societies and social life.

Chapter 8

Questions for Reflection

1   Is nature anything more than the material upon which culture fashions itself?

2   Is the genetic control of crops a step forward in the process of controlling nature?

3   What do the terms "xenophobia" and "heterophobia" refer to?

4   What are the differences between citizenship, state, nation, and nationalism and how do they relate to each other?

Suggested Further Reading

Beck, U. (1992) *Risk Society: Towards a New Modernity* (Thousand Oaks, CA: Sage). Contemporary society is characterized in terms of its propensity to produce risks that have effects upon our everyday lives. Beck's book still generates research and commentary.

Greenfeld, L. (2016) *Advanced Introduction to Nationalism* (Northampton, MA: Edward Elgar). Based on comparative historical research the book charts the rise of nationalism in modernity and its contemporary manifestations.

Jessop, B. (2016) *The State: Past, Present, Future* (Cambridge: Polity). A leading writer on the state provides an exploration of its manifestations over time, forms of governance, and periods of crisis, including austerity and states of emergency.

Meer, N. (2014) *Key Concepts in Race and Ethnicity* (London: Sage). The book takes issues such as anti-Semitism, whiteness, blackness, postcolonialism, and Islamophobia and provides clear definitions of each term along with additional readings.

Chapter 9

Questions for Reflection

1 In what ways are new technologies informing and shaping our lives and with what consequences?

2 Is advertising simply a means of conveying information, or does it determine what we buy?

3 Are public problems increasingly becoming private ills?

4 Can there be more to life than shopping?

Suggested Further Reading

Holmes, D.E. (2017) *Big Data: A Very Short Introduction* (New York: Oxford University Press). A succinct overview of the generation, storage, and security implications of big data, including how developments such as smart homes and cities are shaping the future.

Moran, M. (2015) *Identity and Capitalism* (London: Sage). This study situates how identity has come to mean "personal" with the rise of consumption. It then considers what this means for how we are positioned and its role in political movements.

Turkle, S. (2012) *Alone Together: Why We Expect More From Technology and Less From Each Other* (New York: Basic Books). We are alone together as technology becomes "the architect of our intimacies" and we seem to want robots as companions. This is an in-depth study of computer-mediated interactions and how they affect our lives.

Woodward, I. (2007) *Understanding Material Culture* (London: Sage). How objects play such an important role in our lives through our relations with them and the place of consumption and identity in social life.

Chapter 10

Questions for Reflection

1 What do you hope for in studying sociology and how do you expect that to inform your way of life?

2 What are the issues that have informed the development and practice of sociology as a discipline?

3 What do you think is unique in deploying sociological lenses and is it inevitable that good sociological insights will generate controversy?

4 How do we learn from others without imposing our own ways of life and values?

Suggested Further Reading

Bourdieu, P. (2010) *Sociology Is a Martial Art: Political Writings by Pierre Bourdieu* (New York: The New Press). These are particular writings, from a sociologist whose in-depth studies over so many years yielded unique insights into the dynamics of societies and social relations, born of the "conviction that the most terrible dangers, which today are only visible to a scientifically informed eye, will only emerge slowly, in the long run, when it will be too late to resist."

Levitas, R. (2013) *Utopia as Method: The Imaginary Reconstitution of Society* (New York: Palgrave Macmillan). We often consider knowledge and utopia as speculation, as incompatible. Yet utopia is a practical way of projecting into the future in order to provide a means of examining our present trajectories. Sociology needs to engage with existential questions to remain vibrant, insightful, and relevant.

May, T. and Perry, B. (2017) *Reflexivity: The Essential Guide* (London: Sage). The book looks at the history of knowledge and its relation to the development of the social sciences. It includes contemporary examples to bring alive the use and importance of reflexivity not just for the social sciences, but for understanding ourselves in interaction with others.

Therborn, G. (2013) *The Killing Fields of Inequality* (Cambridge: Polity). Drawing upon a wide range of comparative data, the author explores the types and forms of reproduction of inequalities in societies and their links to race, gender, ethnicity, and class. In the process he identifies the need for a "common civility" that not only allows capabilities to flourish, but support and promote them in all their dimensions.

Index

Thinking Sociologically, Third Edition. Zygmunt Bauman and Tim May.
© 2019 John Wiley & Sons Ltd. Published 2019 by John Wiley & Sons Ltd.